JAZZING

MUSIC IN AMERICAN LIFE

*A list of books in the series appears
at the end of this book.*

JAZZING

New York City's
Unseen Scene

THOMAS H. GREENLAND

University of Illinois Press
Urbana, Chicago, and Springfield

Cover caption: Cover caption: *Save the Children, Yes,* improv-painting (i.e. made live, with the music) by Jeff Schlanger of the Cecil Taylor Corona Ensemble performing at the "Old Knit" (Houston St. Knitting Factory) on December 23, 1989. David S. Ware appears in the upper left-hand corner, his stritch (straight alto saxophone) unfurling down the left margin of the page, and again in the middle foreground playing tenor saxophone. Guitarist John Bruschini is to the right of Ware, over three (or four) images of Cecil Taylor that rise above the piano. Bassist William Parker stands in front of the upturned piano lid, and to the right of his bass appear two heads of vibraphonist Thurman ("T-Bird") Barker, representing his distinctive shifting movement during performances. Above Barker is drummer André Martinez (between two cymbals), and below is vocalist Evelyn Blakey (Art Blakey's daughter) singing *Save the Children, Yes.* Irving Stone is shown in the bottom right-hand corner, his ear taking it all in.

(musicWitness®: *Save the Children, Yes.* Original art 40 x 55" [100 x 140 cm] made Live @ Houston St. Knitting Factory 23 December 1989.)

Publication of this book was supported by a grant from the AMS 75 PAYS Endowment of the American Musicological Society, funded in part by the National Endowment for the Humanities and the Andrew W. Mellon Foundation.

Library of Congress Cataloging-in-Publication Data
Names: Greenland, Thomas H., 1961– author.
Title: Jazzing: New York City's unseen scene /
    Thomas H. Greenland.
Description: Urbana : University of Illinois Press, 2016. |
    Series: Music in American life
Includes bibliographical references and index.
Identifiers: LCCN 2015036943
ISBN 9780252081606 (pbk. : alk. paper)
ISBN 9780252098314 (e-book)
Subjects: LCSH: Jazz—New York (State)—New York—History
    and criticism. | Jazz—Social aspects—New York (State)—
    New York.
Classification: LCC ML3508.8.N5 G74 2016 |
    DDC 781.6509747/1—dc23
LC record available at http://lccn.loc.gov/2015036943

CONTENTS

ACKNOWLEDGMENTS

Ever since my relocation to New York in September 2012, I've variously immersed myself in the city's many jazz scenes as a player, critic, scholar, and fan, going often to live performances and jazz-related events, sitting in on jam sessions, conducting interviews, casually conversing with musicians and other scenesters, writing articles, taking photos, keeping formal records (notes, tapes, photos), and making informal observations. Commentary by the people I consulted for this book is transcribed from interviews, with minimal modifications for readability; I use their actual names (see the next paragraphs and the Appendix).

I would first and foremost like to thank Drs. Tim Cooley, Douglas Daniels, Scott Marcus, and Dolores Hsu for their constructive criticism and moral support, guiding me through the thinking, research, and writing that formed the basis for this book.

Deep gratitude is due my primary consultants, who graciously sat for interviews, offering their valuable time and insight: David Adler, Jeff Arnal, Judy Balos, Rose Bartu, Richard Berger, Peter Bernstein, Steve Bernstein, Seamus Blake, Mitch Borden, Cecil Bridgewater, Chris Byars, Roy Campbell Jr., Tom Chang, Sedric Choukroun, Frank Christopher, Fred Cohen, Lujira Cooper, Jerome Covington, Peter Cox, Bob Cunningham, Steve Dalachinsky, Jonathan Daniel, Margaret Davis Grimes, Mike Davis, Roberta DeNicola, Jim Eigo, Marjorie Eliot, Cecilia Engelhart-Lopez, Dale Fitzgerald, Bruce Gallanter, Matt

Garrison, Lawrence Gibb, Gary Giddins, Jo Gilks, Lorraine Gordon, Zach Hexum, Jessica and Tony Jones, Rachel Kent, Arlee Leonard, Horst Liepolt, Manny Maris, April Matthis, Harold Meiselman, Michael Moreno, Bruce Morris, John Mosca, Todd Nicholson, Yuko Otomo, Harold Ousley, Jeremy Pelt, Gordon Polatnick, Kurt Rosenwinkel, Nick Russo, Jeff Schlanger, Brian Smith, Irving and Stephanie Stone, Tony Suggs, Jerry Sykes, Michael Torsone, Jack Vartoogian, Ryan Weaver, George Wein, and Eri Yamamoto. Their contributions are foundational to this book.

Special thanks go to Jeff Schlanger for the wonderful improv-painting that adorns this book's cover and for two additional images featured inside, and to Jack Vartoogian for his provocative double-photograph of Tommy Flanagan.

Additional appreciation is owed to the following interviewees, who added depth and dimension to my emergent understanding of jazz-making: Ralph Alessi, Ben Allison, Louie Belogenis, Kevin Blancq, George Braith, Michel Camilo, Steve Cannon, Greg Carroll, Bill Charlap, Larry Coryell, Marilyn Crispel, Ted Curson, Joel Dorn, Dave Douglas, Brian Drye, Benny Golson, Dick Griffin, Roy Haynes, Vijay Iyer, Dorthaan Kirk, Yusef Lateef, Harold Mabern, Rudresh Mahanthappa, Michael Marcus, Elaine Martone, Bill McFarlin, Tim McHenry, Charlie Persip, Maria Schneider, Loren Schoenberg, Matt Shipp, Steve Turre, Mike Wilpizeski, Jim Wintner, Richard Wyands, and Eli Yamin.

I am also indebted to various professional colleagues who have kept me abreast of the scene(s) and/or challenged me to refine my work: Ann Braithwaite, Stephen Buono, Jacqueline Edmondson, Scott Friedlander, Charles Hiroshi Garrett, Peter Gershon, Laurence Donohue-Greene, Peter Gannushkin, Kurt Gottschalk, Jason Paul Harmon Byrne, Andrey Henkin, Nancy Hudgins, Nick Kadajski, Howard Mandel, Matt Merewitz, Jon Muchin, Russ Musto, Michael Ricci, Bret Sjerven, Kim Smith, and Greg Thomas.

I am especially grateful to Laurie Matheson, editor extraordinaire, who has been both congenial and constructively critical over the lengthy course of this project. The University of Illinois Press staff—Nancy Albright, Jennifer Clark, Roger Kevin Cunningham, Steven Fast, Jennifer Holzner, Roberta Sparenberg, and Amanda Wicks—patiently fielded my endless questions, providing expert feedback and support. Credit also belongs to editors Elizabeth Branch Dyson, Suzanne Ryan, Ken Prouty, and several anonymous readers for their attention to and feedback on earlier drafts of the manuscript.

Further thanks go to academic associates who, at conferences or over coffee, have variously argued and agreed with me in our common quest for scholarly "truth": Birgit Abels, Ric Alviso, Kara Attrep, Michael Bakan, Eliot Bates, Judith Becker, Michael Beckerman, Harris Berger, Paul Berliner, Michael Birenbaum-

Quintero, Stephen Blum, David Borgo, Bill Boyer, Jamece Brown, Kimasi Browne, Melvin Butler, James Revell Carr, Loren Chuse, Jon Cruz, Scott Currie, Mark De-Witt, Matt Dorman, Sonja Downing, Shannon Dudley, Jane Duran, Eric Ederer, Cornelia Fales, Kai Fikentscher, Meghan Forsyth, Aaron Fox, Arnold Friedman, Steven Friedson, Ofer Gazit, Mina Girgis, Jim Grippo, Jocelyne Guilbault, Ken Habib, John Hajda, Elaine Hayes, Mike Heffley, Michael Heller, Niko Higgins, Juniper Hill, Rob Hodges, Travis Jackson, Max Katz, Cheryl Keyes, Alan Kirk, Scott Lacy, Benjamin Lapidus, Mark Laver, George Lewis, Siv Lie, Mark Lomanno, Ann Lucas, René Lysloff, David Malvini, Peter Manuel, Anthony McCann, Eddie Meadows, Richard Mook, John Murphy, Jon Nathan, Dan Neely, Jeff Packman, Joshua Pilzer, Steven Pond, Ken Prouty, Ali Jihad Racy, Anne Rasmussen, Alex Rodriguez, Matt Sakakeeny, Bobby Sanabria, Justin Scarimbolo, Gibb Schreffler, Charles Sharp, Stephen Slawek, Ted Solis, Alex Stewart, Earl Stewart, Michael Tenzer, Bonnie Wade, Rob Wallace, Chris Washburne, Sean Williams, Chris Wilson, Larry Witzleben, Steve Zeitlin, and Tom Zlabinger.

Finally, I am grateful to my family and friends for being there when I've needed them. My most heartfelt gratitude belongs to Kim, my wife, a good friend and true companion through sunshine and storms, and to Talia, my daughter, a force of nature who daily inspires my admiration and amazement.

I have made every effort to represent and interpret the people and subject matter included here with accuracy, objectivity, and sensitivity. Failing this, I accept full responsibility for any errors of fact or judgment.

JAZZING

PROLOGUE

In March 2013, I received an email announcing that Peter Cox had died. The communication came from Cox's son Andy, who had found my name on his father's "Jazz Friends" email list, and was reaching out to everyone who had "played music for him, listened to music with him, swapped music with him or just knew of him" to alert us to plans for an upcoming memorial concert. The signature at the bottom of the email quoted an Albert Ayler album title: "Music is the healing force of the universe."

The event was held on March 27 at Roulette, a nonprofit performance space that has moved several times in its thirty-five-year history, currently located in downtown Brooklyn. Hosted by Cox's three sons, who were visiting from England, the memorial was attended by musicians, photographers, music professionals, venue proprietors, fans, and friends, most of whom I recognized as active participants in New York City's so-called downtown music or avant-jazz scene, a tight-knit coterie of recognizable faces and names. Projected above and behind the stage was a recent photo of Cox, a gnomelike figure of wizened visage and flowing white beard, his trademark Kufi hat noticeably absent, his face aglow with a mischievous smile (see Figure 1). Musicians and speakers glanced backward and upward at his image throughout the night, as if to acknowledge Cox's ongoing participation in the collective music-making (see Figure 2).

How did Peter Cox, a man who didn't play an instrument or work in a music-related business, become an integral figure in this creative music scene, the subject of a well-attended and heartfelt tribute to his passing? At the memorial,

Bruce Gallanter, owner of Downtown Music Gallery, a record store/perfor-
mance space catering to what he terms "curious listeners," shed some light on
this in describing Cox as a member of a special "family" of music enthusiasts,
reminding the audience that "his appreciation for music and commitment to
the community was unfaltering." Violinist Jason Kao Hwang (see Figure 1) remarked on Cox's ability to be present with the music, to *really* live in the moment." Richard Berger (see Figure 4), a close friend of Cox's who spoke daily
with him on the phone, an equally active fan who had shared many—easily
several hundred—concert experiences with Cox, stated: "If Peter and I didn't
hear music for a day or two, we would get sick; it was like *oxygen*." Berger also
suggested that Cox, in the very act of paying rapt attention to the unfolding
music, was a part of the performance: "For me, his intensity as a listener was
just as important as the musicians that he came to see. . . . You really need both,
like Yin and Yang."

Musicians likewise characterized Cox as a fellow performer, a palpable presence who inspired their best efforts. "Peter was the ultimate *musician* [empha-
sis added] because he was the most noble and profound listener you could
find, anywhere," claimed violinist Mat Maneri; "He completed this symbiotic
circle of life [between musicians and listeners]." "He invited you to open your
door," affirmed bassist Ken Filiano (see Figure 1), 'cause his heart was screa-
min' open!" "He was a one-man packed house," observed tubist Christopher
Meeder, echoing a widely held tenet in the avant-jazz scene that the quality of
an audience's attention is far more important than how many people show up.
Drummer Gerald Cleaver described typical casual encounters he'd had with
Cox before shows, the mysterious feeling he would get that somehow, before
a single note was played, "the music was already going on between us."[1] These
statements allude to the constant intercourse between artists and audiences—
during performances and elsewhere—that is essential for creating meaningful
music and building cohesive communities.

How do we speak about jazz? Most of the time the subject is music and
musicians—what's performed and who performs it. But this virtually ignores
most of the people who attend live musical events: the audience. Largely overlooked, perhaps because they tend to be viewed as passive "receivers" of music,
listeners—whether they are amateur fans, music professionals, or, more often,
some combination of both—are in fact active performers. Consider that much
live jazz is improvised in real time with relatively few "rules" (some performers
try to improvise without *any* preconceptions whatsoever), realized through a
singular conjunction of artists, musical materials, and social ambiance. Everyone gathered in a particular space and time is thus a witness to and participant

in a one-of-a-kind happening. Although our attention is typically drawn to the onstage activities, jazz-making is better understood when our scope is widened to include active participants such as Peter Cox and the various venue proprietors, booking agents, photographers, critics, publicists, painters, amateur musicians, fans, friends, and tourists who create the scene. All of these people "do" jazz, all *are* jazz, an improvised community of listeners and participants who collectively assert their sense of themselves and of each other through the music they make. When we listen to their voices, and try to see through their eyes, an essential but usually overlooked dimension of the jazz scene is revealed, where audiences are part of the artistry.

INTRODUCTION

The Unseen Scene

This book envisions broad, inclusive framework for understanding jazz and for describing how people engage in musical activities. To provide a realistic representation of jazz in New York City I take a somewhat paradoxical and ironic approach: paradoxical because I examine small, specialized scenes to suggest broad-based patterns of jazz participation, ironic because primary attention is directed *away* from the stage, toward the offstage listeners. In challenging the convenient distinction between artists and audiences I call attention to the collaborative interactions of musical performers with the other "nonperforming" participants, arguing that jazz-making is best understood as a communitywide endeavor.

RESEARCH AND DEVELOPMENT

Research on the themes addressed in this book began shortly after I moved to New York in September 2002 and continues to this day. I was originally interested in telling the story of "ordinary" musicians who move to the city to make a career, hoping to demythologize the jazz lifestyle with a realistic portrayal of working conditions for both up-and-coming musicians and established journeymen.[1] To this end, I interviewed musicians I knew from my hometown, from the music schools I'd attended, and others I met sitting in at jam sessions, going to shows, or hanging out at the Local 802 musicians' union hall, record stores, and elsewhere. I also sought out older musicians who had gigged in the city a long time, and female musicians, a noticeable minority. Besides the performers themselves, I looked for people who went out to live music regularly, interviewing various music professionals and fans I met at shows, and identifying other active participants through their referrals. In interviews with jazz people, I tried to avoid steering people with specific questions, preferring instead to open conversations with a general query like "How did you get involved in jazz?" and then allowing the interviewee(s) to broach issues that were most relevant to him or her, hoping I would thus be guided to the most significant themes. As the research unfolded, I became more aware of and interested in those "performers" out in the audience, hence this book's deprioritizing of musicians in favor of the other active participants.

To organize the various viewpoints and participatory activities of the people consulted, I've sorted them into three general categories: musicians, music professionals, and fans. Musicians are instrumentalists and/or singers who perform jazz. Here, they are peripheral characters, chiefly important for their impact on *other* members of the community, who are the primary subjects. Professionals are people who profit—to varying degrees—from jazz-related endeavors, whether or not these are their primary source of income. Professionals interviewed for this book include venue owners and/or operators, concert producers, writers, painters, photographers, tour guides, critics/journalists, publicists, promoters, and record retailers. Note that while there are many other jazz-related occupations, particularly in the recording industry,[2] the people represented here were chosen for their frequent attendance at live jazz performances. Fans include the various aficionados, enthusiasts, and other critical and curious listeners who support jazz in various ways, whether that entails buying tickets and recordings, paying close attention during performances, and/or advocating for it among their associates. In general, fans are amateurs who do not expect or rely on financial compensation for their involvement with jazz. These categories are admittedly imprecise and extremely slippery but will serve to focus the discussion of issues to follow.

SYMBIOSIS AND SYNERGISM

The cooperative nature of jazz practices can't be overemphasized, particularly in the development of "new" or "evolutionary" ideas. Like the emergence of new scientific theories, musical innovations are collectively realized, a culmination and crystallization of concepts and techniques already in circulation.[3] The commonly held notions of reality that generate these shifts, along with the personal relationships and practices that nurture their development, are themselves subject to larger ingrained social forces.[4] In jazz, although iconic figures are often associated with important innovations—a signature style, a landmark composition, or an influential recorded performance—these individuals invariably drew on the work of their (often unaccredited) peers and predecessors. More importantly, their ideas and practices were "in the air," generated within specific artistic and intellectual social environments. Thus, as Ekkehard Jost contends, musical progress doesn't depend on an "individual genius" or even a "small circle of innovators" but rather a "network of interdependencies."[5] The tendency to view jazz history as a cult of individualistic personalities may have a racial subtext,[6] but jazz practices are invariably the collective products of community interactions, generated and developed within particular social environments populated by both great and ordinary men and women.

Performers, however, whether considered as individuals or a collective enterprise, are only a small component of the social gestalt that expresses jazz.[7] Foundational to this approach is Christopher Small's concept of *musicking*, which he defines as musical participation in its broadest sense, from performing and composing to listening, dancing, and other forms of involvement.[8] Here, the emphasis is on processes, not products, and although musical artifacts like compositions and recordings are important, the primary interest lies in how music is created. If jazz is something you *do*, a verb rather than a noun, then *jazzing* (to appropriate Small's term) designates a vast variety of interrelated activities, including performing both in public and private (e.g., rehearsals); practicing alone; composing and arranging pieces; working at concert venues or in the recording industry; producing, promoting, photographing, and writing about jazz; listening to live and prerecorded music; conversing with colleagues about jazz—or anything else. Even silent, seemingly passive nightclub audiences perform by nodding their heads to the beat and making eye contact with musicians, thus creating ambient feedback loops that influence the collective experience. Examining jazz practices therefore requires a flexible framework, one that can contain an entire community of participants, in which any and all members may play significant roles. In this sense, any music scene is an ongoing performance, realized by an eclectic company of actors.

Framing jazz-making as a holistic activity calls attention to the diversity and complexity of local music scenes, the many ways in which individuals engage their communities. The concept of *symbiosis*, defined in biology as "an intimate and protracted association" of dissimilar beings,[9] epitomizes the mutual benefits of cooperative lifestyles. Beings that coevolve and "collaborate," notes Lewis Thomas, "cannot live in any other way; they depend for their survival on each other. They are not really selves, they are specific *others*."[10] Selves *as* others is a powerful metaphor for community collaboration, and the themes of symbiosis (living together) and its companion term synergism (working together) resonate well with the intimate social relationships found in musical scenes, which exhibit interdependent, complementary, and reciprocal qualities. In jazz communities, living and working together help insure the viability of desirable activities such as performing professionally, managing a club, or listening to live music. More importantly, they provide a means for participants to establish collective identities and derive deeper meanings from their experiences.

Communities of painters, sculptors, and other artists and craftspeople customarily network in prescribed social circles—what Howard Becker calls "art worlds"—showing symbiotic and synergistic behavior. To run successfully, a play not only needs actors, but also requires a playwright, an editor, a publisher, a director, set designers, carpenters, costumers, theater managers, publicists, program printers, ticket takers, ushers, and lighting technicians, among others, and last but certainly not least, patrons. The collective efforts of these people not only produce artworks, they bestow them with value and significance. Becker argues that the participants' "mutual appreciation of the conventions they share, and the support they mutually afford one another, convince them that what they are doing is worth doing," and that, "if they act under the definition of 'art,' their interaction convinces them that what they produce are valid works of art."[11] Together, the concepts of musicking and art worlds suggest a more holistic way to understand jazz-making: as a world (or, more accurately, worlds) of overlapping social circles and interrelated activities, all contributing to the production, dispersal, and reception of the music.

Symbiosis and synergism occur in jazz communities in the daily activities of various participants and in the intimate, circumscribed moments of spontaneous performance, where interactions are more concentrated and intense. Victor Turner's and Richard Bauman's formulations of ritual-as-theater[12] offer a useful way to conceive of such events,[13] highlighting the mutual agency of performers and audiences in shared social spaces. In both theater and jazz, successful performances rely on skilled performers and production, but also require sympathetic and knowledgeable audiences to act appropriately—i.e., to co-perform—during the show, whether that entails remaining respectfully silent or making visible and audible responses. The conservative yet malleable formats of ritual activities allow audiences to influence the onstage action in the course of a given performance and over time, as when listeners use performative strategies to effect lasting changes in the nature and format of the ritual process itself.[14] Given their fundamental importance to jazz and other musical performances, it's ironic that relatively little attention has been paid to listeners.[15]

Jazz is predicated on significant levels of flexibility and improvisation, both in moment-to-moment musical developments and in artist-audience interactions. Its spontaneous, indeterminate nature encourages audience input in the sense that both performers and listeners are involved in the process, both "discovering" the music for the first time. When two-way communication is established, social exchanges among artists and audiences may become intimate and intense, leading to experiences of atemporality, trance, *communitas*,[16] transcendence, and spirituality.[17] Similar phenomena have been observed in other improvised musics, including flamenco,[18] *qawwali*,[19] and *tarab*.[20] Significantly, these extramusical experiences seem to depend as much, if not more, on the aptitudes and sensitivities of the listeners—the congregation of "believers"— as they do on those of the musicians. Jazz, as we shall see, often conveys its deeper meanings through coauthored[21] musical events, when both artists and audiences participate in collective improvisation.

ROOTS AND SHOOTS

One of the central ideological debates in jazz occurs between essentialist and universalist positions—the former emphasizing African American cultural values such as the "blues aesthetic,"[22] swing rhythms, physical participation (dancing, call and response, and so forth), and the like, and the latter emphasizing multiculturalism, individual merit, and colorblindness. "It's the lineage that gave birth to it—spirituals were here first—and it's *all* connected," notes pianist Marjorie Eliot, who since 1993 has given free public jazz concerts in her Harlem parlor every Sunday, invariably beginning each with a solemn hymn (see Figures 24 and 25). A gracious hostess who inspires a fiercely loyal following of neighbors, friends, fans, and curious tourists, Eliot is gentle but frank when reminding her racially and culturally mixed audiences where the music comes from:

> There're all these black stories that *have to be told*, and that's what my mission is. And there are *terrible* things that have to be addressed, and if we can address those things in a *beautiful* way, that makes us *all* feel better, it means something. Paul Robeson lived in this building. They took his passport, all because he said, 'This is wrong. Racism is wrong. The way you treat people is wrong.' And he died embittered. And when we [blacks] talk amongst ourselves we say he trusted folks, but he *should* have trusted. So all those things are a piece of it. The music is right there, right there in that. So that's *always* on my mind. You know, it feels good and it's all those things, but *this is serious* stuff to me. This is serious stuff.[23]

Acknowledging the pan-cultural dimensions of jazz, trumpeter/educator Cecil Bridgewater argued that "it's only racial because the races have been so separated. I think it's more a *cultural* thing, so that anybody who feels the blues and plays this music is going to do it as authentically as anybody else." On the other hand, Bridgewater, who describes himself as "not a person that curses," has occasionally surprised himself by the vehemence of his reactions to students who "fool around" in his university ensembles:

> I tell them: "There're too many people who have given their *whole lives* to this music so that you have an opportunity to do this, and you're not going to fuck it up!" And I get real, real serious. . . . And it's not about *me*, it's not about *them*: it's about the respect for the music. 'Cause if you're going to do this, do it well; if you're *not* going to do it, get out of it, 'cause I don't want you to go out misrepresenting what this music is about. There's a *whole history* that goes with this music, people that gave their *lives* to it, went through *hell* so that you could be in this situation and have an opportunity to play.

As performers, pedagogues, and African Americans, both Eliot and Bridgewater confirm the impossibility of separating jazz from its racial and cultural legacies.[24]

Given the historic cycle of black innovation followed by white imitation and exploitation, and the gaping discrepancy in earnings and social privileges for black and white musicians, rarely commensurate with an artist's relative talents or contributions,[25] African American artists have an understandable impulse to protect their cultural resources and empower their communities. For example, although Fletcher Henderson (along with Don Redman) is widely credited for developing the Swing Era orchestral style, he never enjoyed the fame or financial success of Benny Goodman, who used Henderson's arrangements to further his own career. Similarly, Walter Gilbert Fuller, the arranger responsible for Dizzy Gillespie's signature big-band sound, was wary of sharing his techniques: "I refused to write for any other bands. I wouldn't write for no white bands. . . . [Dizzy] had his sound. And whenever I wrote an arrangement for anybody else, I wouldn't voice the same way that I voiced for that band, because I didn't want anybody else to sound like that. That sound was ours, and I wasn't gonna write it down for anybody else, because if you did that, then they could take it and copy it for themselves."[26] African American musical directors, bandleaders, and club owners may even feel obligated to hire other black people. "I often have mixed bands, but I also am *conscious*, and maybe I'm overly conscious of race in some ways," commented Arlee Leonard; "There're a bunch of different factors, but one of them is I wanna give my people jobs! [*laughs*] I wanna represent my people. I want people to *know* I'm representing my people."[27] In his capacity as artistic director of Jazz at Lincoln Center, Wynton Marsalis has been criticized for reverse racist (as well as sexist) hiring practices.[28] Even if racial tensions have eased around certain issues, the legacy of white appropriation of black cultural capital casts a lingering shadow.

Some commentators have observed differences between predominantly black and predominantly white audiences, suggesting that the former bring a unique "energy" to performances.[29] The legendary clarinetist/saxophonist Sidney Bechet's brother Leonard claimed that an audience's character directly affects performers: "You have to play real *hard* when you play for Negroes. You got to *go* some, if you want to avoid their criticism. You got to come up to their mark, you understand? If you do, you get that drive. [Buddy] Bolden had it. Bunk [Johnson] had it. Manuel Perez, the best ragtime Creole trumpet, he didn't have it."[30] Here, Bechet draws a fine color line between darker-skinned "negroes" and lighter-skinned "Creoles." Drummer Johnny Otis maintained that black audiences create a special social ambiance through racially unique forms of participation: "When there are Black people in the audience, African American performers get a special lift. The music takes on a heightened character. White rhythm and blues audiences can be enthusiastic and animated, but it's not the same. With a Black audience the crowd becomes part of the performance in a very unique way. Much as in the Black church, a call and response often develops, and Black magic fills the air."[31] Similarly, saxophonist Steve Wilson asserted, "I think . . . a black person that's . . . familiar with the music can relate to something that comes from the black culture on a much deeper level than someone who doesn't."[32] In 2014, New York jazz performers and audiences could most likely find the "magic" in neighborhood spots such as American Legion Post #398, Bill's Place, Jazz 996, Showman's, or Sistas' Place, as opposed to more formal venues (with more whites in attendance) that discourage talking or calling out during performances.[33] Indeed, tour guide Gordon Polatnick prefers local clubs for their "community and looseness," where his clientele can have a more "authentic" jazz experience.[34]

Musicians themselves seem to be relatively "colorblind" if they respect a colleague's artistic abilities. Even the black-dominated early bebop scene accepted outsiders who had musical "cred." "Johnny Carisi was the only white boy up in Harlem playing at Minton's," noted Dizzy Gillespie; "He'd learn all the tunes. Played all of Thelonious Monk's tunes, all of mine. I'd play a chorus. He'd be right behind me. Roy [Eldridge]? Right behind Roy. Right behind everybody. He was welcome so long as he could blow the way he did."[35] Today, interracial and interethnic groupings are more common than not, though cliques naturally develop around cultural commonalities. As Cecil Bridgewater, Travis Jackson, and others have suggested, the racial divide may only be an outward manifestation of *cultural* differences.[36] In general, jazz performers exhibit considerable tolerance for racial, sexual, and even interpersonal differences among colleagues when their musical collaborations are based on shared cultural aesthetics.

The avant-jazz community is an interesting case study because, although black performers and cultural aesthetics maintain a dominant presence, there is also a relatively large—when compared with mainstream styles—presence of performers who are female and/or members of other ethnic groups.[37] The audience, however, is mostly white, and mostly male (see later in this chapter). This discrepancy was evident on a solo set at ISSUE Project Room by African American alto saxophonist Matana Roberts.[38] With the exception of bassist Henry Grimes, the audience was all white. Mid-set, after she'd publicly acknowledged the presence of longtime scene supporter Margaret Davis Grimes and her renowned husband,[39] Roberts had the audience intone a background drone on an F# note while she sang Oscar Brown Jr.'s slave auction song "Bid 'Em In." In the song's lyric, a slave trader entices prospective buyers by describing a fifteen-year-old slave girl as "black but comely . . . young and ripe . . . full up front and ample behind . . . and well equipped"; "Strip her down Roy, let the gentlemen look," he shouts, boasting that she'll make "a darn good breeder" or "a fine lady's maid when she's properly whipped."[40] On the repeated choruses, Roberts enjoined the audience to sing along. An attractive woman in her midthirties, who acknowledges that "[for] a good portion of my shows, there are rarely people of color in the audience," she was fully aware of the irony of this scenario, one she'd repeated many times during a recent solo tour. "I forget how intense that is for some people," she explained, "and mid-verse I always have to stop and say, 'Listen, this is a *happy* song . . . because . . . without the bidding in of these people, I wouldn't be here right now enjoying my life." Hoping that listeners from diverse cultural backgrounds will understand the angst and pain embodied in her performance art, she asserted, "I'm not damning anyone, but I want to share *this*."[41] At the concert I attended, she amended the song's final lyric to, "Let's dedicate this moment to you and me." In this sense, Roberts's performance can be read as an appropriation of jazz's African American heritage to explore pan-cultural meanings.

In addition to its African American heritage, jazz acquires deeper meanings from its artistic legacy, the standards of musicianship, intelligence, individuality, and emotivity established by venerated forefathers (and -mothers). Indeed, many "gods" of the jazz pantheon enjoy a form of ancestor worship. Following the premature death of Charlie Parker, "Bird Lives" graffiti mushroomed on nightclub and subway walls throughout the city, the symbolic raising of a jazz Lazarus,[42] and Saint John Coltrane continues to be worshipped in weekly services of the African Orthodox church.[43] Referred to as Pops (or Satchmo), Prez, Duke, Bird, Diz, Lady Day, and Trane,[44] jazz's icons are living memories, their given names superfluous in conversations among initiates, their music preserved on seminal recordings and performed by "ghost bands"[45] or at tribute concerts. The aura of this pantheon infuses places like The Village Vanguard, a shrine where many greats once played, their portraits hung along its walls in remembrance, their names mentioned in onstage patter, the room itself a tourist magnet because of their ongoing legacy.[46] Developing players spend hours listening to these musical heroes, analyzing and emulating their styles, trying to absorb the influences even as they search for their own unique sound or "voice," while knowledgeable fans will hear and recognize these ancestral musical personalities in a developing artist's playing.[47]

Artists and audiences alike are acutely aware of jazz's musical legacy. Musicians are both inspired and intimidated by people like Charlie Parker and John Coltrane, feeling the "weight" of these paragon performers, hard-pressed to measure up to their virtuosic artistry and individuality. Gabriel Solis reports that many musicians don't like to perform tunes like Thelonious Monk's "'Round Midnight" because of "the panoply of voices associated with it": the performer's own, the composer's, Miles Davis's iconic recording, and others.[48] Veteran players that have had personal and musical relationships with jazz legends mention these with pride, a cherished part of their pedigree. As we've seen, Cecil Bridgewater has been strongly affected by the important artists who've mentored him and feels obligated to instill his students with respect for the music. He himself is now a father figure, a mentor to and role model for the next generation of torchbearers.

As jazz continues to extend its global reach, adopted and adapted in many parts of the world as a specialized yet flexible approach to music-making, outside cultures increasingly influence how local New Yorkers play the music. The city's extremely diverse demographics support many jazz scenes, often clustered around certain venues and/or artistic cliques and their support groups. Under the umbrella of "Latin jazz," for example, come a host of musical styles influenced by Afro-Cuban, Argentinean, Brazilian, Iberian American, and other cultures. New York's Israeli jazz scene has been strongly associated with certain immigrant musicians, but here too, ethnic, cultural, and geographic boundaries are blurred. Bassist/oudist Omer Avital, one of the scene's central figures, is of Moroccan and Yemenite heritage and has collaborated with many non-Israeli and non-Jewish musicians to develop a distinctive style that incorporates Israeli, North African, and Eastern Mediterranean musical traditions. Similarly, the highly eclectic downtown/avant-jazz scene displays strong influences of African American free jazz and Western European free-improv (nonidiomatic improvisation),[49] but ultimately resists categorization. All of these sub-scenes can trace their roots to certain aspects of the jazz "mainstream," but the proliferation of self-determined local practices has increasingly muddied the idea of a centralized tradition.

Although it's been embraced by many different cultures, jazz remains a heterosexual male-dominated domain, where men (including performers, industry professionals, and fans) far outnumber women,[50] and only a handful of gays have come out.[51] Out of a hundred-plus formal interviews conducted for this book, for instance, only twenty were given by women, and only seven of these aspired to careers as performers.[52] As in professional sports, jazz's gender hierarchies are particularly pronounced, and female performers, especially instrumentalists, continue to struggle for inclusion and respect. Although the standout successes of arranger/composer Maria Schneider or clarinetist Anat Cohen—both winners of numerous awards and critics' polls—might suggest that times are changing, the entrenched social structures and cultural conditioning that confront female musicians remain pervasive and tenacious. Gender politics in the downtown/avant-jazz community are relatively progressive in this respect, due to the tangible presence of women on stage and in the audience—yet even here their participation is limited. Harold Meiselman, an active fan (see Figure 6), observed that participants are "predominantly male"; Bruce Gallanter, proprietor of Downtown Music Gallery (see Figure 12), reported that his clientele is "mostly guys"; and Roberta DeNicola (see Figure 4), another active fan, stated: "It's basically a very male-oriented scene; I don't see women with these guys when they're playing, or hanging out with them, or coming with them." In spite of their smaller numbers, however, a select group of highly committed female fans, including DeNicola, Judy Balos (see Figure 7), Margaret Davis Grimes, Yuko Otomo (see Figure 5), and the late Stephanie Stone (see Figure 3), have been central figures in this scene, crucial to its vitality and to its sense of what "good" music is. Their voices, included here, will provide a much needed counterpoint to the historic prevalence of male perspectives.

JAZZ IN NEW YORK AND NEW YORK IN JAZZ

The density and intensity of jazz activity in the city is unique and nonpareil, with legions of accomplished artists in residence, over eight hundred active performance venues,[53] and continual recording sessions, all located in a geographically compact area. Although the growth of distinctive musical scenes elsewhere has diminished its predominance, New York remains a magnet for cutting-edge artists and dedicated enthusiasts, a prime conduit for jazz's global cultural flow.[54] In spite of New York's singular status in popular perceptions, it must be emphasized that the city's many live jazz sub-scenes are ultimately a *local* phenomenon, specific to individual people and places. As such, observations made here are not intended to present stereotyped views of jazz practices in general or privilege New York's preeminence but should be read as a highly qualitative selection of individual oral histories and case studies that offer complementary insights into various facets of local jazz-making.

In a city of economic extremes, where drastic class disparities coexist in close proximity, jazz forms a sound track to diverse lifestyles. Bassist Bob Cunningham (see Figure 24) described how the music nimbly accommodates the spectrum of New York society:

> People from almost every walk of life come to hear jazz: you get the clergy, businessmen, people from Wall Street—or from *the* street [*laughs*]—pimps, prostitutes, gangsters. That's one of the beautiful things about music. I've played in sewers, so to speak, lousy little holes in some basement, all boarded up and no ventilation, because it's an illegal spot, and people are drinking, enjoying the music, and doing whatever else they want to do to have fun. And I'd leave there and go to 59th Street or 57th Street, get in a little private elevator, and go up to someone's apartment in a penthouse. On the street level it might be sweltering hot, like August in New York—it's rough. And it's amazing how, when you get up to the penthouse, there's a breeze like you get on the beach, blowing the tablecloths off the table, and the butler has to put clips on the table, nail everything down, and put door stops to keep them from slamming.

Like Cunningham's elevator, jazz traverses New York's lower and upper classes, from subterranean dives to the tops of skyscrapers, providing everything from danceable beats at boisterous events to sonic wallpaper in reserved milieux. "The music takes you through almost every echelon of life," Cunningham concludes: "So you meet all kinds of people. We played for presidents, politicians, and so on and so forth, and at the same time I've played for underworld people, and played in church, the *same day!*" The flexible, spontaneous nature of the music allows it to adapt to and connect with a variety of audience communities.

New York's historical prominence, multicultural demographics, industrial infrastructure, and compact geography all combine to support thriving local live music scenes. Jazz musicians—everyone from established veterans to up-and-comers—move to and through the city in a steady stream: gigging, recording, jamming, networking, and going out to hear their peers play. "They're all here," observed keyboardist Ryan Weaver, referring to the top-shelf players, "and if they're not here, they stop through here." "There's not one night in a year that you can't hear a major jazz superstar playing in this city, never one night where you can't choose between, usually, four or five," noted critic Gary Giddins (see Figure 16); "There are still seven or eight major, major clubs here—they *all* have stars." Manhattan Island probably has the highest concentration of jazz venues and performance spaces anywhere, roughly twenty-eight per square mile.[55] Ranging from premiere establishments like Jazz at Lincoln Center and Carnegie Hall complexes, to iconic clubs like the Village Vanguard and Blue Note, to nonprofit performance spaces and lesser-known local hangouts, there are settings to sustain all manner of sub-scenes and artistic cliques. One constant, however, is change: venues continuously open, close, relocate, and initiate or terminate jazz programming.

The city's proliferation of artists and venues likewise attracts all manner of listeners, from active enthusiasts to casual tourists, often seated together in the same room. Audience members also typically include publicists, critics, photographers, and other music professionals, as well as venue staff—all habitués of a scene by virtue of their occupations. Many (but not necessarily all) of these jazz jobbers are avid fans as well. They form a persistent and familiar presence on the scene, readily recognizable to other denizens. Amateur fans, in contrast, typically cannot afford to frequent the pricier clubs but can afford to put in regular appearances at more economically priced venues, such as those with lower overheads featuring less expensive artists. Neighborhood clubs may attract patrons who live nearby, while venues catering to niche audiences will draw fans of particular artists or musical styles. While jazz undoubtedly plays well in concert halls and other formal environments, such large-scale events limit opportunities for artist-audience interactions and generally do not attract a regular, identifiable fan base. Small, informal venues, in contrast, are more conducive to social intercourse: close proximity permits eye contact between performers and listeners; a more relaxed atmosphere encourages audiences to express visual and audio feedback, or even to dance; and the greater chance of seeing familiar faces fosters a sense of community.[56]

The so-called New York jazz scene is not a single, unified community, but many separate and overlapping communities, a multitude of porously bordered, constantly changing micro-scenes and social circles. Where, then, are the "regulars"? Although out-of-town and overseas tourists make up a major part of the audience in the most prominent Manhattan clubs, they are only familiar as an anonymous populace, not as individuals. Jazz professionals are a consistent presence at high-profile events but less likely to show up at neighborhood clubs or at restaurants and other low-profile performance venues. And, while it is not difficult to recognize certain club owners and other professionals, familiar faces you can count on to be there, regular fans are far more difficult to identify—with one very important exception: the most visible, most active amateur fans congregate around the downtown/avant-jazz scene.

"Downtown music," so named in the early sixties to differentiate it from contemporary classical music featured "uptown" at Lincoln Center,[57] is a broad, ambiguous category historically referring to New York composer/performers working within a cluster of avant-garde performance-art genres including free improvisation, electronica, deejaying, aleatoric composition, progressive rock, contemporary classical music, multimedia, improvisatory dance and video, and sound painting.[58] Jazz-related genres falling under this umbrella have been variously labeled free jazz, avant-garde jazz, ecstatic jazz (European), free improv(isation), avant-jazz, experimental jazz, new (improvised) music, and so forth. Such terms are elastic and somewhat interchangeable because artists and projects in this arena typically resist pat labels. Tellingly, Manny Maris (see Figure 13) once ran a record store named Lunch for Your Ears that displayed merchandise in only two categories: "Instrumental" and "Vocal." If downtown music is difficult to define, the live music scene supporting it is not, populated by a small but highly visible and constant group of people who regularly gather at a handful of venues specializing in this music.[59]

I use the term *avant-jazz* as a shorthand to denote the music associated with the live downtown music scene: "avant" because it tries above all to achieve something "new," *sui generis*, and of-its-moment; something that will—paradoxically—defy categorization; and "jazz" because it is generally traceable to the music of Ornette Coleman, Cecil Taylor (see cover painting), Sun Ra, Albert Ayler, late-period John Coltrane, and other free jazz musicians. The downtown scene is also influenced by avant-garde music and free improvisation, as developed by New York artists such as Bill Laswell, George Lewis, Pauline Oliveros, Terry Riley, Elliott Sharpe, and John Zorn; by members of the Chicago-based Association for the Advancement of Creative Musicians (AACM); and by European improvisers such as Derek Bailey, Han Bennink, Peter Brötzmann, Misha Mengelberg, Evan Parker, and members of the AMM group. These artists have tended to eschew swing rhythms, blues aesthetics, and other traditional elements of jazz in favor of radical experimentation, though this is not always the case. In general, avant-jazz emphasizes spontaneous improvisation over precomposition[60] (though predetermined structures or improvisational concepts may be used), and fans overwhelmingly agree that it's best experienced in live performance rather than through recorded media.[61]

Communitywide social interactions and performance-based artist-audience interactions are important to any staging of jazz, but these elements are particularly pronounced in the avant-jazz scene. Characterized by irregularity, high sonic density, and a lack of obvious referents to rhythm, melody, and harmony, avant-jazz often sounds noisy—even harsh or nonmusical—to those who haven't developed the taste or tolerance for it. It demands a lot of its audience, quickly weeding out casual listeners to leave a nucleus of dedicated aficionados. In this tight-knit sub-scene, a core group of extremely active and committed fans have typically attended over a hundred shows a year each over the course of two, three, or more decades, a level of amateur group participation unmatched by any other jazz community in the city.[62] Here, in contrast to the city's many other jazz sub-scenes, the audience is an identifiable, palpable presence that profoundly influences the onstage action, a critical factor in any performance's success.

Tourists and fans of mainstream jazz styles are typically infrequent or sporadic concertgoers. For example, in a review of his 1995 study based on the NEA's Survey for Public Participation in the Arts, Scott DeVeaux noted that only about 10 percent of the North American adult population attends a jazz show during the year, and that "the real hard-core [fans], those who go to hear jazz at least once a month, form a tiny fraction of this total, probably less than 0.5 percent."[63] These relatively low attendance levels mean that many jazz fans are not likely to be recognized as regulars by other scenesters, though there are rare exceptions like "Jazz Judy" Balos, who can often be spotted at many different types of jazz performances around New York City.[64] Although I was able to identify and interview a few occasional and/or nonlocal concertgoers—e.g., I consulted a trio of English fans taking one of Gordon Polatnick's jazz tours (see Figure 26)—the prime focus of this book is on active concertgoers, whether they are amateur fans or music professionals, or some combination of the two. In sections that deal with fans, as well as those that deal with interactions between artists and audiences during performances, much of the commentary is dominated by denizens of the avant-jazz scene—a result of their extremely prolific concert attendance. Elsewhere in the book, however, the focus moves through a number of jazz's sub-scenes, avant-jazz and otherwise, to provide a broader sampling of the ideas and activities of venue operators, music professionals, and other active participants and scene supporters (see Figure 27).

*   *   *

How then to interpret and understand the communitywide participation that produces the shared meanings and expressions of jazz? In reconciling the diverse viewpoints of the various professional and amateur listeners who congregate in jazz performance spaces—heard here in a mixed chorus of distinctive individual voices—a clearer picture of the intricacies and intangibles of jazz-making will hopefully emerge. It should soon be evident that the rapport established among participants during improvised performances closely models the collaborative social transactions taking place in local jazz scenes.

LISTENING TO JAZZ

What someone hears is in large part determined by *how* one hears. To the extent that a listener is actively engaged in the perception of music and in the construction of musical meanings, he or she is an actor, a *performer*, of music. Even in the privacy of one's home or headphones, a listener performs by exacting order and symbolic value from auditory vibrations and by self-identifying with these sounds. In a second, more obvious, sense the act of listening becomes a performance when it is *presented* in the public domain, as when jazz fans gather at concerts—a subject to be further explored in the following chapter. This chapter highlights some of the ways in which individual listeners interface with, understand, and thereby appreciate improvised performances.

HEARING THE "FACTS"

The subject of musical perception and, more specifically, the role of listener agency in the act of musical perception, is complex. Some theories maintain there are objective musical "facts" to be heard and recognized,[1] others suggest that musical understanding is situated and subjective, while others argue that meanings are co-constructed by both communicators and interpreters. In some sense, all of these explanations are relevant to how jazz is heard and construed.

Most people can agree on certain characteristics or properties of a given performance, such as the name of a song, the literal meaning of its lyrics (if any), the rhythmic grouping of its beats (though a listener may impose alternate groupings),[2] the pitch sequence of a melody, the harmonic progression of a composition (though here again we're on shaky ground),[3] or other specifiable musical features. Because jazz musicians usually improvise together, making split-second choices in response to each other's playing, they must attune to any operative parameters such as key area, harmonic progression, and rhythmic structure. Audience members, especially those with musical training, may listen for and be aware of these features, while others will not—not that they necessarily need to. Many listeners can identify a tune like "Over the Rainbow," even when its melody and/or harmony have been radically reinterpreted, if they are provided with sufficient "clues." On the other hand, there is always some leeway for individuals to derive different interpretations of the same event. If someone is daydreaming or under the influence of drugs during a concert, for example, his or her perception of it may be significantly preempted or altered by internal psychological processes.

Even when we concede the existence of certain basic musical facts, matters soon become more complicated when the facts themselves are fuzzy. Most jazz performance is purely instrumental, so the music doesn't directly refer to anything, and therefore meanings must derive from the association of musical sounds with other objects and concepts, a highly individual and unpredictable process.[4] How does G♭ minor sound: happy, sad, both, or neither? How would you characterize a chord combining a "dark" minor third with a "bright" major sixth or seventh scale degree? How much dissonance is pleasurable, tolerable, or intolerable? The crux of the issue lies in the difficulty/impossibility of translating musical sound into words.[5] Using speech to describe music implies that musical meanings are, at best, imprecisely and incompletely conveyed through language and, furthermore, that there are fundamental semiotic and philosophical biases inherent in the very use of language, but it does not therefore invalidate a listener's perceptions and interpretations.

Some theorists would argue that looking for meaning in jazz is like shopping for apples in the orange bin. At one extreme, music philosopher Peter Kivy maintains that meaning can be expressed only through language,[6] which effectively removes most jazz, a mostly instrumental music, from the equation. Many contend that music derives its meanings from its associations with other objects and events.[7] Ethnomusicologist Thomas Turino suggests that listeners not only connect music to particular people, places, and experiences in their lives but often perceive music as a product of these factors, as when a screeching high note during a saxophone solo is assumed to embody the peaking emotions of the improvising musician.[8] The protean and relational qualities

21

afforded to musical sounds through these various associations accounts for the many distinct, even incongruent, ways that individuals engage with and derive meanings from jazz. To be sure, experienced listeners invariably develop subtle and complex understandings of the music, even if, paradoxically, they are unable to articulate these awarenesses. To appreciate their insights, one must listen "between the lines" for meanings indirectly stated, perhaps unconsciously understood.[9]

Musical elements that resist analysis and classification include timbre (the "color" of sound), nonstandard pitches or tunings, and rhythmic flexibility. While the pitch of a "blue note"[10] or the placement of "swung" eighth-notes[11] can be objectively measured,[12] timbre is much more difficult to quantify; it is usually described in metaphorical terms that are, by definition, imprecise and highly subjective. Furthermore, these elements are always situated in a specific musical environment. Hence a musician can only "rush" or "drag" (i.e., play ahead of or behind the beat, respectively) in relation to a commonly established pulse. Avant-jazz generally avoids or eliminates the harmonic and rhythmic cycles prevalent in mainstream jazz; melodic continuity may be deliberately obtuse, and emergent structures are likely to depend on group interaction, cues, and/or timbral manipulation. Indeed, the aesthetic impact of avant-jazz is partly predicated upon its ability to resist "parsing" via the grammar and syntax of conventional musical analysis. A few analysts have used computer-generated diagrams to map and analyze changes in sound density and complexity during musical performances,[13] but these and other valuations add little to our intuitive understandings of and emotional responses to the musical phenomena in question. Despite the difficulty of describing these attributes, however, experienced listeners can often agree that a particular performance was "soulful" or "swinging," suggesting that these qualities are, if not measurable, at least observable and, to some extent, commonly understood within certain communities.

In order to respond swiftly and appropriately to emergent developments in a group improvisation, jazz musicians must cultivate their aural skills—they need to know what they're hearing—along with "ear-to-hand" coordination (i.e., the ability to instantly reproduce any overheard sounds on their instrument).[14] If a pianist plays some unusual chords behind a solo, for example, the soloist may want to alter his or her improvised melody line to fit the new harmonies. Advanced musicians can often pick out quite sophisticated elements of music, particularly if they've "woodshedded" (practiced) these same ideas on their instruments. The acquisition of these requisite skills may predispose them to listen analytically, even when they are "off duty" (not performing), just as people respond reflexively to the sound of their own name.[15] A harmony instructor at Berklee College of Music once joked that his wife won't go to movies with him anymore because he invariably gets distracted by the sound track. Listening competency doesn't depend on formal musical training, however, as many experienced nonmusicians develop considerable aural acumen and fluency without necessarily being able to label, analyze, or discuss what they "know."

As jazz artists develop new forms and approaches, listeners must find ways to track these changes. Those who try to follow a song's form by counting beats, feeling metrical subdivisions internally, or silently singing the melody might be baffled by the latest innovations. For example, musicians associated with the M-Base collective[16] often use through-composed rhythmic claves (or "drum chants")[17] to structure their compositions and improvisations, and though it may be possible for a listener to hear these chants as symmetric cycles of evenly spaced pulses, such perceptions are not necessarily in sync with how M-Base musicians conceive of and generate their music. Traditional listening techniques may not "work" for jazz's more radical developments, which require new modes of attention and perception.

CREATING CONTEXTS

The saying "I don't know anything about art, but I know what I like" implies that even casual or indifferent listeners *do* understand something of what they hear, even if they have difficulty articulating what that is. To complicate matters, people's ways of comprehending jazz vary considerably. In addition to the musical content (or "facts"), their perceptions are informed by the various contexts of listening. This ability to connect music to past and present experiences enables listeners to create individualized meanings for improvised jazz.

While some forms of communication are one-sided, as when someone reads a book, music performances are often mutually influential exchanges between actors and "actees." Musical perception is not a hard-wired mechanism of the human nervous system because it varies with focus of attention, historical context, situated social conduct, and other factors. Consider Rubin's Goblet: with effort a viewer can consciously switch between two mutually incompatible images (either a goblet, or two faces in profile), a condition Gestalt psychologists designate as multistability. If perception is active, then listening to and participating in music is an *act*, a practice, a performance. This isn't meant to imply that each listener reinvents reality but emphasizes the situated nature of his or her musical experiences.

Because they occur within a broader social arena, where collective and historical forces are at play, individual acts of perception may have important ramifications. Although large-scale social structures and politico-economic forces may appear hegemonic, local activities can and do influence these formations. Individual actions, though heavily informed by and mediated through the past and present dimensions of society, may effect both deliberate and inadvertent changes in present and future societies.[18] The plurality of perception insures that musical traditions in general and musical performances in particular are always the collective production of individual participants—the musicians who play and the audience members who listen. How then do jazz listeners exercise their individuality of perception? And by extension, how are perceptual acts made manifest, or *performed*, in broader social contexts? Finally, to what extent do shared understandings in jazz communities mediate the ways individual participants hear and interpret the music?

To better understand and appreciate jazz, listeners develop unique aesthetic criteria, self-taught vernaculars based on their perceptual "toolkit" and past experiences. Fans learn about jazz by attending concerts and through other, less immediate sources such as recordings, YouTube videos, podcasts, radio and television programs, album liner notes, fan and trade magazines, internet blogs and interest sites, and conversations with fellow fans. Utilizing these resources, listeners acquire knowledge of artists, recordings, and repertoire; increase their sensitivity to the emotional, psychological, and metacommunicative aspects of jazz performances; and enhance their ability to detect other context-dependent cues.

Knowledge of repertoire—whether that refers to the canon of frequently played standards or to original compositions associated with particular artists—gives listeners an important frame of reference for understanding performances. Much of traditional, mainstream, bebop, and many contemporary jazz styles is built on the rhythmic, melodic, and harmonic structure of specific songs, most featuring a recognizable melody and a regularly cycling harmonic progression (the "changes") that accompanies it and serves as a model for improvised solos.[19] Familiarity with previous performances or recordings of a particular song lets listeners compare and assess live performances of it: How radical or conservative is the interpretation? How do the performers express uniqueness, creativity, and immediacy in their rendition of the song? Furthermore, knowing the tune allows listeners to track improvisations by humming the melody or singing the words in their heads, repeating this theme for each complete harmonic cycle (or "chorus").[20] On commonly used chord progressions like George Gershwin's "I Got Rhythm," listeners can superimpose either the original song or a new one written to the same harmonies (e.g., "The Flintstones Theme"). Lujira Cooper (see Figure 17) uses standard melodies to map her listening experiences: "Some musicians like to get off on these long solos [and] you forget what the melody is, or they play songs you've never heard, and it sounds like noise. Some guys'll do a solo, and it's long, and it's involved, but they'll give you a hint of the melody." On several occasions I have overheard audience members humming snatches of a tune during a solo, demonstrating not only that they can correctly imagine the melody in relation to the harmonic accompaniment, but also that they can accurately monitor the song form during an improvisation.[21] Standard songs thus provide an anchor of familiarity: a point of departure for the musicians and a point of reference for listeners.

One of the most basic ways listeners contextualize a jazz performance is by following its progress through the arrangement (or "roadmap"). A typical template might look like this: 1) intro section; 2) statement of the theme (or "head"); 3) sequence of solos, each a chorus or more in length; 4) "trading fours" (four-bar solos alternating between the drummer and other musicians); 5) reprise of the theme; and 6) outro section, often a vamp or a triple repeat (or "tag") based on the tune's terminal harmonies.[22] Despite many variations on this prototype, its general form is consistent enough to provide listeners with the musical equivalent of a narrative arc.

Listeners may also recognize the stylistic precursors of and influences on an artist's style. For example, two of the most copied tenor saxophonists of their time were Coleman Hawkins and Lester Young. Experienced fans can usually hear the differences between their styles and may also recognize the influence of Hawkins in Sonny Rollins's playing or the influence of Young in Stan Getz's, though both of these younger tenor players eventually developed distinctive styles of their own.[23] Some listeners can identify artists on an unknown recording purely by their "sound" (a combination of their musical style and instrumental timbre). *DownBeat* magazine's long-running "Blindfold Test" challenges musicians—presumably the experts—to do just that. The tone of John Coltrane's stark, vibratoless tenor saxophone, Miles Davis's Harmonmuted (*sans* stem) trumpet, or Wes Montgomery's thumb-picked guitar (often voiced in octaves) are iconic sonic signatures that knowledgeable fans recognize after only a few notes or phrases, though the proliferation of skillful imitators makes this ever trickier.

In addition to their knowledge of songs, recordings, and musicians, listeners create contexts for understanding jazz by observing the emotional, psychological, and metacommunicative (e.g., performer body language, staging, and so forth) aspects of performances. Critic Gary Giddins attested that he responds first and foremost to the emotional impact of music, while Lujira Cooper appreciates the physicality and visual spectacle of jazz making: "There was an upright bass player—I'd just sit there and watch his *hands*! I didn't even know half the time, what he may have been playing, but I was just so *mesmerized*, because it was a fascination just to see somebody's hands; they're so fluid, and they just move so nicely." Jazz tour guide Gordon Polatnick takes in the total ambiance of a performance space: "Half of the fun for me, as a fan, is the atmosphere and the element of possibilities. Am I walking in off the street? Or are people shouting back at the band?" Polatnick steers clients to informal neighborhood venues where audience participation is encouraged and "just about anything goes." Each of these participants privileges distinctive reference points—emotional impact, graphic imagery, or a room's "vibe"—to frame their listening experiences.

Instrumentalists develop kinesthetic understandings of music they hear. For example, pianists who've seen videos of Thelonious Monk playing right-hand accompaniment chords while his left hand crosses over to peck out treble melodies may be able to recognize and visualize this unorthodox technique while listening to his recordings. Similarly, horn and woodwind players are alert to certain musical ideas that lay well on their horns or "trick" effects made possible by alternate fingerings. Guitarists using vibrato, slides, hammer-ons, pull-offs, electronic signal processors, and other instrumental techniques will have a physical familiarity of how these sounds are realized. "I have an arsenal of immediate classifications for guitar players," noted critic David Adler (see Figure 18), "'cause I've heard lots and lots of them and I have spent a lot of time myself investigating jazz guitar and the sound and the style and whatever. So I can really peg a guitar player very easily: 'He's *this* kind of player, or *that* kind of player.'"

The ability to recognize repertoire, follow a performance's dramatic curve, identify an artist's stylistic influences and signature sound, attend to extramusical cues, and form kinesthetic images of sound are all measures of a listener's knowledge, experience, and aesthetic discernment of the jazz idiom. Accumulated expertise with these perceptual tools allows individuals to compare what they're hearing with what they've already heard and assimilated, adding to the depth and sophistication of their subjective impressions. As Ralph Ellison observed, "[T]here's no inherent problem which prohibits understanding [jazz] but the assumptions brought to it."[24] Consequently, any active and attentive listener can develop meaningful modes for engaging with jazz, the possibilities as unlimited as his or her imagination.

SOUNDS OF SURPRISE

What makes a jazz performance "good" or "bad"? Beyond specific musical features and associated contexts, what other aspects do listeners respond to? How do individual perceptions engender critical reflection and/or emotional responses? Such questions target an audience's sensitivities, tastes, and values, the character and quality of which vary dramatically among individuals and social cohorts. Furthermore, these criteria and orientations may change in response to new circumstances, evolving tastes, or broadscale sociocultural changes. There are no absolute standards, but jazz participants often concur that certain parameters are of paramount importance, including technical proficiency, intellectual interest, originality, emotional impact, unpredictability, and immediacy. Jazz's artistic impact thus hinges on a balance of contradictory factors: tradition and innovation, order and chaos, consistency and surprise.[25]

The term *virtuoso* is so bandied about in jazz contexts that one editor extirpates it from his newspaper's articles on principle.[26] Nevertheless, like Western European and Indian classical musics, jazz requires considerable training and skill, and contemporary musicians are inevitably measured against previously established standards. Benefiting from a comprehensive educational system and an explosion of recorded resources via internet file-sharing, new generations of musicians arrive on the scene better prepared to handle the technical challenges of the art form, many developing formidable skill-sets (or "chops").[27] Some artists develop extended techniques: vocalists incorporate yodeling, Tuvan-style throat singing, horn imitations, and/or digital looping devices; instrumentalists find unusual ways to vary their tone and timbre. Many audiences have come to expect adept craftsmanship, even virtuosity, in performers, typically manifested by the ability to play complex ideas higher, faster, and louder.[28] While many fans respond positively to this "sports" ethos, wowed by spectacular technical displays, others view technique as merely a means to express other aspects of the jazz art form. In avant-jazz and other forms of experimental improvisation, the manifestation of virtuosity may be less obvious. Thus, while Ornette Coleman was roundly criticized in some quarters for his "harsh" tone and "faulty" intonation, other listeners have responded to his musical charisma, a type of emotional virtuosity that, for some, supersedes instrumental facility.

A dense, content-rich music, jazz stimulates intellectual appreciation on many levels, permitting trained and/or experienced listeners to assess the cleverness and creativity of a performance. Any of the musical elements discussed earlier can be criteria for aesthetic judgments. For example, a reinterpreted melody, reharmonized chord progression, or superimposed polyrhythm all demonstrate an artist's ingenuity. Original compositions are valued for their structural elegance or the interrelationship of their melody, harmony, and lyrics. Improvisers are appreciated for clever use of musical sequences, quotations from other compositions, polyrhythmic variations, juxtaposed harmonic and nonharmonic passages, manipulation of intervallic structures, rigorous melodic development, and other aptitudes. The more listeners know about underlying improvisational models, the more they can assess the degree to which performances conform to such models or introduce innovations. Some fans will monitor how soloists "make the changes" (i.e., improvise melodies harmonically appropriate to the underlying chords); others prefer improvisers who bend or break "the rules" in artful ways. Artists working on jazz's experimental fringe often use highly esoteric concepts for composing and improvising—John Zorn, for example, has used numerology and classical music techniques like retrograde and inversion in his compositions[29]—though these may be difficult or impossible for listeners to aurally identify without recourse to liner notes or other contextualizing information.

Many jazz audiences put a high premium on originality. While performers are obliged to know and honor the tradition, they are further expected to develop a personal "voice," or signature style, whether that entails innovation within extant praxes, or better yet developing a new personalized praxis. Practitioners of New Orleans jazz, swing, bebop, and members of the neoclassicist movement generally share a conservative, repertory-centered ethos that strives for stylistic accuracy and authenticity. Although such retrospective approaches might seem to stifle originality, musicians working in these subgenres express their individuality through spontaneous improvisations and original compositions. As jazz continues to develop, the challenge to invent new concepts and approaches escalates, placing pressure on up-and-coming artists to generate original means and material. Many have responded by looking to other musical cultures for ideas and inspiration, blending and fusing these influences with the tenets and techniques of jazz to form hybrid musical styles.

Listeners who place high value on novelty and innovation are likely to look to jazz's experimental fringes. Although many avant-jazz fans reported that they listen to recordings of earlier jazz styles, most much prefer to see "new" music live. Harold Meiselman maintained that he's not interested in seeing a musician who plays like Sonny Rollins: "You're not going to play what *he* does better than he did it, so do something *different*; do something creative. I don't think jazz should be a repertory music." Margaret Davis Grimes, who calls her favorite music "ecstatic jazz," holds similar views: "I *love* old-fashioned jazz, but I don't want to hear somebody playing it *now*, the same stuff, and try to make it the same, because it's not. It was new, it was original—*then*—and now it's not. And I don't wanna hear it! [*laughs*]." Davis Grimes is drawn to "great improvising musicians of the prophetic, as opposed to *pathetic* [*laughs*], level—as opposed to retreads and imitators and corporate, bureaucratic-approved, system endorsers and endorse*ments*."[30] Record retailer Manny Maris uses the term "ironic mode" to describe work that revisits previously explored styles, arguing that such an approach sacrifices a sense of immediacy.[31] Longtime fan Peter Cox rejected labels on principle, subscribing to Duke Ellington's adage that there are only two types of music, good and bad:[32] "I try to have my mind open to all sorts of different musics; some of them I might reject, but at least I've tried to listen to it. So I'm happy listening to Ornette and Cecil, as I am listening to Louie, Fletcher Henderson, and Duke Ellington.[33] It's good or it's bad. They all have a sense of creativity—that's the most important thing—[and] are contributing, are creating this great art form which we know as jazz." For these avant-jazz fans especially, originality and creativity take precedence over technical and intellectual aspects of music.

But what's "new," and *how* new is it? Avant-jazz, hypothetically unconstrained by restrictive improvisational models, nevertheless is sometimes criticized for sounding noisy, random, predictable, monotonous, or too similar to the pioneering work of Ornette Coleman, Cecil Taylor, Albert Ayler, and others. On the other hand, many mainstream artists experimenting with emergent technologies, unusual instrumentation, multimedia presentations, novel algorithms for improvisation and composition, or the music of etic musi-cultures have developed distinctive individual sounds and styles. Some players display a chameleonlike penchant for experimentation and change, seeming to generate novel approaches with every new release. Miles Davis, an outstanding example of this, helped develop cool, modal, jazz-rock fusion and Third Stream styles, as well as new paradigms for group interaction.[34] The rampant eclecticism and mercurial curiosity of some contemporary performers make it difficult to pigeonhole them as uptown or downtown, mainstream or avant-jazz.[35] The perceived newness of a musical offering therefore hinges on the aesthetic criteria of individual artists and listeners.

Like all musics, jazz has the ability to evoke psychological states and trigger emotional responses. Exactly how this is accomplished varies among musicians and stylistic clusters of jazz. Performers drawing on African American traditions, for example, endeavor to suffuse their audiences with the soul of blues and spirituality of gospel; others try to move listeners with compellingly propulsive Latin or electronic grooves. Jazz singers communicate through the subtle sounds of their voice and the intimate delivery of the lyrics, while a sensitively rendered instrumental ballad can induce audible silences in a crowded room. Fans may be aroused by flashy displays of technical prowess, by bold inharmonic passages that eventually resolve to a tonality, by humorous inserted quotations, or by instruments emulating human speech. They can also pick up emotional cues from artists' facial expressions, body language, and other environmental factors. For example, the audience at a concert Bobby Hutcherson gave to benefit the Jazz Foundation of America[36] was audibly amused by his onstage shtick, which included exaggerated facial mugging and pretending to fumble for the "right" notes with his vibraphone mallets.

For many listeners, the emotional impact of a performance takes precedence over its technical or intellectual dimensions. Avant-jazz fan Stephanie Stone criticized Steve Coleman's work, often touted for its innovative compositional and improvisational approaches, as "head music," explaining that although she found it "very interesting, that somebody thought of this thing, and it's very bright, it doesn't move me, all—except it's interesting." What "gets to" her, she explained, is "what comes out of your heart and what comes out of your gut." Her husband Irving (see Figure 3), an extremely active and influential fan on the downtown scene,[37] agreed: "I'm not impressed with technique, really." He recounted hearing pianist Oscar Peterson at Carnegie Hall: "I sat through an hour of [it]. I know what he's doing; I understand what he's doing. It doesn't get to me." Tellingly, Stone held even less respect for Peterson's fans. By way of comparison he championed Ike Rodgers, a "primitive" musician who "probably plays about three notes, and *can't play* by any standards," but nonetheless delivers emotionally. "It's what I hear," he clarified, "it's what it makes me feel, that matters. I don't care how you know how to do it."

For many fans, the most crucial attributes of jazz presentation are surprise and immediacy, the sense that artists and audience have assembled for a one-time-only, who-knows-what-will-happen-next event. Because jazz is predicated on improvisation, each performance is unique, with a high degree of spontaneity and unexpectedness inherent in its realization. Audience members take part in this unfolding as witnesses to a voyage of discovery, coauthors of the collective experience. Although it's possible to isolate the bits and pieces of a particular performance—the various musical elements in their broader contexts—successful jazz ultimately eludes facile analyses: what is produced isn't nearly so important as *how* it was produced. In other words, it's all about process, not products; about delivery, not goods delivered.

Listeners have differing tolerance levels—and predilections for—unfamiliar and/or random elements in jazz performances. Surprise, like humor, is created when audience expectations are courted, then thwarted.[38] The less ordered the music, the less capacity it has to surprise audiences, because there are fewer established patterns to disrupt.[39] Similarly, overly dense and complex music risks frustrating listeners who can't comprehend its ordering principles (i.e., it's not random, but it might as well be).[40] In contrast, highly repetitive, predictable music is not surprising either and may bore some listeners. Effective jazz, like any other art form, contains a balance of foreign and familiar materials, though different styles prioritize these elements in different ways. Relative to other jazz genres, so-called "smooth jazz" is fairly repetitive, while avant-jazz is more variable. New Orleans/traditional jazz, bebop, and other repertory styles are both ordered and complex, with the chief elements of surprise occurring during improvised solos. Interestingly, many of the long-term fans I spoke with—though they typically expressed affection for all different kinds of jazz—had, over time, developed higher tolerance for its more radical forms.

The element of surprise contributes to the overall immediacy of a performance, the quality of here-and-nowness. Artists can achieve this on several scales: writing original compositions and developing new approaches, playing with different combinations of musicians or in changing circumstances, and finding fresh ways to improvise on a gig-by-gig, song-by-song, moment-to-moment basis. When performing recent compositions or developing new ideas, musicians are still in the process of discovering the material for themselves, experimenting with the form, thinking (musically) on their feet—and fans may be especially curious to follow their progress. Different combinations of musicians—whether a pickup group formed for a one-off gig, a combo formed for a short tour, or an ongoing association between players—also generate excitement because each new reconfiguration changes the interpersonal and musical chemistry in unpredictable ways. Subbing out the third trombone chair on a big-band date is not as drastic as replacing the drummer in a trio, but each participant contributes to the overall sound. Musicians who have sustained long-term professional relationships, such as Keith Jarrett, Gary Peacock, and Jack DeJohnette, become like old married couples who can finish each others' sentences, interacting on intuitive, seemingly telepathic levels. On the other hand, too much familiarity can lead to routinized performances. In the avant-jazz scene, for example, musicians may regroup frequently or forego rehearsing in order to enhance the unpredictability of each performance.

Avant-jazz fans like Margaret Davis Grimes embrace the indeterminate and inchoate qualities of live music: "If I know the next three notes, I get up and go home. I don't mean the melody, but the next three things the musician's going to do in an improvisation. And there's way, way, way too much of that. And that's what the system *loves*, because it's not dangerous anymore, it's not threatening anymore. Art is supposed to upset the status quo—that's what it's *for*. It's not supposed to *be* the status quo." Inveterate concertgoer Peter Cox savored the element of unpredictability: "And that, to me, is really what it's all about—the sound of surprise—because you never know what's going to happen. It could really go someplace else, but you don't really know, and to me that's the beauty of it. It's not stereotyped in any way, shape, or form." He admired artists who could avoid falling into ruts: "You're listening to a musician like Ras Moshe one night, and you say, 'Oh, I know what this guy's going to do,' but then the next night he could do something completely off-the-wall. It's still gonna to be recognizable Ras Moshe, but it's gonna be a bit of a different take on it." Harold Meiselman opined that jazz should be "forever evolving and looking for new connections and creative outlets. Certain things just become predictable to listen to, for *me*—not that there can't be tremendous creativity and things of interest within chord changes—but it just doesn't engage me in the same way as a player who goes outside the chord changes, or in and out, or totally out." He conceded that even "out" playing can become predictable. In contrast to these avant-jazz aficionados, more conservatively minded fans may have difficulty embracing the radical tenets of free improvisation.

The quality of immediacy in a jazz performance may acquire extramusical dimensions, a sense that something deep, even spiritual, is happening. When artists and audiences are attuned in time and place, when both are willing to take chances, to leave their respective comfort zones, the experience can become a collectively mediated meditation, a ritualistic communion. When experimental composer/producer/saxophonist John Zorn once queried Irving Stone why he was continually "chasing the dog" (going to hundreds of concerts), Stone replied, "I'm looking for the perfect set," musing, "It's never gonna happen, but I'm willing to keep trying." On a similar note, Stone related a conversation he'd had with violinist Mark Feldman: "One night at a gig he says, 'What do you think of my new bow?' I said, 'Uhh?' He says, 'You mean you can't tell the difference between a two-thousand-dollar bow and a hundred-dollar bow?' I said, 'Uh *huh*, but I also can tell if you're playing or you're full of shit.'" "Right, that's the criterion, really," Stephanie Stone concurred; "That's what *matters*." Irving concluded; "As somebody once said: 'You want *blood*; that's what *you* want.' *Yes!* I want blood." Stone's elusive "perfect set" and his thirst for "blood" epitomizes the holy grail of creative immediacy sought for and exalted by these avant-jazz fans.

*   *   *

In New York City's local jazz scenes, professionals, amateurs, and various other "nonperformers" listen to recordings and gather in venues to participate in improvised performances. Jazz "speaks" to these people in many ways, on many levels. Closely attuned to the intellectual, emotional, and imaginative dimensions of performances, their most meaningful experiences are derived not from the music's products but from its process, the journey taken rather than the destination attained. They want to go somewhere they've never been before, with plenty of surprises along the way.

DEVELOPING "BIG EARS"

Jazz Fans

If we accept, metaphorically, that an entire village raises the child, and if our desire is to understand and appreciate jazz people and doings in the most holistic and representative context possible, then fans, amateurs, and other jazz community participants must be recognized for their important contributions. This chapter pans the camera 180 degrees, from an illumined stage of improvising musicians over to the darkened house, where an audience of active listeners responds to the performance. Recall the memorial tribute to fan Peter Cox described in the Prologue: in addition to onstage musicians, the performance space was filled with an event producer, a journalist (myself), several photographers, a videographer, two sound/recording technicians, nonperforming musicians (some waiting to perform, others just hanging out), Cox's friends, and members of his family. If it had been a commercial event, there likely would have been tourists and casual listeners attending as well. These offstage participants are also "performing" jazz; they constitute the unseen jazz scene, the silent and not-so-silent majority that forms an integral part of communal music-making. Their attitudes and activities, rarely scrutinized, come into full focus here: How do their musical tastes develop? How do they view performers and performances? How do their private and public listening practices inform their understandings of and appreciation for jazz?

COMMUNITIES AND SCENES

What, exactly, do we mean by jazz community? And how are fans a part of it? If we define the community as an occupational subgroup, as many early sociological studies did, then, as we've seen, fans are severely marginalized. If we define it as an art world—or associated communities of practice, as Becker and others have[1]—then fans are largely regulated to the role of patrons—active supporters but passive participants in the creation and/or dissemination of artworks. If we subscribe to Christopher Small's concept of musicking,[2] incorporating activities such as active listening and concertgoing within our definition of jazz-making, then fans can now be seen as part of a larger community of interest *and practice*. And if, as Benedict Anderson, Arjun Appadurai, and others have suggested,[3] our definition of community is further expanded to encompass translocal and global identities based on shared interests and/or enculturation mediated through information technology and other cultural flows, then a large number of self-identified wide-ranging communities are also possible.

The vast majority of fans engages and self-identifies with jazz through the medium of recordings—to a much greater extent than through concert attendance. Private record-listening practices, when shared through social media and other digital platforms, facilitate interaction and learning within delocalized virtual and global jazz communities.[4] My interest here, however, is in the local, face-to-face communities of active concertgoers, specific to New York City, and further specific to particular venues, artistic cliques, and/or subgenres of jazz. While record-listening is a quintessential practice for most of these fans as well, I have deliberately consulted people who maintain an active presence on the scene(s), for whom live music takes on a proportionately greater significance. The communities I describe thus have an overtly physical component, manifested in the spaces where people gather and in participants' conceptions of these spaces.[5] There is a temporal component to these groupings as well due to the ephemerality of collective musical experiences. Like jazz improvisations, these communities are transient yet durable, spontaneous yet structured, each created (and re-created) through a singular concurrence of people, place, and time.

When people talk about music scenes, they're usually referring to certain local or regional musical styles and the people—musicians, fans, and others—who participate in them. Interestingly, the term was first used in the 1940s to describe the "bohemian demiworld" of jazz[6] but is now more often associated with youth and popular music subcultures. Scenes are usually linked to specific geographical locales that embody important historical events[7] and are often characterized as sites of independence from and resistance to mainstream culture.[8] We can think of jazz activity in New York as a scene—or, more accurately, a constellation of scenes—not only because it represents a form of alternative culture, but because it exemplifies the face-to-face networks of artists, entrepreneurs, and enthusiasts who collectively create music. Most importantly, it is self-constituting, realized through the cooperative actions of its various stakeholders.[9]

Although local scenes are typically clustered around and articulated within specific geographic loci, locality itself is a construction, often erected in reaction to incursion by outsiders.[10] Spaces can derive their identities only through serial emplacements of music scenes that imbue them with material and symbolic value. Furthermore, no group can remain an island, especially in the aftermath of the 1980s digital and mid-1990s internet revolutions, so all scenes must contain some circulation of ideas, transience of population, and complementary degrees of localization and globalization. A number of scholars have focused on what Holly Kruse has called "translocal" scenes that, unconfined to local spaces, expand into larger cultural domains where music producers, players, and fans can express their collective tastes and identity.[11] Her case studies of indie pop/rock scenes in San Francisco, Champaign-Urbana, Illinois, and Athens, Georgia, illustrate how bands, record label employees, record retailers, college radio personnel, and fans form a web of practices and relationships that support local and national manifestations of each scene. Like earlier theorists, she positions these scenes in opposition to mainstream musics, locating them in specific spaces that have acquired their symbolic resonance through affective associations.[12]

Similar circulation occurs when New York–based jazz musicians tour nationally and abroad, plugging into simpatico scenes clustered around urban areas and festival sites; or when, for example, improvisers from Europe's free-improv scene come to New York to collaborate with local avant-jazz practitioners, exchanges facilitated by the two groups' closely overlapping aesthetic values and praxes. Considering the size, spread, and wealth of diverse jazz activity, the city's many sub-scenes can also be characterized as local emplacements, demarcated from the jazz "mainstream" *within* the five-borough area. For example, members of the Sidney Bechet Society, a trad(itional) jazz fan group, usually circulate among a half-dozen or so Manhattan venues but occasionally trek out to Flushing Hall in Queens or the Nassau County Bar Association in Mineola, New York, where presumably they mingle with traditional-jazz fans from those neighborhoods. Like Ruth Finnegan's physical and metaphorical "pathways" trodden by amateur musicians in Milton Keynes,[13] New York City's various venues, neighborhoods, and transportation systems have become the well-worn conduits of jazz scenesters who plot their courses to and from certain artists, musical genres, and venues.

The digital revolution continues to exert a profound influence on how music is produced and disseminated, how bands market themselves, how fans communicate with musicians and among each other, spawning bottom-up, no-middleman business models and extensive, niche-based networks that facilitate new forms of grassroots "activism" among participants.[14] An increasing number of studies have examined how the complementary processes of digitalization and globalization allow local participants in niche communities to connect and collaborate (or not) with their counterparts living elsewhere.[15] An exciting upshot of this research is that chat rooms, listservs, Skype, and other social internetworks[16] enable expressions of individual and collective fan agency never possible before. Many of the people consulted for this book engage with these larger webworks, but here our primary interest in online scenes lies in their ability to foster *off*line (i.e., face-to-face) activity.

To better understand fans and general audiences, this book adopts a participant-driven approach. In other words, what do fans themselves have to say? How do they understand music? Frankfort School theorists like Theodor Adorno characterized them as passive and commodifiable, and cultural studies scholars depicted them as reactive,[17] both top-down orientations that restrict audience autonomy and agency. Contemporary social scholars continue to overlook the importance of active listeners, seldom consulting them for ethnographies.[18] In cyber communities, audiences are separated in time (even if it's only the fraction of a second needed to tweet a response) and physical space,[19] whereas audience agency in jazz relies on face-to-face communication. If we see local scenes as self-constituting, however, it opens possibilities for grassroots agency in the social infrastructures of musical practices.[20] This is not to suggest that individual agency takes precedence over social structuring, but to acknowledge that human actions are contextualized by and mediated through both past actions and present activities, resulting in a combination of intended and unintended outcomes.[21] My methodology is therefore consciously bottom-up, emphasizing the perspectives and activities of individual actors at the local level.

Who are these fans?[22] In the broadest sense, *all* jazz community members, whatever their personal or professional pursuits, are fans. Musicians, venue operators, and various other music professionals must be accounted for, but in the next two chapters the focus is on amateurs: people who pursue a jazz lifestyle out of love for the music and who are not principally motivated by potential profits. This includes historians, hobbyists, record collectors, swing dancers, laypeople, aficionados, and any other avid listeners and active concertgoers who devote significant time, money, and energy to be with the music.

In fan communities, amateur activities often overlap with professional ones. Some of the people consulted for this chapter have worked part-time or provisionally in jazz-related jobs, but none have made it a career. Lujira Cooper wrote a newsletter for Pumpkins; Peter Cox curated a monthly event at Brecht Forum; Steve Dalachinsky (see Figure 5) writes and performs avant-jazz poetry; Margaret Davis Grimes is a publicist for (and married to) bassist Henry Grimes and edits *Art Attack!*, an electronic newsletter;[23] Peter Gannushkin maintains a photo-blog of downtown musical events;[24] April Matthis is an actress and amateur jazz singer; Yuko Otomo is a poet and visual artist; Irving Stone produced a concert for Ornette Coleman; and Stephanie Stone (Irving's wife) worked as a pianist/singer in 52nd Street jazz nightclubs during World War II. These amateur participants have worked in music at one time or another—as performers, producers, venue staff, or fine artists—for pay, for bartered goods and services, or as a favor to friends. For example, the organizers of Vision Festival, an important annual event in the avant-jazz community, utilize volunteer staff to check tickets, serve food, sell merchandise, record performances, and other tasks; in return, volunteers receive free admission to events and enjoy the satisfaction of helping a nonprofit cause. Amateur status, then, is not absolute but a matter of degree. In this book, amateur fans are defined as people who make improvised music a central pursuit in their daily lives, without relying on it for their livelihoods.

What does an "ordinary" jazz enthusiast look like? Are there different types?[25] During the Swing Era, when jazz enjoyed its highest level of popularity, some fans came out to dance to it, while others gathered by the stage to watch their favorite musicians, whom they often knew by name. Today, people still dance to traditional and swing jazz styles, but the emphasis is on listening, and fans have diverse criteria for judging what they hear. Daniel Cavicchi distinguishes between fans and nonfans, arguing that they have different expectations and experiences of live music; the former see it as a temporary departure—a form of escape or entertainment—from their ordinary lives, while the latter experience it as an affirmation and continuation of their everyday lives.[26] Thus, for "true" fans, musical participation is more than record collecting or occasional concert attendance: it is an ongoing pursuit, a way of life. Instead of using oversimplified typologies, however, it's probably more productive to describe fan participation as "idiocultural" (i.e., individual and idiosyncratic),[27] varying in the degree of personal commitment and activity. Occasional concertgoers, transient tourists, and other less active and/or recognizable participants in New York's jazz communities are all included here, but I have paid special attention to the most active concertgoers (the regulars).

LISTENING IN

Fans vary in musical tastes, acuity, levels of experience, commitment, activity, and sociability with artists and/or other fans. Active, long-term fans, for example, might be differentiated from dilettantes or newcomers. Some favor subgenres such as New Orleans (aka "trad"), mainstream, or contemporary (aka "smooth") jazz, while a smaller number prefer avant-jazz and more experimental forms of improvisation. Most will own a record and/or CD collection representative of their particular tastes and will frequent specific venues that reflect their preferences. They tend to follow particular artists: collectors amass recordings by icons like John Coltrane and Miles Davis, concertgoers go to see favorite performers when they appear locally, and hard-core followers might try to attend every available show by a particular artist. Although they can be differentiated by taste—followers of a certain artist or group, habitués of a particular venue, or aficionados of a specific style—most fans are interested in a wide range of musics and musicians, jazz and otherwise. In this sense they are as difficult to pigeonhole as the creative artists they listen to.[28]

Many, perhaps most, fans are semiregulars—those who come out when a favorite musician plays in town or tourists visiting from out of town or abroad—and therefore make the scene less frequently, maybe only a few times a year. Although tourists are a dominant presence in high-profile clubs like Blue Note and Iridium, usually accounting for a majority of the attendees,[29] to locals they are a generic mass of unfamiliar faces. It is far easier to identify individual fans in the intimate, specialized sub-scenes clustered around neighborhood venues and subgenres of jazz.[30]

All of the extremely active fans I spoke with stated that they appreciate many kinds of jazz,[31] but about half prefer avant-jazz concerts when going out.[32] Of this latter group, almost all are college-educated European Americans. In contrast, jazz performers (especially avant-jazz performers) are more diverse: although many of the most respected musicians are African Americans, European and Asian Americans are highly visible, and many performing groups are of mixed ethnicity.[33] Similarly, jazz audiences are predominantly male. Interestingly, almost half of the most hard-core fans I interviewed were female, including Judy Balos, Roberta DeNicola, Margaret Davis Grimes, Yuko Otomo, and Stephanie Stone. Note, too, that while female performers are underrepresented in mainstream jazz, the avant-jazz scene seems to be relatively progressive in this respect, with a more tangible presence of female performers and mixed gender groups. In spite of the scene's marginality, I have privileged the viewpoints of avant-jazz fans in this and the next chapter because, as a group, they are far and away the most active and consistent concert attendees, highly visible as individuals.[34] Labeling them "avant-jazz fans," however, doesn't account for the many other types of music, jazz and otherwise, that they attend. Their tastes tend to be expansive, not exclusive.[35] Their hyperactivity—demonstrated in both the frequency and longevity of their concertgoing—has imbued them with deep experiential knowledge of performers and performances, making them invaluable resources. Thus, while my consultant pool can't claim to represent the average jazz fan (whoever that might be), the perspectives provided by these expert fans are appropriate for a qualitative study of common practices in active local fan communities.

Fans almost always remember their first time, when a particular record or performance caught their attention and gave them "the jazz bug."[36] Former proprietor of Sweet Basil, Horst Liepolt (see Figure 14) described his teenaged reaction to *Savoy Blues* by Louis Armstrong & the Hot Five: "That day I came home, and this guy played me this record, and he had a lot [of others] but he couldn't play me anything because I insisted that he play that record, that side, over and over and over. So he played it about twenty times and said, 'That's enough now!' So that's how the jazz got me, and today, sixty years later, it's still got me. It's never left me."[37] At fourteen, former Smalls manager Mitch Borden heard *Diz and Bird*: "It was never the same after that. . . . I actually felt that the wool had been pulled down over my eyes, and I was *angry*. . . . How could the world just ignore this and keep me in the dark? [It] turned me in a direction and I never went back. . . . I was just *shocked!*"[38] Borden then "hunt[ed] down every Charlie Parker record," becoming a champion of bebop. Most fans can relate similar accounts of their first experience of recorded jazz: for some it clicked immediately, for others it left an unresolved impression, piquing their curiosity.

Other fans become interested in jazz through their own attempts to learn to play music. Several I spoke with studied band instruments in school and/or took lessons. Stephanie Stone taught herself to sing and play piano, working in nightclubs for a short period as a young woman. Starting at age three, Margaret Davis Grimes studied classical piano for ten years, then spent several years each on flute and trumpet. "I wanted to be a musician—of *course*," she explained, "as a small child I played a *lot*, a long time, and *very* seriously. I practiced, re-hearsed, transcribed, transposed, studied, took lessons, and cried myself to sleep at night, because I never could get it to sound like I heard it in my head." Frustrated by her perceived limitations, Davis Grimes stopped playing in her twenties, transferring her passion for music to supporting live performances: "As soon as I quit, I discovered I had this incredibly urgent need to go and hear music, to hear other people playing." Her former experiences as a musician translated into deep appreciation for other musicians: "The more I listened, the more I fell in love, the more I wanted to know how it happens, how it's possible, where it comes from, where it goes. . . . So I got to know musicians who were doing it, see what their lives are like, and understand some of the mystical aspects of it." Other amateur musicians, such as rock guitarists, develop a taste for jazz through crossover artists like George Benson or John McLaughlin who merge R&B, rock, and/or pop with jazz. Often, having hands-on experience with a musical instrument attunes fans to the technical challenges of playing and fosters their appreciation for proficient musicians.

Once jazz has caught their attention, fans develop tastes for different artists and styles through further exposure to live performances, recordings, radio,[39] and other media. They read album liner notes, trade magazines, fan websites and blogs, critical reviews, books on music, and follow suggestions from peers to check out certain musicians, recordings, or concerts. Lujira Cooper got interested in jazz hearing local performers at Brooklyn's Pumpkins and Jazz 966 senior center,[40] and then familiarized herself with its history via radio: "I hear a lot of it here [at work] because we listen to a lot of [W]BGO,[41] so I'm now getting the chance to go backward and hear those people who set the standard." Like the marketing tactics of consumer websites such as Amazon.com ("Customers Who Bought This Item Also Bought") or Pandora Radio ("personalized radio that plays music you'll love")[42] to introduce music to listeners that company analysts have rated as similar to music they already like, fans use music that sparks their curiosity as a catalyst to trace stylistic lineages in all directions. If a particular subgenre or performer inspires them, they can seek out artistic antecedents, contemporaries, and descendants of that music or musician.

Recordings—whether digital files, CDs, DVDs, vinyl records, even bootleg cassette or reel-to-reel tapes—are a quintessential medium for helping fans understand and appreciate what they hear.[43] Many jazz enthusiasts are avid collectors who research, expand, and refine their individual preferences through active private listening.[44] Because records can be replayed and subjected to close scrutiny and analysis, they allow fans to "learn" the music and develop subjective aesthetic criteria.[45] Furthermore, although recorded jazz is a *fait accompli* and so hasn't the immediacy of experiencing live improvisation, even old recordings are new to first-time listeners, engaging their active awareness and satisfying their appetites for novelty and surprise. Record collecting and collectors is a fascinating topic, warranting a book-length treatment of its own, but a few observations here will suffice to show the relevancy of collector culture to other forms of musical participation.

Jazz's historical legacy—its legendary players and influential styles—stays alive via tribute concerts and neotraditionalism, when modern artists honor and emulate the past. Records are even more specific: sonic time capsules of improvised musical moments frozen and preserved for posterity, inspiring future artists and fans. Curators of major jazz record labels like Columbia, Blue Note, Prestige, Verve, Riverside, and Impulse! regularly exhume lost treasures from their vaults; while archival labels like Mosaic repackage artists' works—often adding previously unpublished alternate takes—into new comprehensive and/or definitive collections that will be of particular interest to completist collectors and aficionados.[46] Advances in audio fidelity, remastering, and digital restoration techniques have resulted in reissues that sound "better" than the originals. Thus, while the music on recordings remains virtually unchanged, it may gain new currency when reintroduced to the jazz community and utilized in active ways by its membership.[47]

Collectors in New York used to be able to browse through prodigious inventory at Tower Records store near Lincoln Center, the Union Square Virgin Megastore, and the financial district's J&R Music World, all of which contained enormous and comprehensive jazz collections, all of which, in the aftermath of the digital revolution, were eventually forced to close due to competition from online shopping and illegal file-sharing.[48] Jazz enthusiasts can still shop, however, at small niche stores like Fred Cohen's (see Figure 15) Jazz Record Center and Bruce Gallanter's Downtown Music Gallery. Cohen's store, hidden away on the eighth floor of an unsigned, nondescript office building, is a true aficionados' hangout, stocking vinyl and digital collectors' items and an extensive scholarly book selection that includes complete scores and comprehensive discographies. Gallanter's venue caters to avant-jazz and experimental music fans, featuring an extremely eclectic selection of aurally challenging, independently produced, and/or hard-to-find recordings, supplemented by in-store performances on Sundays. Consumers can still get personalized assistance from Cohen, Gallanter, Manny Maris, and other knowledgeable retailers,[49] who often function as arbiters of taste by recommending appropriate recordings or playing sample tracks over the sound system at patrons' requests.[50] In this sense, record outlets serve as community centers where fans can come to research and talk shop.

In their continuing quest for new sounds, some fans amass considerable collections. Publicist Jim Eigo estimates he once owned fifty-five thousand records of jazz and other music, later sold off (except, he noted, for a few "choice things") and supplanted by a jazz CD collection that covers an entire wall of his home/office. Eigo differentiated between collectors and those who "have a lot of stuff": "If you're a jazz record collector, *serious*, you have your favorite artists, so you basically collect everything that that artist does: bootlegs, anything you can get your hands on. And you want it all; you're a completist. If you like Eric Dolphy, you have every Eric Dolphy record: the box sets, the European bootleg, the whole nine yards." In addition to in-store stock, Bruce Gallanter estimated he's got forty thousand CDs in his private collection.[51] Horst Liepolt accrued eight thousand vinyl LPs while living in Melbourne, Australia, augmenting these with hard-to-find items acquired during yearly forages to Manhattan, eventually selling the lot when he immigrated to the city. Peter Cox bought over three thousand CDs. Steve Dalachinsky and Yuko Otomo's small apartment overflows with LPs, CDs, and an archive of reel-to-reel tapes that Dalachinsky recorded live, mostly of saxophonist Charles Gayle. Harold Meiselman owns at least fifteen hundred CDs, including, he estimates, sixty to seventy apiece by favorite artists like Derek Bailey, Peter Brötzmann, Ornette Coleman, Evan Parker, and Cecil Taylor. Irving Stone sold most of his eight thousand LPs, only to accumulate fifteen hundred CDs before he died. Comprehensive collections such as these underline the considerable depth and breadth of fans' private listening practices.

In collector cultures, acquiring and displaying objects may take precedence over actually listening to them,[52] but many jazz fans report that they do actively listen to and learn from their records. "Collecting is a different thing than listening!" noted Irving Stone, "I do both. But look, I bought the records to listen to." Roberta DeNicola described her routine: "In the morning I meditate and then I listen to music. I have certain things—like now I listen to *Luminescence* a lot. That's Daniel and Reuben, right after 9/11, in Seattle. It's beautiful."[53] She likened her listening to the Buddhist practice of concentrating on one thing at a time: "I really like being simple, pure, and total saturation; I don't like mixing and overlapping things. . . . I want clear ground." "I can't do other things, and I like to focus," noted Harold Meiselman; "Frequently, if I've become distracted and I've lost focus on the music at a certain point, I'll go back to the point or I'll play it over again, because I wanna absorb it. Because this kind of music isn't aural wallpaper: it's there to engage with; it demands your attention. You get out of it what you put into it." He estimated that at least two hundred of his CDs were still in shrink-wrap, earmarked for future listening sessions when he could give them his undivided attention. For these and other fans, private listening is active and intense, a form of ritual practice.

Deep, focused listening can bring fans closer to the music. Irving Stone, a self-defined "compulsive," followed a carefully balanced program: "I have five records that I'm [usually] working on: two of so-called avant-garde, two bebops, and one pre-bop." He would listen to part of each album in rotation—"I can't play a whole LP, I get bored"—often taking three separate sittings to finish a forty-minute to hour-long recording. Stone reported that he used "whatever time I can sneak" to concentrate on the music: "I figure that if I'm going to scratch it with a needle, then I *have* to listen. There're certain things I could hear without paying attention, but no, I'd rather listen: there may be something there I haven't heard the first ten times."[54] Harold Meiselman also budgets his listening time: "I have this dilemma, or conflict, about wanting to absorb and revisit many recordings that really *require* repeated listenings to really understand—or not really 'understand,' but appreciate—and start to hear what's actually occurring. And then there's this feeling that, 'Oh, I have to make progress listening to these recordings that I haven't yet listened to, that I'm interested in listening to, because I purchased them.' So they're all of interest to me, and then finding time to listen is difficult as well." Stone's "working on" and Meiselman's "making progress" point to the agency and urgency they and others bring to listening practices.

Many fans use private record-listening to explore and experiment with new music, often that of a more radical or "difficult" character. Bruce Gallanter uses the terms "serious listeners" or "curious listeners" to identify enthusiasts of experimental improvised musics who are willing to engage with unfamiliar and challenging sonic experiences. Similarly, Peter Cox used the term "big ears" to describe fans that are "open to every kind of listening experience . . . all sorts of musics." Collectors typically use favorite artists and styles to discover musical lineages backward, forward, and sideways along extended-family trees of aesthetic influences. Cox was attracted to traditional New Orleans jazz as a preteen after hearing his cousin's albums from the 1920s and 1930s, and subsequently bought 78 rpm records of Louis Armstrong, Sidney Bechet, and Jelly Roll Morton. "From then on in I started to listen to it more intently and I got into other schools of the music," he reported; "I started with the early guys, and I went through the swing bands, and it was a natural progression into the modern jazz—the bebop revolution—then into more avant-garde stuff." Irving Stone began by listening to popular swing artists, and then researched "ancestors" like Joe "King" Oliver and "cousins" like Duke Ellington, eventually expanding his interests to encompass radical new-breed improvisers. Stephanie Stone had been listening to swing saxophonists Lester Young and Coleman Hawkins when a friend played her a recording of Charlie Parker's "Red Cross": "I said, 'What? Play that again!' He played it two times, three times. I went out and bought the record, but I had to hear it a couple of times before I knew something was really happening there [with] Bird. It was very strange."[55] "Everything that you have introduces you to something else," explained Harold Meiselman, "and then you discover a whole *other* musician's body of work that becomes interesting to you."

Listening to a series of recordings by the same artist or group can give fans contexts for understanding those sounds. Harold Meiselman has studied the music of Evan Parker, who plays in a sonically dense, "sheets of sound"[56] style influenced by John Coltrane, further thickened by a breathing technique that produces a continuous airstream. "That circular breathing," Meiselman observed, "if you're not attuned to the fine detail of what's happening *within* it, then it's all going to *sound* like he's always doing the same thing. Like, people on that bulletin board[57] were saying, 'Oh, Evan Parker's always doing the same thing! Now he just goes into the circular breathing.' But that's as if saying 'Oh, he did the circular breathing' is all you need to hear to know what he was doing." Meiselman's interest in and familiarity with Parker's recordings allows him to distinguish details of the improviser's style that may be lost on others: "He's got six or eight recordings of solo soprano saxophone improvisations, and it's mostly all the circular breathing, but it's just so complex and varied in terms of where it goes and what it does and the way it spirals. So I guess if you don't find that style or that sound engaging then you're not willing to hear the nuances in it."[58] Comparison of recordings also allow fans to chart changes over the course of an artist's career.

Besides record-listening, fans' tastes are influenced by what they read and overhear about records. An anecdote from Irving Stone illustrates how printed and word-of-mouth sources may influence listener perception:

How did I start? I went to the corner of the block [where] you could get into a discussion about [music]. It was the Swing Era, so I started out with Benny Goodman and Artie Shaw. And then somebody hipped me: "You seem like an intelligent guy; you should realize that Duke Ellington is infinitely superior to this shit." And I listened to Duke Ellington—didn't quite understand it. Artie Shaw had printed an article in the *Saturday Evening Post* that said, basically, what this guy had said to me: "Why is there a contest between me [Shaw] and Benny Goodman about who has the best band in the world when there's a man named Duke Ellington who has an orchestra that's infinitely superior?" So I listened again and I got to it.[59]

Stone also diligently consulted album liner notes, referring back to them when he wished to identify a particular soloist who had caught his ear. Written and oral sources may therefore influence how fans hear music, but for Stone and similarly committed fans, active listening and critical acumen are the most important factors in "getting to it."

Like a relay baton, appreciation for music can be passed forward. Just as reading Artie Shaw's article influenced Irving Stone's friend to embrace Ellington's music, so that friend influenced Stone, who in turn influenced many downtown scenesters to embrace strange new musics. For example, one of Bruce Gallanter's favorite stories relates the first few times he saw Eugene Chadbourne and John Zorn performing at Studio Henry,[60] noting his perplexed reaction to their unusual sounds and "ridiculous" stage mannerisms. Spotting an elderly couple, who turned out to be Irving and Stephanie Stone, in the audience at all of these gigs, Gallanter was "flabbergasted" to discover that they "loved" these musicians, but soon he too became a staunch fan and supporter of these same artists and others like them.[61]

Given that deep, focused listening is central to jazz, critical for gaining knowledge of and experience in the idiom, crucial for full immersion in a musical moment, it's not surprising that serious fans devote significant time and energy to developing "big ears." "Big" here not only implies that one is open-minded to new and challenging musics, but also that one's auditory acumen is both concentrated and comprehensive.[62] The active private listening practices of jazz devotees whet their appetites for improvised surprises, appetites that are further whetted through experiences of live jazz.

LISTENING OUT

Private record-listening, whether cursory or deeply focused, may be sufficient for many jazz fans, but the active concertgoers I spoke with, not surprisingly, prefer to experience the music live. Certainly recordings, videos, and other media facilitate understanding and appreciation of the art, enabling listeners to create strong intellectual and emotional bonds to an artist.[63] They are, however, removed in time and place from the act of musical creation itself, which can be directly experienced and engaged with only in person, in real time. This section examines what happens when fans are in the house, attending to and interacting with live music and musicians.

Listeners who haven't had formal musical training rely on their knowledge of repertoire (i.e., song structures and melodies), recordings, historical trends (i.e., styles and interpretive practices), and specific artists to develop contexts and criteria for evaluating jazz. While previous exposure helps many fans expand their tastes, it may equally well bias them against particular artists or styles, the auditory equivalent of tunnel vision. Interestingly, Lujira Cooper submitted that, although she is very knowledgeable about blues music, her relative ignorance of jazz is an advantage because it allows her to listen with impartiality: "[T]here is freedom within a structure, and you'd like to hear some of the freedom. You don't want to hear people playing note-for-note-for-note-for-note. And for me, having *not* spent a lot of time listening to the [jazz] masters, I've got the advantage of being able to appreciate whether people can play, not who they sound like. . . . If I'm listening to blues on the other hand, I could hear [a player's influences]; with jazz, I don't have that 'misfortune.'"[64] Fans who've heard Billie Holiday's rendition of "Strange Fruit" or Miles Davis's iconic recording of "So What," for example, may have trouble accepting alternate versions, either because they are deemed too derivative, too radical, or simply inferior. Similarly, fans may hold tenor saxophonists to the technical and artistic standards set by John Coltrane, Michael Brecker, Evan Parker, or others. In this sense, previous experience may introduce aesthetic biases that hinder listeners from judging performers or performances on their own merits.

Painter/drawer Jonathan Daniel (see Figure 21) developed a deep understanding of live jazz through active association with certain performers. For almost a year he regularly attended the Chris Byars Octet's late-night (usually 2:30–4:30 A.M.) sets at Smalls, and developed a deeper sense of how the musicians were communicating with each other:

> I listen quite a bit to the guys on Sunday night at Smalls. I *do* know the [band] well, better than anyone else, and I can definitely hear their dialogue. Now, that kind of clicked for me about six months ago—of course, there's always a dialogue between the musicians—but I really tuned in to it about six months ago. All of a sudden it happened: one night I could just hear every word they were saying to each other. It was really a nice experience, to hit that level. I never really heard that before. I mean, jazz pretty much operates where everyone gets their turn to say what they wanna say, right? I don't know how it's structured, exactly, but that *seems* to be—in my observation—what jazz is: people playing and having a dialogue, a *conversation*. So, if you listen long enough, you really hear. At least, it occurred to me that I could just pick up/ tune in to that conversation.[65]

Daniel's commentary is a compelling example of how a layman listener can "pick up" and "tune in to" jazz on a deep level.

In general, familiarity with jazz artists, artworks, and idiomatic practices augments fans' appreciation of performances. For example, even a cursory understanding of blues structure allows listeners to recognize the chorus structures and anticipate call-and-response phrases; humming or internally hearing a song's melody helps them to track the song-form during improvisations; awareness of historical trends, stylistic approaches, and artists' careers attunes them to various details of a performance and situates it within a broader social context. Experienced fans of mainstream jazz generally expect performers to play—and may even request—standard tunes. "There're some songs you just automatically expect musicians to know," observed Lujira Cooper; "I mean, it would be pretty hard [if] somebody tells you they don't know 'Caravan,' or '[A] Night in Tunisia,' or 'Sophisticated Lady,' or those kinds of things. And it *happens*. You ask if they know a song, and they don't know it. But then, that means you're not following the history."[66] The canonized standards serve as a lingua franca, allowing artists to speak to and be understood by audiences, even when there are significant language and/or cultural barriers. "There's a group that plays down at Pumpkins," Cooper illustrated, "a contingent of Japanese, and it's very interesting that, when they play, they predominantly play or sing standards. They may not be able to speak English, but they *know* their music. They'll come up to the bar and they'll whisper, [*whispering*] 'Can I have a ginger ale?' and then they get up there, and you listen to them, and you go: [*makes gesture of amazement*]!" Like Cooper, fans often build their understandings of and appreciation for artistic expression on a foundation of common core knowledge of jazz's forms, history, and performance practices.

With deeper initiation and immersion into the jazz world, listeners may become highly discerning and emotionally responsive, recognized by their peers as virtuoso listeners. In the avant-jazz scene, Irving Stone was commonly regarded as an exceptionally talented listener—an inveterate concertgoer who had developed rich contexts for comprehending live performances, evinced strong passion for the music, and was thought to be a shrewd judge of its quality. Like the *sammiʿah* of Arabic *ṭarab* music,[67] or flamenco *cabales*,[68] jazz has its dedicated connoisseurs who think and *feel* music on a deep level. At concerts, their charismatic presence serves as a role model for and an inspiration to other members of the listening community.[69]

Being with jazz, at the place and in the moment of its creation, adds an essential element of immediacy (literally, a *lack* of mediation), an experiential dimension impossible to replicate through record-listening.[70] Indeed, a few fans reported that they *only* like to hear jazz live and generally eschew recordings or other media. All of the fans I spoke with preferred live to "canned" music.[71] "When I'm at home," observed Peter Cox, "I have my CD collection. I listen to a lot of different stuff, like [traditional] and middle period [jazz], but when I go *out*—let's face it, people aren't playing that sort of stuff so much anymore in clubs—so I'm listening to more 'out' stuff, like Joe McPhee and Roy Campbell [Jr.]. . . . If you're listening to somebody in a club playing, and they're communicating to you, then it's much more immediate and more viable and more responsive and of the moment than listening to a record. After all, a record is just like something that's been recorded that's now in the past."[72] Similarly, Margaret Davis Grimes noted: "I love to listen to the radio and the recordings I have, but most of all I love to go out and hear music—I need to be there. I have to listen to a CD probably twenty times before I start to hear it. I *never* have that problem in person." Being there, she elaborated, opens up a spiritual dimension: "Recorded music just doesn't reach me. And there are no spirits. I mean, I've seen so many spirits around the music when I've *been* there; not seen in the visual sense, but there's a whole other world happening that you just don't get on a little round thing that's made out of metal, that's in your kitchen."

Concertgoing permits the listener to witness the process of improvisation firsthand, without filtration or postproduction editing; to observe body language and other visual cues accompanying the music; to absorb the sensorial ambiance of the performance space with its various smells, tastes, and tactile stimuli; and to interact with other participants in real time. Concerts also function as progress reports on a musician's or group's work, a "breaking news" bulletin on the state of the art, giving fans a sense of being in-the-loop at the scene of the action. Most importantly, attending live events allows audiences to become coauthors of collective improvisations in a living jazz scene.

Many of the fans consulted for this book reported that watching performances was pivotal in developing their tastes. Irving and Stephanie Stone witnessed the latest developments in jazz over seven decades, going to see Coleman Hawkins, Duke Ellington, Charlie Parker, Miles Davis, Thelonious Monk, Charles Mingus, Ornette Coleman, Cecil Taylor, John Zorn, and other seminal innovators. Even in his last years, increasingly debilitated by diabetes, Stone attended countless concerts by lesser known artists active on the downtown scene. Like many curious listeners, he continued to learn about earlier forms of jazz through recordings, but developed an increasing interest in contemporary players after going to their gigs: "Really, what brought me back [to modern jazz] was Thelonious Monk. He had a gig at the Five Spot with John Coltrane and Wilbur Ware and I used to go three or four times a week."[73] Peter Cox, acknowledging that "a great motivation" for moving to New York from England was "because the music scene here was so great," recollected that his initial taste for trad(itional) jazz and swing-band recordings expanded into bebop and the avant-garde when he began attending shows: "Later on I got to go to jazz clubs in London, like the 100 Club and Ronnie Scott's. So I heard people like Joe Harriot, Tubby Hayes, Johnny Dankworth, and people like that who were the forefront of the London scene at that time, playing bebop, modern stuff. . . . They were all influential to my music listening experience. . . . And then I met and heard Joe Harriot, a free jazz player from Jamaica, who was another turnaround for me. And it went from there, just a natural progression." For fans like Stone and Cox, live music initiated their interest in contemporary and progressive jazz.

In contrast to less improvised musical styles, jazz concerts can vary radically from set to set or night to night, even when musicians repeat the same tunes in the same order. Artists seek to sustain maximum musical interest, not only for their audiences, but also for their bandmates and themselves, by injecting elements of innovation and surprise whenever possible. Because it's difficult for improvisers to avoid repeating themselves—there are only twelve notes, and certain musical ideas and physical gestures invariably become engrained habits of thought and action[74]—loyal fans will be especially inspired if they sense that a performer is "stretching out." For infrequent concertgoers, much of what they hear will be new to them. Fans who've attended a series of concerts by the same artist or group, on the other hand, will be able to assess whether a musician is transcending his or her own artistic clichés, whether the group is transcending its usual patterns of interaction, and/or whether the music is going somewhere "new."

The challenge to continually come up with new ideas and periodically reinvent oneself is thus compounded when playing for regular listeners intimately familiar with the artists' work and methods. In the avant-jazz scene, where free improvisation is emphasized over preconceived musical structures, musicians employ strategies such as radical compositional approaches or novel combinations of participants to foster spontaneity. John Zorn composed a series of game pieces (e.g., "Cobra") that use hand gestures and cue cards to prompt improvising groups to role-play and think outside of the box. Similarly, downtown musicians frequently perform with new people or new combinations of collaborators to change up the social and musical chemistry. All of these practices seek to minimize established habits of exchange. "Some musicians will go to extreme ends to stay fresh," noted Harold Meiselman, citing guitarist Derek Bailey: "I think his concept is: avoid repetition in all [ways]; never establish any groove or any pattern or any sound or any[thing]—as soon as something is established it's obliterated." He suggested, however, that avoiding clichés can become a cliché: "[Bailey's] stuff is all unique, but it's all of a type, but that in it*self* has developed this recognizable sound that you could pinpoint in a second. ... There're a lot of Derek Bailey clones out [there]."[75] In trying to avoid the obvious, Bailey nevertheless developed a signature style, a way of playing—or rather a way of *not* playing—distinctive enough to be copied by others. Inveterate fans realize that artists cannot completely reinvent themselves with each performance and so will wait patiently for moments of spontaneity and surprise.

To illustrate these general points, consider Harold Meiselman's appreciation for Cecil Taylor, a free jazz pioneer whose music is notoriously dense and dissonant. Meiselman has immersed himself in the pianist's music, on record and in concert, once attending six back-to-back concerts given by Taylor. Although uninitiated fans might find Taylor's music to be repetitive, noisy, even opaque, Meiselman actively listens for nuances in the seemingly homogenous musical textures: "You definitely recognize characteristic sounds, tone, and technique. And in long-standing groupings [of musicians] there are patterns of communication that represent their history." Nevertheless, he argues, within these established patterns are opportunities for spontaneity: "People have described him as always playing the same piece of music, refining and playing variations on the same composition. And *some*times it feels that way, but other times it feels different." The difference, he believes, lies in Taylor's unpredictability—"that's something to look for ... the *lack* of recognition of patterns and stuff"—and in the group dynamics: "*Some* performances are more inspired than others, and some achieve a greater degree of communication or interaction between the performers—you can tell. Like, I frequently heard people say after a Cecil Taylor performance, 'Oh, it sounded like he was really listening to the other musicians.' Sometimes he just goes his own way, and then sometimes you have more of a sense that he's responding to what the other musicians are doing." Meiselman's diligent attention to Taylor's relatively inscrutable music demonstrates that he's as fully committed to listening as Taylor is to performing.

An improviser's musical style is expanded and transformed when he or she switches up instruments, collaborates with different combinations of colleagues, or experiments with different approaches to improvisation. Open-minded artists who adapt effectively to changing circumstances are especially inspiring to listen to (and perform with) because their music embodies an ethos of adventure; fans (and fellow musicians) that covet surprise reserve their highest praise for such artists.

As in baseball and other professional sports, avid jazz fans follow the careers of favorite players, cheering them on through triumphs and tribulations. A number of the fans I spoke with had developed close relationships with musicians. "We've done that with a few people," Steve Dalachinsky observed, "because once we start to pay attention to certain artists, we want to see how they change, how they flourish, and how they derail, or crumble—musically I'm talking about. So we can't miss anything, we follow as far as we can go, and then, whatever happens, then we'll stop. So in a way we get hooked with certain people." "We get hooked," agreed Yuko Otomo, his wife, "and unfortunately we sometimes get disappointed with their direction." By closely following artists for an extended period, fans feel they are part of history in the making, witnesses to and participants in a voyage of discovery. Dalachinsky and Otomo befriended artists like Rob Brown, William Parker, and Matthew Shipp in the earlier stages of their careers, then watched, as Otomo put it, "how they blossomed, or how they withered—all those changes." "We've had the privilege," Dalachinsky explained, "of seeing people like Charles Gayle—who had a chance to be *the* most famous guy, as an avant-garde sax player—almost undermine his entire career, which gave room for a guy like David Ware to be *the* saxophone guy on the avant-garde jazz scene. . . . So we *did* see these guys who either lived in New York or came here to make it. We saw everything they went through." As veterans of the local scene, Dalachinsky and Otomo traced its long-term changes, and were inspired—*compelled*—to watch and listen for new developments.

Artist-audience social relationships occur along a continuum: from brief eye contact across a crowded venue, to a face-to-face conversation after a set, to more intimate associations cultivated through frequent contact over time. In most cases performers and audiences *don't* develop enduring relationships. Most concertgoers are satisfied to watch an artist perform, but extroverted enthusiasts may approach performers to chat or have a favorite recording autographed. Musicians, who rely on fans financially (via CD and concert ticket sales)[76] and artistically (via active listening/feedback during performances), make a point of showing their gratitude to audiences—"Thanks for supporting live jazz! We couldn't do this without you!" and so forth—and usually make themselves available to fans between sets. "I think all musicians scuffle, and you might say that jazz musicians seem to scuffle a little more," noted Richard Berger; "They're struggling to make it, to make money, to make the scene, to get by, and I think that makes them more accessible because they know how hard it is to make it, and they appreciate whoever's there that comes to hear them."

Affinity for an artist's work often translates to a desire to possess it, whether that means owning recorded copies of it, acquiring deep knowledge of it, or establishing a special relationship with the artist him- or herself. Fans often refer to favorite musicians by their first name or nicknames (e.g., Miles, Wynton, Bird, Trane),[77] presuming a level of intimacy. "Scenes are funny things in that the price of admission includes buying a piece of the artist," asserted arts photographer Jack Vartoogian (see Figure 19). "For those people who *really* love the stuff, it's not *just* the music, it's the personalities," he elaborated, describing how collectors approach artists: "In a lot of cases jazz fans bring in old LPs. If you bring in a CD it's okay, but it's not really cool. But if you've got an old LP—the older the better—of some of the old guys, or something from when a contemporary guy was *young*, you bring it in—or sometimes two or three—and have it *signed*. It's a great thing to do, because you love that particular thing. And if a guy looks at it and says, 'Oh man, where'd you get *that*?' it's a real connection." This doesn't insure, he cautions, that the fan's feelings are reciprocated: "The artist is being *polite*, being friendly, but they're not gonna remember *that*. And a *lot* of the fans take that as: 'Well, we're not best friends in the world, but yeah, sure, I've talked to them.' And *I* do that; I've talked to these guys." Fans may feel enriched acquiring a "piece" of an artist—a record, signature, or personal acknowledgment—because it makes them partial "owners" of the art form.

Name artists who frequently tour out of town and whose stature dictates that they perform for large crowds in rigorously secured venues are less accessible than local musicians who play small informal venues, but even top-tier artists are often available to interested fans.[78] "There's a lack of ego with a lot of these musicians," noted Richard Berger, "plus—I don't know if it's the music or where it's played—the musicians are very accessible. Most of the musicians we've ever seen—rock, opera—you can't get near them: you're in a big stadium or concert hall; you can't touch them. But these places where we go to hear them, they're right there." "It's more intimate," added Roberta DeNicola, Berger's wife; "They get off the stage and they're right there, you're hanging out with them, talking to them, brushing shoulders with them. . . . Even when we've seen our idols, they'll talk to you when you're in a little [club]—we talked to Dexter Gordon, Sonny Rollins, Sonny Fortune—they're just so human, so accessible, and so open!" In contrast to large, formal clubs and concert halls, in smaller, informal venues performers often linger near the stage between sets: selling and signing CDs, talking shop with colleagues, conducting business with club owners and other music professionals, and chatting with fans. Journeymen musicians with regular gigs around town become familiar faces, so participants in the various micro-scenes clustered around particular venues and artistic cliques have ample opportunities to interact with them.

Small insular scenes promote a sense of solidarity and insiderness because regulars—fans and/or artists—constantly bump into each other. Fans' relationships with performers often evolve through frequent contact and shared interests. "It's not like you try, it just happens by chance," Roberta DeNicola claimed; "I don't think these [downtown] guys are particularly into socializing, per se, just to socialize. They're not trying to win you over to go to more of their stuff. They're really into the music." Rather, she believes such relationships are built on mutual passion for free improvisation: "If they see you understand the music, they open up to you—if they see you really feel it. I really didn't expect these people to open up to us.[79] I mean, I love the music for what it was, but they could see how much you loved it. And then I would just say something sometimes, and then they'd answer back, and that was the start." DeNicola started exchanging emails and poems with certain musicians, "and now I feel like they're extended family." Richard Berger, DeNicola's husband, noted that artists respond positively to active fans: "When they start seeing the same faces—because we go to a lot of things—when they start seeing you a lot, they say, 'Hey, these people really dig the music! They're cool, they're allright!' And then you become friendly with them, and it breaks down the barriers, and that's when you can really touch somebody." Several fans of saxophonist Steve Lacy, after going to many of his concerts, became fast friends with him: Lacy would notify them of upcoming local gigs, offer complimentary tickets, and meet them for dinner and other social outings.[80] In these and other cases, musical bonds between fans and artists extended into other parts of their lives.

Mutual interests among fans and artists don't necessarily translate to shared understandings because of an inherent "language barrier": fans often don't understand the technical elements of music (e.g., rhythms, harmonies, instrumental techniques) and so can't "talk shop" with performers. "I never discuss music with them. I don't feel that I'm qualified enough," reported Peter Cox. "I chat with them off the gig, as friends—'Hey, I thought it was great, Roy!'[81]— but after that, we just split; they go home and I go home. It's not like we hang out at a bar, or go to have a meal, or something like that." Similarly, although Harold Meiselman shares a sense of camaraderie with other avant-jazz aficionados—"people that know each other and are friendly because they see each other all the time at shows"—he feels partially excluded from musician circles: "There's *definitely* a sense of community with all the musicians that network, interact, and are personally involved with each other, but I don't really feel part of it—and I'll *never* be, because I'm not a musician and I'm not involved with them on any level like that. . . . I rarely feel comfortable engaging musicians in conversation about their music, about what they do musically or creatively. I don't know if I'm intimidated, but maybe I don't feel qualified." On the other hand, his avid appreciation and active attendance forges a meaningful connection with artists: "I say hello to many of them, shake their hands. . . . I tell them that I enjoyed their performance, or ask, 'What are you going to be doing in the future?' or if there's anything nonmusical to discuss." Presumably, any language barrier separating fans and musicians can be surmounted by their shared aesthetic values.

Because jazz is highly variable, co-improvised by a group of idiosyncratic artists, fans often hear the music as an extension of the artist him- or herself.[82] Like other art forms, jazz has produced its share of distinctive, even eccentric musical personalities. Certainly many audiences appreciate artist-entertainers who attempt to engage them with patter and shtick or by performing familiar and/or accessible material, seeking to give them what they want or expect. But other listeners adopt an art-for-art's-sake ethos, preferring performers who doggedly follow the dictates of their muse at the risk of alienating all but the most adventurous aficionados. Historically, fans forgave Miles Davis's scowling mien and averted posture, Thelonious Monk's quirky reticence, and Charles Mingus's violent temper because their music was so compelling. Some fans may even be *drawn* to misanthropic behavior: "People came not only to hear Charlie [Mingus] but to see him in action," noted club owner Max Gordon; "They'd sit and wait for him to throw one of his fits, stop the music cold, right in the middle of a number, rage and fume at his men because he heard something he didn't like. They'd sit fascinated."[83] Likewise, Irving Stone didn't seem to mind that his long-standing relationship with Cecil Taylor never graduated to a first-name basis: "I've known this motherfucker for fifty years and he can't call me by my name! I don't think he even *remembers* my name. He calls me 'the historian.'"[84] While some fans want to be entertained (perhaps by the spectacle of melodramatic personalities), charm and theatrics may carry less weight with other fans, for whom the music itself comes first.[85]

Over their lifetimes, Stephanie and especially Irving Stone achieved a uniquely prominent status among downtown musicians and fans. John Zorn described them as "surrogate parents for me, and for an entire musical scene . . . instrumental in nurturing a group of young musicians who were passionate yet misunderstood"; Bruce Gallanter referred to them as "the spiritual parents of this vast downtown family"; and guitarist Joe Morris avowed they "were the most important witnesses to the music anywhere."[86] Zorn recounted how the couple had attended a concert in his apartment back in 1976, and "after that . . . saw just about everything I did in New York," adding, "They were the first people to care."[87] Irving's passing at age eighty was felt throughout the community, which honored him with a ten-hour memorial at Tonic on July 5, 2003,[88] beginning early in the afternoon with spoken reminiscences and tributes by musicians, friends, and fans—some of whom had known him for sixty years—with performances lasting late into the night. "It was overwhelming," recalled Harold Meiselman; "Everybody learned something about him that they didn't know. . . . Musicians talked about what it meant for them: how they first learned who he was, and when they saw him there all the time, and then came to feel that, 'Oh, if the Stones are in the audience it's gonna be a good performance'; or, 'This is the place to be'; or, 'There's gonna be something worth hearing happening.'" Stone's legacy lives on: in the music played at the club/house Zorn named for him, and in the ears of his "children."[89]

Stephanie Stone survived her husband by more than a decade, living to the age of ninety-three. Despite her advancing years and the debilitating effects of cancer, she maintained an active presence at avant-jazz events and occasionally performed in public, singing and playing (piano) her favorite Tin Pan Alley standards, alone or in a duo with saxophonist Dave Sewellson. Her last gig was on February 2014 at a memorial tribute for trumpeter Roy Campbell Jr.,[90] which she pulled off with aplomb despite the fact that she was confined to a wheelchair and breathing from an oxygen tank. Two separate memorial concerts were held after she passed in April 2014, one at the Stone and a second at Roulette, where musicians, fans, friends, and other members of her extended family gathered to improvise in honor of her living memory.

Early champions of the seventies avant-garde loft era,[91] the Stones witnessed many up-and-coming artists at the beginning of their careers, forming lasting personal relationships with important innovators such as Ornette Coleman, Cecil Taylor, and John Zorn. "Stone and Ornette were friends for quite a while," Stephanie claimed; "I mean, they were *friends*, you know? Stone used to hang out at his loft." "I spent a *long* time talking to that man," Irving confirmed.[92] Harold Meiselman, who had grown close to the elderly couple while driving them to shows, noted that, "The Stones bridged that gap between the musicians and the fans because they had personal relationships with *many*, if not most, of the musicians." "The Stone's *really* know how to become friends with those people," asserted Steve Dalachinsky, who is close to many artists himself; "When they met someone like Tony Malaby, say, the *first* thing that intrigued them was that they really loved the way he played saxophone, and they *listened* to him. And then, because they're the Stones—which is *enough*—they become *more* than just a listener to a guy playing a saxophone: they became *friends*."[93] Some musicians even went to Irving Stone for advice or assistance. When Coleman's bassist Charlie Haden grew concerned about changes in band personnel and artistic direction, he entreated Stone to intervene: "For Christ's sake! *This* isn't what we should be doing. Talk to him! [Coleman]—he sometimes listens to you—and tell him this is bullshit!"[94]

All fans want to leave a performance feeling touched, moved, or changed somehow, whether they were soothed or stimulated, their expectations met or confounded, their tastes reaffirmed or challenged. Most jazz fans respond to driving rhythms, catchy tunes, skillful playing, clever ideas, or engaging entertainers, but serious listeners may also covet originality and spontaneity, holding out for what some have called "blood"—an artist's utter immersion in the present musical moment.[95] Harold Meiselman wants music to lead him somewhere new: "I want it to tell me a story or make me feel a certain way. If you're falling back on repeated patterns or habits, then you haven't taken me anywhere, because I've been there before, or I recognize that you're just going through the motions, and you haven't really attempted to find the source of your creativity, at that moment—you didn't live up to *your* part of the bargain when I come out to hear you, which is to be sincere in your effort to be creative and engage." He differentiates between entertainers and musical artists: "Those people that *usually* do patterned stuff, or can do it in their sleep, they're being *entertainers*; they're not being creative; they're not being *musicians*." Musical art, he maintains, is "beyond entertaining. . . . I could be entertained for the moment—you could have my attention—and then there's nothing beyond that, because I'm not going to remember it, or I'm not going to feel that I've experienced something I haven't before, or that I was present at a creative moment. You played me your greatest hits, I enjoyed it, but I wasn't present at anything new, or [wasn't] part of your experience of being an artist."[96] For such fans, jazz isn't art without "blood."

* * *

For all of the active concertgoers I consulted, live performance is the fullest, most immediate expression of jazz. Certainly record-listening can be a crucial component of their jazz participation, but it's not the same as being an eye and ear witness to the music in the moment of its creation. Even so, going out to see musicians cover classics from the jazz cannon in a traditional style, or repeat themselves night after night, and/or fail to "take you where you've never been before," can feel like a trip to the museum. These avid fans seek, above all, the impact and immediacy of "living" jazz, created by innovative improvisers fully committed to the moment of music-making. The more adventurous of them typically gravitate to avant-jazz and experimental music concerts, where performers attempt to reinvent music every time they play. When an audience with "big ears" is in the house, it creates a sympathetic environment where jazz can come alive. And when the music is both "new" and "now," fans and artists share a unique moment in space and time—just before history becomes history.

Chapter 3

MAKING THE SCENE

Fan Communities

In addition to their individual contributions as financial, aesthetic, and moral supporters of music, jazz fans are members of a larger community comprised of musicians, venue operators, music professionals, and fellow fans. Their activities and interactions with these other jazz-makers contribute to the web of social synergism that collectively expresses jazz. This chapter examines how intimate social correspondence between active participants in New York City's avant-jazz scene engenders individual and group identities—a sense of who we are, where we go, what we love, and how we live.

FAN FELLOWSHIP

Do concurrent tastes and concert attendance necessarily create communality? And if so, to what degree? At one extreme, audiences in large formal performance venues are restricted to relatively passive roles, like moviegoers in a darkened theater who laugh or cry en masse, but leave as strangers. "Jazz is like painting," observed Roberta DeNicola; "I see people react totally different ways and be totally different when it's over, where in a great rock concert you're all in the same mood when it's over. [In jazz] there're no words, so you are *seeing your own pictures*." Jazz has always championed individuality within a group context, for both performers and fans. In intimate settings, however, where the demarcation between stage and house is less pronounced, where certain musicians and fans assemble with more regularity, and where the atmosphere is more conducive to social exchanges among fellow enthusiasts, there is significantly more potential for familiarity and even familiality. Such scenes can become clannish and claustrophobic, subject to the same interpersonal politics endemic to extended families and niche social groups. Actress and part-time jazz singer April Matthis described habitués of Marjorie Eliot's parlor concerts as "family": "If I don't go, every week, I always feel like I miss something." Fellowship is therefore a relative term, encompassing a broad range of possible relationships among jazz concertgoers.

Passions for jazz, like politics and religion, can run high enough to cause rifts in relationships. One active concertgoer reported: "We had some friends, and went to this club with them, and Horace Silver was playing. They didn't like it, and insisted we leave. . . . I was *mortified*, and they didn't last as friends. That's just not the thing to do, you know? If it was *really* horrible, okay, but it's Horace *Silver*. So we left and then we never stayed in touch much after that."[1] A musician I once lived with used to play loud bebop on his boombox at all hours, prompting a call from our upstairs neighbor threatening to summon the police if the music wasn't turned down. When I related this warning to my flatmate, he replied, "But it's *Dizzy!*" as if to say, Who *wouldn't* like this music? At a concert I attended in July 2014, tempers heated and words were exchanged when a talkative group refused to comply with my companion's request to quiet down during the performance—a not-so-unusual occurrence when "serious listeners" mingle with less attentive concertgoers in public spaces. In all of these cases, jazz appreciation was a defining criterion for social compatibility.

The previous chapter focused on fans' relationships with musicians, but in many cases concertgoers create their own sub-scenes, based on relationships with peers. An avant-jazz scene, for example, contains an identifiable nucleus of active fans, mostly longtime participants, and a few relative newcomers. "As you go to more and more shows, and you see the same people playing, you slowly get to know them," noted Richard Berger, "and you see the same group of people in the audience, the same faces. We've gotten to know some of these people. There're a lot of people I don't know at all, but then every time we go to a show, I'll see that girl Abby there, or Steve the postman, or Peter, or Kurt. There's a core group of people that go to a lot of the same shows we go to."[2] "You can count the hard-core listeners, who've been listening to downtown music ongoing, nonstop, on [two hands]," observed Yuko Otomo: "The Stones, of course; Peter Cox; a young listener we call 'Mailman Steve'; Larry, who's a manager in Tower Records; Kurt; and of course Bruce Gallanter. The so-called core—I call them the family members because it is like a small family—is maybe ten people. . . . But the Stones are like the mom and dad of the whole thing: parents for the musicians and for the listeners."[3] "There's definitely a camaraderie, or a sense of sharing an experience, because it's a relatively small number of people that regularly *subject* themselves to this kind of music that isn't appreciated by most," Harold Meiselman wryly remarked; "It's almost like a little exclusive club, because there's a certain amount of pride in liking and being involved with something that is out of the mainstream; or that you see something—or at least *think* you see something—that other people don't." The esoteric nature of avant-jazz weeds out casual fans, paring down participants to a double-handful of insiders.

In intimate musical circles, when there are limited places to go and fewer folks interested, the core group is essential to the very existence of the scene. "Those people are always there to support this," noted Yuko Otomo; "If they didn't exist, to listen to or witness this whole scene, I don't know how it could support itself, because you need a balance of giving and taking." Inveterate downtown concertgoers like Irving and Stephanie Stone, Bruce Gallanter, Steve Dalachinsky, and Yuko Otomo have witnessed much change in the music, musicians, and fellow fans over time. "Karen Burdick was one of them and J. D.—they both withdrew from the scene in the midnineties for personal reasons, and also, I guess, they had a little problem with the music—and Peter Cox is now part of it," observed Otomo; "This small family is very, very open, so new people come in, like Roberta and Richard. We are open arms [*sic*] and we welcome people. But people come in and out, so we've seen some people that *came* into the scene as a listener, and stayed in the core, then left." Despite the transience inherent to the downtown scene—evolving "styles," constant regroupings of musicians, venue openings and closings, fan turnover—a small core group has always been there to support it: "Those ten people continuously took everything in, and they have been a perpetual witness of the whole scene," marveled Otomo.[4] Her use of the singular subject, "witness," emphasizes the unity and stability of this fan nucleus.

Even in tight-knit scenes, a certain degree of privacy and autonomy is maintained. Roberta DeNicola described downtown fans as "very interior people, in their minds a lot, and very serious about the music. It's not a casual music crowd." She separates "fringe people" who come to socialize or hear friends perform from hard-core regulars: "It's a very personal thing for these people. It feeds something, gives them something they need, but it's very individual." Three married couples have been core participants—Dalachinsky and Otomo, Berger and DeNicola, and, until their deaths, the Stones—but they're exceptions; most avant-jazz concertgoers are white males attending without significant others.[5] DeNicola often sits with Berger at shows, but nevertheless likens her experience to "a solo flight": "I'm very open and I let it in a lot, so I can't just snap back that fast; I need time to feel it. I can't just digest it and put it in words right away. I don't like it when people immediately start talking about something or change the subject; I don't like trading all those opinions right away—later I can. I'm not a big experience-it-with-a-crowd person." Irving Stone agreed: "One of the things I like about Tonic is nobody talks. I really can't stand people who talk while music is going on, and then have an opinion."[6] DeNicola characterized avant-jazz audiences as "individuals listening": "On a certain level there's a group, but basically it's personal, even *though* it's a group. It's a group of separates." "We don't go out or have a drink together," Berger added. "It's almost too intense to be a positive social thing," DeNicola continued; "It's almost like going to a spiritual experience and leaving, and I think a lot of them feel that way." Avant-jazz fans, Matthew Somoroff suggests, "want to bring their interiority into contact with those of the musicians and other listeners, to experience an interiority that paradoxically gains intensity from its grounding in social and/or public situations of performance and audition that enable a shared feeling of '"we-ness."'[7] Like churchgoers, ardent fans develop personal relationships with inspirational music, and though they congregate with fellow believers, their communion is private.

Judy Balos often confers with Berger and DeNicola during the day to determine which shows they're likely to attend that night. Peter Cox was a former member of this coterie of fans.[8] Typically, the earliest arrival(s) saves seats for the others so that everyone will be near the musical action, where distractions are minimal. "I like to be up close," Balos commented, "because I feel more involved, and I like to watch all the interaction . . . the whole relationship, as well as listening to the sound. Even though you think of music as an auditory experience . . . a lot of it's a visual experience." She notes, however, that if a seat with better acoustics or sightlines becomes available (e.g., one in the "reserved section"), she'll desert her companions to take advantage of it, and this is socially acceptable, she explains, because she and her fan-friends come to listen, not talk, during performances. She claims it is the musician-fans and music professionals who tend to talk the most during performances, and makes it a point to sit away from them. Matthew Somoroff made a similar observation about the avant-jazz musicians hanging out and talking during Brecht Forum performances: "I sometimes wonder if they listen to the music."[9]

In spite of their "interiority," repeated contact in close quarters breaks down barriers and forges bonds between listeners. Although some fans embrace these social aspects of the scene, others may view it as a distraction. "It's like Irving says: he's still waiting for the perfect set," commented Steve Dalachinsky; "We've *seen* a lot of perfect sets, and then the music got really *shitty* again, and a lot of new people started moving into the music, a new audience, new players, a younger generation." He embraces change, but prefers to maintain critical distance. "There *are* people who are very lovey-dovey about the scene, nothing wrong with that—it's great because people like to be very magnanimous—but there's a lot of *shit* in the scene, because it's a *scene*. Any scene is built upon how people kiss each other's asses, and for me that's a very uncomfortable part of it, how people are always in a revelatory and communicative sense." Like other core participants, his primary interest is the music itself. "For *me*, it was never about community; it was a very personal thing. If you're a listener, you're a listener; if you're an artist, you're an artist. After a while, the whole idea of community—and even for Yuko—became very burdensome, because then you can't just go and listen to the music."[10] His comments point to self-affirming biases inherent to social groups, suggesting that peer pressure can dull critical faculties, encouraging the proliferation of "shitty" music.

Other fans embrace camaraderie, sharing and acknowledging musical moments during and after performances. Yuko Otomo has had experiences where audiences "hit the same note" at musical "high spots," and Richard Berger notices "groups of people within the whole group that are really groovin' on the same level and moving the same way." He demonstrated how he communicated with Peter Cox during performances: "We go through these things: we point and then we go like this [*gestures*]. We have our little sign language. I'll point at a musician, or he'll point at a musician, or if someone's doing something special, a great solo, I'll go [*gestures*] and then Peter'll go like that [*gestures*], or we'll start rocking together, and you'll see somebody else rocking. It's reciprocal." He notices that performers pick up on these exchanges—"Musicians probably tune into it also, especially Roy [Campbell Jr.]; he watches everything"—then use this feedback to "tune" their improvisations to the social ambiance. Rather than being a distraction, such communication fosters fan fellowship, though there are occasional breaches of etiquette. "[Ms. X] is known for the semiorgasmic sounds that come out of her mouth during performances, sighs of ecstasy, and she's on many a [live] recording. Some people get really pissed off. It's—well—distracting: you want to hear the performance, not oohing and aahing."[11] Camaraderie among fans, during and after concerts, may range from solitary contemplation to mutual correspondence, from feelings of annoyance or confliction to mutual affection and intimacy.

MUSICAL CHAIRS: IN SEARCH OF A CLUB/HOUSE

Fans need a place to gather, preferably an accessible, affordable, and otherwise fan-friendly venue that regularly presents the music and musicians they love. Often, a particular club becomes the nexus of activity, functioning as a home-away-from-home or "club/house" where fans go to establish their scene. This section looks at how fans interface with these adopted spaces and the people that run them.

At first glance, the activities of venue operators and other music professionals are peripheral to a fan's principal interest, which is music. Concertgoers generally disregard the ticket-takers, ushers, waiters, technical crew, press, and other support staff at a performance. They may, however, develop fierce loyalties for certain venues and be grateful for the club owners, managers, curators, artistic directors, and booking agents that present the music they want at prices they can afford. Fans' experiences are significantly impacted by the venue management's artistic and economic policies. Artistic policies determine what kind of music is featured, which artists are hired and how often, and how shows are staged (lighting, noise levels, sound quality, set lengths, tolerance for talking during performances, and so forth); economic policies determine door charges, drink minimums, and guest list policies. Fans in turn create a demand for certain artists and musics, raising revenues when management accommodates them.

Fans who've tried their hand at jazz production can identify with the inherent challenge of the jazz business. Irving Stone confessed that his production of Ornette Coleman's 1966 Town Hall concert was "a disaster." Peter Cox served on a volunteer ad hoc committee staging monthly avant-jazz performances: "We have to pay the Brecht Forum 20 percent of the door for use of the room, but the other 80 percent goes straight to the musicians. We don't get anything ourselves, but it's great for the music." Jazz performers and venues depend on a relatively small but loyal fanbase, but the fans themselves are often unaware of the economic difficulties club owners must overcome in order to retain jazz programming.

Venues that consistently feature certain artists and subgenres of jazz attract regular clientele, becoming bases of operation for musical cliques and scenes. Record stores, community centers, and other public spaces may also serve as rendezvous spots for jazz people to drop in and hang out. Lujira Cooper listed three favorite mingling spots: Jazz 966, a senior center in Brooklyn's Fort Greene neighborhood; Pumpkins, a local bar with live jazz every night; and Nizam Fatah's store, an informal hub for the Jazz Associates and other Brooklyn-based musicians. "That's the advantage of being down here," she remarked of the latter, "so many musicians float through."[12] For almost two decades, Marjorie Eliot's parlor has been a Sunday afternoon gathering place for faithful friends and followers.[13] Before they closed, the city's two Tower Records outlets, the Virgin Megastore, and J&R Music World were known for their comprehensive selections of jazz recordings, and one could often overhear CD collectors soliciting recommendations from knowledgeable staff members such as Larry Isacson. A few small specialty stores like Fred Cohen's Jazz Record Center or Bruce Gallanter's Downtown Music Gallery still provide face-to-face contact for the niche communities they serve, but the bulk of their trade is (e)mail order.[14] Gallanter's store/performance space is a crossroads for avant-jazz enthusiasts: stacks of flyers and posted bulletins announce upcoming events; local musicians perform at free Sunday afternoon concerts, or drop off copies of their CDs to be sold on consignment; fans browse bins for hard-to-find items; while Gallanter and his staff[15] play newly released music over the store's sound system and dispense news, recommendations, and well-cultivated opinions.

Concertgoers must be budget-conscious: even with modest cover charges, the additional cost of transportation, food, and drinks can easily add up to an expensive evening out. Tourists with disposable funds can afford the upscale Manhattan clubs featuring name acts—indeed, such venues are priced toward foreign, not local, trade[16]—but borough-based fans seeking a regular diet of live jazz may prefer to patronize the less expensive neighborhood bars. "For a long time the Brooklyn [jazz] scene did not have to worry about covers, because they had an underground economy," observed Lujira Cooper; "If you could avoid [charging for music] because you were making money in other ways, legally or illegally, then you didn't have to worry about trying to get people to come in." Increased police surveillance led to "a crack-down," she noted; "It became a problem of *having* to charge covers. And I think that's one of the things that's most resented—especially in Brooklyn—is that cover charge. It's hard to try and get people to understand that the cover pays the musician." Brooklynites, Harlemites, and other locals have congregated at Bar 4, Barbès, Chez Oskar, Freddy's Backroom, Lenox Lounge, Lucky Cat Lounge, Pumpkins, Puppet's Jazz Bar, Showman's Lounge, Sistas' Place, Up-Over Jazz Café, and other haunts (many now defunct) that feature journeymen musicians at reasonable rates. Small clubs constantly mushroom and die throughout the five boroughs, especially in Brooklyn's Park Slope, Williamsburg, and Fort Greene neighborhoods, changing their names, locations, and music formats. Relentless turnover forces fans to abandon former favorites and transfer their loyalty to current hot spots.

In tight-knit scenes where fans become friendly with musicians and/or club staff, regulars may be extended special privileges. Several people I spoke with claimed they'd been on the "permanent guest list" at the former Knitting Factory through their associations with owner Michael Dorf and musicians who played there, others were allowed into CBGB's Sunday night "Freestyle Events" without paying a cover charge,[17] and at least four people claimed that their connections could almost always get them into shows they wanted to see. "I'm not in a position to pay several hundred dollars each time I want to see a musician, but I feel strongly about *paying* my way," Harold Meiselman reported, "whereas a lot of people that I know don't *have* to, if they choose, because they know the people of the club or the musicians. I'm in a position to pay the ten or fifteen dollars to get in. It's not so much, and I wanna be supportive of the musicians, and I know that half the people here didn't pay to get in." Some well-connected fans stated that they always pay their way, on principal, while others find creative ways to contribute. Richard Berger and Roberta DeNicola met Vision Festival founders William and Patricia Parker through jazz publicist Jim Eigo, joining the festival's "extended family" and volunteering their services at various events. In such scenes, favors are traded among the participants,[18] but these barter systems have limits: musicians want to be paid and proprietors have business expenses.

Although fans form affection for certain venues, ultimately the music and musicians come first, so loyalties shift when a club changes programming, goes out of business, or when the action moves elsewhere. "People who get to be listeners like we are follow the music, wherever it goes," maintained Steve Dalachinsky; "If it's a nice venue, that's really wonderful, but the music comes first, the venue second." As a local on a budget, he prefers to stay in the city, but can cite colleagues who trek great distances to see favorite artists: "I know people who follow Evan Parker from Tonic to upstate New York, and then to some other places. It depends on how crazy you are and how much money you want to spend to do it." Venues are only means to an end. Proprietors cannot *create* a scene, but they can provide an appropriate space, then *allow* the scene to invent itself.

Conflicts of artistic and economic interest within the avant-jazz community are dramatically illustrated in the history of the Knitting Factory. At its former location on Houston Street,[19] "The Knit" was an epicenter of new improvised music from the early eighties to the midnineties.[20] Tensions developing between owner Michael Dorf and certain musicians were exacerbated when journalist Steven Mirkin lauded Dorf in a article,[21] prompting John Lurie, leader of one of the Knit's "house bands," to refute Mirkin's praise in a letter to the magazine's editor. "Take the time and actually call John Zorn, Marc Ribot, James Blood Ulmer, [or] Steven Bernstein," Lurie wrote, "anybody who helped the little creep get his club off the ground, and ask them. These people that I've listed are the ones who got top treatment from Dorf because he needed them. The way he treats lesser-known musicians is criminal." Lurie called for a boycott of the venue, believing Dorf had "gotten rich off the backs of a lot of musicians who, mostly, still can't afford to pay their phone bills."[22] In a subsequent letter to the editor, Dorf rejoined that, although he respected Lurie's talent, "John can also be difficult to work with and sometimes goes overboard with criticism. A few years ago he participated in our jazz festival and to a half-full theater he said, 'Fuck the Knitting Factory and Michael Dorf.' At first I was hurt, then shrugged it off as an eccentric genius who likes to complain, as he often does, but seems to smile and be my 'friend' when we pay him (often at financial loss) or go to lunch to plan the next gig."[23] Discord between Dorf and musicians eventually affected the entire avant-jazz community.

Fans loved the Knit for its music, and many took advantage of its lenient admission policies, but they sympathized with the plight of performers. "The Knitting Factory was still very much a part of the scene, up until a few years ago, when the focus shifted," Harold Meiselman reported; "A large part of that was based on the shitty treatment that musicians got from the owner, the fact that he would take advantage—or they felt that he would—of them financially and provide very poor working conditions, while they had made his club successful by adopting it as a place to have their scene and then developed this following. A lot of musicians felt that there was no appreciation or sense of gratitude." Irving Stone, a personal friend of John Zorn, watched as the latter's eight-year-plus relationship with Dorf steadily eroded, until "one day Dorf taped a rehearsal, without telling anybody he was doing it, and that was the straw that broke the camel's back." The action raised flags because Dorf ran an in-house label that released live recordings of venue performances. Zorn had previously complained to Stone, "Every time I talk to him, I see dollar signs dancing in his eyes," to which Stone had replied, "Well, you ain't got no place else to play, really. *Tolerate* it," reminding Zorn that he was lucky to have a place to perform his (Zorn's) highly experimental, marginally profitable music. As a friend, Stone empathized with Zorn and other musicians; as a fan, he benefited from Dorn's willingness to present radical, defiantly "*anti*-popular" music; and as a pragmatist he realized that both Zorn and Dorf made sacrifices for the music and would benefit from cooperation. "Since I'm looking for music," he concluded wryly, "I sometimes don't realize that my answers are prejudiced."[24]

Venue operators can benefit from the input of experienced fans who've got their fingers on the pulse. "Michael Dorf didn't know anything," Stephanie Stone maintained. "He didn't have *no* taste!" agreed her husband; "We all told him who to book, pretty much, at the beginning." Harold Meiselman independently confirmed the Stones' claims: "Stephanie and [Irving] Stone and Bruce [Gallanter] and Steve Dalachinsky really *taught* this guy about the music and who to book and whatnot." Irving Stone described how Dorf had consulted him about contracting a musician for his annual festival: "He [Dorf] said, 'Who's Archie Shepp?' and I said: 'Hire him. He hasn't played in New York for eight years. Don't give him the store, but hire him.' And then, after the thing, he said, 'He drew the best of anybody,' and I said, 'Next time, you listen to *me!*'"[25] Stone correctly surmised that fans would come out of the woodwork when someone of Shepp's stature came to town. He knew, however, that avant-jazz "prophets" don't always turn profits for those presenting them, so his warning to Dorf to not overpay Shepp may reflect his self-interest in keeping Dorf's "store" solvent for future shows.

Downtown fans demonstrated their loyalty to music (over venues) with a mass exodus from the Knitting Factory, following in the wake of John Zorn and other disgruntled musicians. According to Irving Stone, the unauthorized taping incident prompted Zorn to look for a new venue: "So [he] went out on his bicycle and found Tonic." As he'd done for Dorf, Stone offered Zorn some advice on booking acts:

> He [Zorn] calls me: "I found a place." I says, "Where is it?" and he tells me where it is. And I says, "Is there a subway near there?" "Yeah." "Okay, good." [He] calls back the next day: "I'm booking the first month. . . . This is the list: we have this and this and this and this." And I said: "That's nice. What's this, a *white* club? You ain't got no black people." I mean, the whole list was white players. He says, "You know I'm straight about that." I says, "I know you're straight about that, but what if somebody comes by and says, 'You got thirty acts and they're all white acts?' What're you going to tell them: 'Stone'll vouch for you?' You're out of your mind!" "Okay, let me think on it." Next day he calls up—maybe a day was skipped—he says, "Okay." He's going to get some black acts. He's also got some acts with women leaders. Good boy! I gave you one, you got the other. We're straight now with society as it exists and we can go on.

Tonic owners John and Melissa Caruso Scott adopted a progressive policy in which guest curators (usually musicians) booked each month, resulting in highly eclectic programming. The Knitting Factory continued to present avant-jazz in its Old Office lounge, but mainly featured rock acts. Soon avant-jazz activity at Tonic had reached a critical mass and it became the scene's new epicenter (see Figures 28 and 29).

For a nine-year period, beginning with John Zorn's two-month curatorship in Spring 1998, Tonic filled the void created when "the Old Knit" closed, but gradually lost some of its hard-core downtown fanbase when programming expanded to include electronica, deejays, indie rock, and pop musics. In an interview given when Tonic was the most prominent downtown venue, Steve Dalachinsky cautioned: "Tonic is a very nice place, *but*, if the entire crew, if Zorn took up his entourage, everybody took up *their* entourage, and if Zorn had a fight with Tonic and moved everybody he loves out of Tonic like he moved them out of the Knitting Factory." Pausing to let the idea sink in, Dalachinsky reiterated his earlier point: "People like us *follow* the *music*! The venue is *secondary*." Yuko Otomo concurred with him: "We're like cockroaches following crumbs!"[26] Sure enough, audience attendance was diverted from Tonic when Zorn opened The Stone, a no-frills performance space named in honor of Irving Stone, who had recently passed. Like Tonic, it featured a (mostly) musician-curated calendar of avant-jazz and other experimental music. In spite of widespread efforts by fans and musicians, which included a series of benefit concerts and grassroots activism, Tonic closed in April 2007, victim to rapidly rising overhead costs (doubled rent, tripled insurance, required structural repairs, and theft). Its closing caused much consternation in the community: the Caruso Scotts had been sympathetic and knowledgeable supporters of the experimental music, their venue the largest (180 seats) to support the scene(s). Although the couple has continued to present occasional concerts in cooperation with Abrons Art Center, Tonic now exists only in cyberspace and memory.

For lack of a "club/house" downtown, fans have been even more peripatetic in the ensuing years, spreading their attendance across a larger number of smaller venues.[27] The Stone remains an important hub but has not dominated the scene to the extent that the Old Knit and Tonic did. Set up by John Zorn as a nonprofit organization, it pays performers all of the door receipts (Tonic's owners retained 25 percent of the door), but has limited seating, no food or bar, and a bathroom directly behind the stage, impossible to visit during sets. Photographer Peter Gannushkin's *Downtown Music* photo-blog[28] provides informal evidence of the decentralization of the scene(s) in recent years. The Russian-born avant-jazz fan/photographer has been an exceptionally prolific concert attendee whose online photo diary contains thousands of images of avant-jazz musicians performing. Beginning in June 2000, a majority of his shots were taken at Tonic concerts; five years later, almost from the day it opened, The Stone became a clear favorite in his postings. Later on, he apportioned coverage to other venues like Barbès, Douglass Street Music Collective, I-Beam, ISSUE Project Room, Littlefield, Local 269, Le Poisson Rouge, and Roulette.

His blog also covers local and international festivals, most notably the annual Vision Festival, which one fan called "The World Series" of downtown music, an event that has moved through many different venues since its inception in 1996.[29] By comparison, mainstream jazz's "corporate headquarters" is at Lincoln Center, its ancestral "home" at the Village Vanguard, New York's oldest jazz clubhouse/shrine, whose location and importance haven't changed since 1935.

WHAT IS HIP? SOCIAL DETERMINANTS OF TASTE

"What is hip?" asks the Tower of Power song, "Do you think you know?"[30] Beauty may lie in the eyes and ears of beholders but, as the parable of "The Emperor's New Clothes"[31] suggests, it can also be what others convince us to see, or what we convince our*selves* to see. So what separates hip from hype? To what extent are our tastes in and experiences of music mediated by outside influences? While people respond to music autonomously and instinctively, they also bring certain preconceptions and predispositions to their listening experiences. Some hear beauty where others hear a beast—and vice versa. In the avant-jazz scene, fans in search of "blood" or "the perfect set" tolerate extremely dissonant and chaotic music, yet still hold performances to rigorous critical standards.[32] In other scenes, such as the Sidney Bechet Society, a consortium of trad(itional) jazz fans, musical structures are often more codified and canonized. Whatever their aesthetic criteria, fan communities typically reach a consensus in their evaluations of particular performances, suggesting a degree of social intersubjectivity, an inextricable intertwining of public and private tastes.[33]

Music, and information about music, is filtered to fans through myriad sources: mass media and commercial recordings; live concerts; ambient music in business establishments or performance venues; internet sources (blogs, chat rooms, YouTube, Pandora radio, shared playlists, artist websites, feeds, top-ten lists, and so forth); concert flyers, pamphlets, or postings; and word of mouth. The entertainment industry invests significant promotional machinery behind potential moneymakers, priming target audiences to preapprove their products; although they cannot ultimately dictate public taste,[34] record companies and advertising media do influence listeners in terms of what's available, what's exposed, and how it's presented. Fans may also be influenced by various "authorities," public arbiters of taste such as radio deejays, critics, journalists, publicists, and venue proprietors, among others, whose opinions carry weight because of their experience, status, and/or charisma. Anyone in a jazz community can influence others' tastes: a respected artist revealing his or her favorite artists, a prominent venue featuring unknown "talent deserving of wider recognition,"[35] a critic panning a recording, or a fan raving about a concert.

In the popular imagination, jazz is often thought to be cool/hip, earthy/funky, original/unconventional, and/or deep/sophisticated. "Jazz represents quality, it represents art," ventured producer George Wein (see Figure 11), "it represents Culture-with-a-capital-C." Restaurants use jazz (canned or live) to create an elegant or artsy ambiance, usually at low volumes that won't disturb patrons. Visitors to New York often seek a "jazz experience," so heavily touristed venues announce and enforce no-talking policies during shows to insure that neophyte listeners won't breach etiquette. Some fans may respond to the *sight*—not the sound—of jazz, as in Lujira Cooper's earlier recollection of being transfixed by the movements of a bass player's fingers.[36] Singer Patricia Barber pokes fun at pseudohipsters in her song "Company": "I go to the club, talk through the show; I'm so hip there's nothing about jazz that I don't know; I read the critic[']s evaluation. . . . I like a loud and noisy tune if that's what everyone else thinks is cool."[37] Underlying her humor is the suggestion that some people "wear" jazz like a lifestyle accessory in order to appear à la mode or impress their friends (or perhaps them*selves*). As Andy Bennett and Richard Peterson note, "A few at the core of [a] scene may live that life entirely, but, in keeping with a late-modern context in which identities are increasingly fluid and interchangeable, most participants regularly put on and take off the scene identity."[38]

To explore and evolve their tastes, collectors consult liner notes to discover salient elements of a recording; Irving Stone often checked them to identify a particular soloist who had caught his ear. Curious listeners can research the internet. AllMusic.com lists an artist or group's biography, discography (rated by the website and by viewers on a one- to five-star scale), similar-sounding artists, artists they've been influenced by, and artists they've had an influence on. Search algorithms on Amazon.com or Pandora radio suggest music to potential shoppers based on previous purchasing patterns or "recently viewed items." A fan of, say, saxophonist Hank Mobley can create a Pandora station that plays Mobley's recordings and also introduces "similar" artists (as determined by staff raters).[39] Tourists use the internet to find local clubs, tours, and other information. Harold Meiselman illustrated how one source leads to another: "I was into Frank Zappa. I read about him, and he discussed being interested in a wide range of musicians, including Webern, Boulez, Ornette Coleman, and I sought out those artists and listened to them. And a local record store near the college would recommend things, so I started listening to Coltrane and discovered I had a taste for more "outside" jazz.[40] Then my taste expanded exponentially into most of the 1960s avant-garde artists, then European free jazz, and I found reading books like *Penguin Guide*[41] tremendously useful, and seeking recommendations for things I might be interested in." Proactive fans have infinite avenues to discover new musical experiences, limited only by their enthusiasm.

Interpersonal relationships can play a strong role in developing taste. The internet has opened new channels of communication among fans—friends share playlists on Facebook and other social networking sites; people blog or chat about recordings, musicians, and performances—but face-to-face interactions are especially important. Record retailer Manny Maris reported that he enjoys sussing out customers' musical preferences and making recommendations based on what he thinks they'll like, and feels especially gratified if they return to verify his predictions. English jazz fans Jo Gilks, Lawrence Gibb, and Jerry Sykes, intrigued by tours and favorable client reviews posted on Gordon Polatnick's *Big Apple Jazz* website, hired him to take them to various "under-the-radar" spots they couldn't have found on their own. Steve Dalachinsky described how Bruce Gallanter helped him overcome his initial bias against Rudolph Grey and other guitarists: "[He] gave me very good advice. I said, 'Bruce, you know I'm not into electric guitars, unless it's some rock'n'roll group I happen to like,' and he says, 'Well, you love to listen to saxophone players. Why don't you try to listen to Rudolph like he's a saxophone player? Listen to the sheets of sound[42] like you'd listen to Coltrane.' I was still very open, so I said, 'Great, I'll try it out.' I went and heard the music, thinking, I'm going to listen like Bruce suggested—and *PHWHAHH*!! 'Wow, that's not so bad! That *works*!'" Richard Berger consults his fan-friends to find out where the action is: "We talk: 'Oh, you going to Tonic tonight?' 'Yeah, I'll see you at Roulette tomorrow, and Saturday we'll be at the Knitting Factory, alright?' You go over the schedule with people: where you're going, who you're gonna see next, that kind of stuff." In all of the above examples, fans' tastes are strongly influenced by interpersonal rapport.

Not everyone is amenable to peers' suggestions, however; as fans sharpen and refine their critical faculties they may simultaneously lose some peripheral perspective. Historically, heated altercations between diehard trad-jazz fans (aka "moldy figs") and those who embraced bebop (aka "modernists") were a result of insular aesthetic criteria. Even an innovator like Duke Ellington—whose big-band arrangements broke many "rules"—had trouble accepting bop, comparing it to "playing Scrabble with all the vowels missing."[43] More recently, Jazz at Lincoln Center artistic director Wynton Marsalis and documentary filmmaker Ken Burns have been roundly criticized for advancing similarly conservative viewpoints. Irving Stone poked fun at his friend Jack Farrell, the author of a book on jazz,[44] for his doctrinaire attitudes: "[Jack] had a theory that a trumpet player plays the lead, the trombone plays contrapuntal parts, the clarinet plays [decorations][45]—and there you have Dixieland. Okay. [But] Jack Farrell won't listen to anything else; that's against some deep-set principle." Stone decided to play a friendly trick on Farrell to test his orthodoxy. "Farrell comes over to a mutual friend's house, [who says] "Jack is coming." I say, "Play him Art Tatum's *Tiger Rag*." Farrell listens to it, and there's a huge smile on his face, and then he figures out that it's Art Tatum—and he's not supposed to like Art Tatum. Therefore, the smile comes off and he has no comment to make, because he enjoyed it, *motherfucker*! [*laughs*] Until he found out he wasn't supposed to enjoy it in accordance with his theory of music."[46] Stone's gambit exposes how listeners, especially those with cultivated tastes, can develop strong preconceptions about music, aesthetic filters that prevent them from hearing new music with open ears.

Even so-called progressive fans may adopt orthodox opinions. When I spoke with webpage editor Margaret Davis Grimes, she asked me who my favorite musicians were, and upon hearing my list,[47] chided me that they were all dead. I quickly amended the roster to include contemporary artists like Peter Bernstein, Seamus Blake, Kurt Rosenwinkel, Josh Redman, and Mark Turner (all of whom hew closer to jazz's "mainstream" than its avant-garde), but she still wasn't impressed: "Nobody wants a Peter Bernstein album—I'm *sorry*! [*laughs*] I don't know how to break this to you, but nobody *wants* it! He sounds like people who played fifty years ago." I countered that Redman's CDs were selling relatively well. "Yeah," she replied, "people who don't like jazz want a Joshua Redman album; people who love jazz want a *Dewey* Redman album [*laughs*]." Dewey, Joshua's father, was most noted for his collaborations with free jazz pioneer Ornette Coleman. He, not his son, measures up to Davis Grimes's standards: that an artist must represent—and revolutionize—his or her times.[48]

Peer interactions within scenes can encourage peers to accept unfamiliar artists and music. "It's pretty *un*common for somebody that I would see at Evan Parker, Peter Brötzmann, and Cecil Taylor *not* to like other musicians in that vein, even though they're all very different and unique," observed Harold Meiselman; "It's rare that somebody who appreciates *them* would say, 'I *like* Cecil Taylor, but I *don't* like Derek Bailey'—because it's a *sensibility*. I mean—if you're familiar with it—the sensibility you have that allows you to appreciate *one* is there to let you hear the merit in the *other*, or find something interesting in it." When fans share such sensibilities, they learn to trust each other's judgment. Like Richard Berger and other avant-jazz fans, Meiselman often consults his circle, confident they'll steer him straight: "These people are not trying to put one over on me, so I'm going to go. And that's what I frequently do with Irving Stone, Bruce [Gallanter], Peter Cox, or Steve Dalachinsky. It's like: 'Where are you going next?' 'Oh, I didn't think about *that*, but *yeah*, that sounds like a good idea!' Frequently it's a *choice*: 'Are you going *here*, or *there*?' And on any given night in New York there could be a choice of half a dozen things to go to!" He's also noticed similar exchanges on internet posts: "They're saying: 'Are you going *here*?' 'No, I'm going to see *this* person, or *that* person,' or, 'No, I didn't like him the *last* time he played.'"

Several fans claimed that positive feedback and favoritism can be taken too far. "We also had a quality that the Stones had, which I think is very important, which a lot of listeners are *missing*," alleged Steve Dalachinsky, citing a hypothetical example: "I won't name any names, because this is where we'll get in *more* trouble, but Mr. Y is a real fan of Mr. X. Mr. Y goes to every gig Mr. X does, records it, loves Mr. X." "He becomes biased," added Yuko Otomo. "Right," confirmed Dalachinsky, "the problem with Mr. Y is Mr. X can do no wrong." Understandably, Dalachinsky's outspokenness has not always been well received, by musicians or fans: "We *saw* these guys who either lived in New York or came here to make it, everything they went through: how they—*I* think—corrupted and weakened their own music. And, you know, we don't have a right to *say* those things out loud, so it's very frustrating. A lot of them stopped communicating with me because they would ask my opinion and I would *tell* them! After a while, people don't want to hear 'How was I last night?'—because they always tell you they really want to know, but they *don't* really want to know."[49] Candor can be risky when one's opinions oppose positively "biased" community consensus.

The more intimate the scene, the more difficult it may be for individuals to express dissension. As a music photographer who prefers to "maintain a certain amount of journalistic distance," Jack Vartoogian is well familiar with a number of jazz scenes. "The downtown thing has a bit of the outsider quality to it," he asserted; "They're very friendly and all this, but if you wander outside of the line of *their* thinking they get mad and storm away. There's a little bit of a circling-the-wagons mentality. I've seen it happen in a couple of situations, when people who write about this stuff *don't* toe the line properly. You know, you can't really be critical sometimes." He notices a difference between tourist-based mainstream jazz venues and the partisan-based experimental jazz scene: "You can be critical *up*town all the time and people'll take potshots at you, but it doesn't *matter*, because there's *not* that community in the way that it sort of exists down there, with everybody loving this stuff."[50] He singled out Dalachinsky and Otomo as exceptions: "This does not *apply* to people like Steve and Yuko.

They're part of that—he's totally opinionated—but he does it in the proper way, where we can talk and disagree, and it doesn't *matter*—*that's* what's so special about them. Steve will come out and say, 'Oh man! Boy! *That* was a waste of time!' You don't hear that much." While fans experience relative anonymity in "uptown" venues, the more intimate downtown venues foster close social cohesion, along with peer pressure, even prejudice.[51]

"Irving [Stone] was also very vocal about it," Dalachinsky reported, "but he's an older guy and it was a different story." As a venerated "elder statesman," Stone held a unique status in the downtown community. Musicians and fans alike respected his judgment, to the point that his very presence at concerts (usually accompanied by Stephanie, his wife) was generally seen as an omen of good musical things to come. Consider the following statements: "If the Stones were in the house you knew you were in the right place" (Jim Eigo); "When the Stones were in the audience for a gig, you knew something special was about to happen" (Bruce Gallanter); and, "If Stone liked [my music], I knew I was on the right track" (Joe Morris).[52] Stone himself strongly rejected this imposed role of arbiter of community taste, believing people should judge for themselves. "It's nobody's business how I feel. I'm not hiding it, but this is *dumb*. What did *you* hear? Fundamentally it's between *you* and the people up there that are doing it." He likewise rejected the idea that community consensus signifies quality: "[A] young Asian guy came up to me and said, 'I see you all the time; whenever's [*sic*] good gig, I see you. We have good taste!' I said, 'No, we have the *same* taste'—and that was the end of that conversation." Pressed for clarification, he elaborated: "We go to the same things! *So*? [*laughs*] We may be fucked up in the same way!—is another way to look at it. Somebody once said to me, 'I have good taste,' and I said, 'Whaddya mean? You *agree* with yourself?' What *else* can it mean?" Stone believed that musical taste should be autonomous and authentic, not socially derived or intellectually contrived: "It's what I hear, it's what it makes me feel, that matters."

Stone's influence on his peers entailed more than being a guru of "good" taste and independent thinking; his devotion to listening instilled in others a sense of the music's profundity. John Zorn claimed that the Stones' "support and enthusiasm gave a newly emerging scene the feeling that what we were creating had value and meaning."[53] Yuko Otomo stated that, "To be able to listen to this kind of music, in this amount, for *me*, is such a privilege, and I feel this privilege should be shared. So I naturally formed a certain sense of responsibility: not just an on-and-off listener, I have to be a *serious* listener." It was Stone, she claimed, who inspired her to go even deeper: "Irving Stone has the same sense of mission, as a listener—they do, but especially *he* does—because he's been with the music from Duke Ellington, Charlie Parker, Monk, and Ornette Coleman. He *really* lived through the history of this so-called jazz music, so he has a clear sense. . . . He doesn't *talk* about it. He will never have a pretension to tell you that he has that obsessive mission, but he *does*, and very deep inside. That's one thing I've learned from him."[54] "I loved Stone for his love of the music. . . . He was the muse," asserted trumpeter Herb Robertson; saxophonist Oliver Lake was more succinct: "Stone was music."[55] Whether he changed anyone's taste is open to question, but there's no doubt that Stone showed his extended avant-jazz "family" *how* to listen: with deep intent.

Can someone truly "know thyself"—as Socrates charged—in terms of taste? How do listeners learn to appreciate radically experimental improvisation? More bluntly, what separates such "music" from noise? "To the untrained ear, the thing with Derek Bailey is: 'Oh, any *child* could mess around with the guitar to produce what he's producing—totally random abstract sounds and scrapings and everything *but* the traditional use of the instrument,'" observed Harold Meiselman; "The difference is that everything he does, to an extremely large degree, is *intentional*; he knows exactly what sound he's going to get. Cecil Taylor can rattle off a ninety-minute improvisation, and someone not familiar with his music, or that *style* of music, could think he's just *banging* on the piano for two hours! But he's got such technical facility. When he takes his elbow and smashes it, he *knows*, to the exact key and pressure on each key— *I* believe—what it's going to sound like, and there's nothing random there." Not everyone shares Meiselman's appraisal of Taylor's playing style. "I took my cousin to see [him]," he mused, "and she said: '*I* think this is all a big con! Everybody's *fooling* themselves! You don't *like* this! You *can't* like this! What is there to *like? They* don't know what they're doing! They don't know how to play.'" Meiselman disclosed that, although he doesn't understand what Taylor does, he nevertheless enjoys the process: "I challenge myself to try to hear the structure in a Cecil Taylor improvisation, because I know it's there, but it's just so complex." Under closer scrutiny, seemingly unorganized or aleatoric music may reveal underlying structures and schema, but where one person hears "intention" another may hear "a big con."

Conversations with avant-jazz and other fans reveal their deep awareness of musical nuances, however difficult these may be to describe. We've seen in the previous chapter how some fans identify certain significant elements (e.g., musical structure, instrumental timbres) or contexts (e.g., an artist's previous work or stylistic lineage). Other aspects of their listening experience, however, are less easily identified, remaining perhaps in the realm of the subconscious.

There is no question, however, that these inarticulable understandings form part of the listener's perceptual paradigm, affecting what and how he or she hears. Furthermore, fans connected to intimate scenes become part of its collective consciousness of music, a shared awareness mediated through each participant's input, where beauty, truth, and what is hip reveal themselves through a subtle synthesis of personal and interpersonal factors.

FAN VERSUS HIMSELF: DIVIDED NIGHTS

One of the occupational hazards associated with jazz fandom in New York City was dubbed "divided nights" by Steve Dalachinsky, denoting the desire to be in two different places at once.[56] Judy Balos, Roberta DeNicola, Yuko Otomo, Stephanie Stone, Jack Vartoogian, and others spoke of the anxiety created when simultaneously scheduled events force fans to choose between them or try to attend both. Cinephiles and art enthusiasts have repeated opportunities to watch films or visit an exhibition, but jazz performances are of-the-moment and therefore impossible to revisit; even high fidelity recordings can't reproduce the experience of being there. The problem is aggravated by the plethora of jazz performances offered in New York City. In addition to a couple dozen full-time jazz venues, there are hundreds of other clubs and performance spaces presenting live music.[57] A glance through available listings[58] reveals dozens of options on any given night; even more unlisted performances occur at neighborhood bars and other low profile venues. Even specialized genres like avant-jazz or traditional jazz often offer a choice between concurrent events. Avid fans want to be present for these events—especially when a legendary performer makes a rare appearance—and will experience a sense of loss if they can't go.

Deciding between two shows produces "conflict" in a fan's mind. Yuko Otomo compared it to an addict's cravings: "You can talk about addiction, but it's *beyond* addiction. I don't like to use that terminology, but this is like you want to be in three different places at the same time. There's a conflict, a *huge* conflict, a dilemma; it's like a life and death pain that they go through." On May 21, 2003, for example, avant-jazz fans could choose between seeing English saxophonist Paul Dunmall at "the old Knit" or vocalist Patty Waters at the opening night of Vision Festival VIII. "Roberta and Richard will be sitting here at the Vision Festival, but all these other guys—Peter, Bruce—they'll all be going over here," predicted Steve Dalachinsky; "So that's going to be a very divided night." Dunmall rarely performed in the city, while Waters was returning to concertizing after a long hiatus, making it difficult to choose between the two historically important events. "It fucks your brain up more than anything," noted Dalachinsky; "Some of us go through it more. *I* do: I go nuts; I'm *to*tally mentally ill." "Some people *really* suffer," laughed Otomo; "This is like you have a complete split, and you are *forced* to be this twisted, and it's very difficult." She admitted that she suffers too, but resigns herself once she's made a decision: "I kind of precalculate the value, the *possible* values: 'This might happen, this might happen.' So I set my mind and I settle in." Others however, including her husband, have difficulty "settling in": "Steve's schizo. He can't do that. He goes crazy. So many people go through the same thing. They just can't help it."

Some fans go to great lengths to contend with divided nights, traveling to two, three, or more different venues in the same evening. Richard Berger and Roberta DeNicola once went to Sunday evening in-store concerts at Bruce Gallanter's Downtown Music Gallery, leaving early to see Dee Pop's Freestyle Events in the basement of CBGB's, walking distance away. For years, they'd catch at least three sets every Sunday, return to their Staten Island residence, and go to work Monday morning. "That's hard," noted DeNicola; "We give up a lot because day gigs get in the way."[59] Late- or all-night gigs, especially during the week, are not a good option for elderly fans or those with early jobs. "In the beginning I used to run back and forth: jump on the train, or walk at top speed from one place to the other, [or] I'd ride a bike—usually the top limit was three gigs a night," reported Steve Dalachinsky; "I'd say, 'Come on, Yuko, it's only across town,' and we'd *walk*, all the way from the Knitting Factory to The Cooler."[60] He cited a similarly active associate: "This kid, 'Steve the Mailman,' you'll see him: 'Where you coming from, Steve?' 'Oh, I just came from Tonic.' 'Where're you going Steve? Are you going to *work*?' 'Uh, yeah, I gotta go; I've got a late-night shift at the post office,' or it will be, 'Oh no, I want to go see the last set at the Jazz Gallery,' and he'd go all the way across town." Both Steves, the poet and the postman, are just two examples of a more prevalent pattern: "There're a *lot* of people that do it," Dalachinsky attested; "Richard and Roberta'll go to a couple of places a night, Bruce has done it, [though] he doesn't do it as much anymore; I *still* do it, but I really try not to, I'm trying to cut down."[61] The vigorous club-hopping described here is possible only because of the city's unique topography—i.e., the (relatively) large number of avant-jazz venues in close proximity. As another scenester surmised, "It's a New York thing."[62]

In spite of yeoman efforts to cover all bases, zealous concertgoers are apt to suffer some level of frustration or disappointment. Steve Dalachinsky described how he rushed from a poetry reading with pianist Matthew Shipp to see Anthony Braxton play a solo saxophone concert uptown: "The gig [with Shipp] was *beau*tiful! [but] I wouldn't have *done* it this night if I knew about the Braxton thing in advance. . . . The minute the gig is over, instead of even waiting to get my check, or sitting to hear Billy Bang play what I heard was a really glorious set, I *ran* out of the fuckin' place, *ran* uptown, to catch as much of Braxton's solo concert as I could." "He disappeared!" interjected Yuko Otomo, "and then he came *back*." "It's the middle of the concert," Dalachinsky continued; "I got to see forty-odd minutes of Braxton, which was—in its own way—heaven. But then I'm thinking, 'How could I leave the Vision Festival like that? What am I, crazy?' And when I came back, it was, 'Aaay, Steve, you missed a really great set. Man, Joe Morris really played his ass off!' And I said, 'Oh yeah? Well, maybe I should've stayed. *Ah*, no, I saw Braxton, so that was okay.'" Dalachinsky was "divided," physically and mentally, between uptown and downtown, between Braxton's music and Bang's, but resolved his conflict by rationalizing that "heaven" trumps "a really great set."

A week later, a similar incident occurred when Peter Brötzmann's tentet played Tonic the same night Sonny Simmons appeared at the Vision Festival. A group of fans made a plan to catch Brötzmann's first set and then leave to see Simmons. "We go to Tonic and see the first Brötzmann set," related Steve Dalachinsky; "*Ah*, it's a good set. Yuko said, 'It's good, but it could be better.' I said, 'Look, I'm going back to the Vision Festival; I gotta work the concession table, and I wanna see Sonny Simmons.' Yuko, for the first time in her *life*, said, 'I'm not going; I'm staying here; I want to see Brötzmann's second set.'" "I didn't want to go back and forth," Otomo explained. Once he got to the festival, Dalachinsky second-guessed his decision, ultimately deciding to stay: "I'm sitting there, in the middle of Sonny Simmons, saying, 'Yeah, they're playing really good, but man, I betcha Brötzmann's playing much better this set. I gotta get back there!' I thought, 'No, no, stay here. Do the table. You'll sell CDs for people, they'll be happy.'" When the rest of the fans joined him an hour later, someone remarked, "Wow Steve, the second set was *so* much better than the first; you have *no* idea!" Otomo agreed: "The second set was phe*nom*enal. *Everybody* said that. Ten people in chorus said that [to Steve]: 'You missed the *best* show *ever*!!'" She laughed amiably remembering her husband's distress and imitated his forlorn expression. Dalachinsky conceded her point, with reservations: "I bet you're right. But, you know, it's always the best show when you're not there. Someone finally burned me a CD of it and sent it to me. I listened to it and it's a very, very good set. Whether it would've been the best show ever, I don't know, because for me, I would probably've been sitting there saying, 'Wow, they're playing much better than the first set, but I sure want to see Sonny Simmons. I *love* Sonny Simmons.'"[63]

"I do have that," commented Judy Balos when I asked her about the divided nights syndrome; "I don't want to miss anything! How can I choose? Why do they both have to be at the same time?!" She related an experience that had been particularly disappointing:

> Craig Harris—I happen to love his playing, he's a friend—was playing at the Rubin [Museum of Art], which I really wanted to see him play in, and I knew he was bringing his didgeridoo, which I *love*. And that was my plan: to go there. Then I saw that this bass choir thing had Richard Davis, who is an old friend, and Richard never comes to New York anymore. And it's like, "Oh, what do I *do*?" One starts at seven, one starts at eight, but they're both open-seating. If I go to the Rubin for half an hour—I don't wanna pay twenty dollars for half an hour, but Craig would put me on the guest list if I asked him—but then I really can't stay long enough to leave to get to the other one and get a decent seat, 'cause it's open-seating. So I gave up Craig, and it turned out the bass concert was the worst I'd been to in years and years and years—maybe *ever*—and it was *so* disappointing. It was really painful, and then I missed something really good that I wanted to see. But, you know, I *try*. But I haven't learned how to calm myself.

She claimed that it used to be easier to go to several shows a night in the city, but when certain clubs started opening earlier "it made it harder," adding an additional level of frustration. "You can still do it," she said; "I try not to *over*do it, you know, but by many people's standards I do."

These anecdotes illustrate the conflicted emotions of committed concertgoers, the frustration of missing an important event coupled with a willingness to laugh at their own fanatic/"fan-addict" behavior. "It's very tragicomic: for the person who's suffering, it's a tragedy; but from outside, it's a comedy," mused Yuko Otomo; "We're like students who go to the music department to get a poetry degree—so we never get it." "We still talk about a Japanese film we didn't see because we chose the music over the film," said Steve Dalachinsky, "and the funny thing is, we have no remembrance of what the music was [*laughs*], but we remember the exact film we didn't go to see." He has tried a longanimous approach—"I made a determination last year: if you've got a conflict, you pick *one thing*; and then that's what you've picked, and just dig it to it fullest"—but found the mindset difficult to maintain: "I *still* couldn't do it." Irving Stone reported that he had observed Dalachinsky ducking out of performances during a midsong lull only to return shortly afterward, hoping thereby to catch highlights from simultaneous shows *in the same building*: "There're two rooms at the Knitting Factory. During a bass solo upstairs, he will run downstairs to see if there's something happening over there." "He's afraid to miss anything," reflected Stephanie Stone, "so he misses a lot."[64]

Commentary by avant-jazz aficionados in this section reveals an intimate knowledge of fellow fans and themselves. Beneath their dubiety and humor lie mutual empathy and respect. The prolific club-hopping induced by "divided nights" is more than tragicomic theater: it reveals fans' desire and felt duty to witness music in its moments of creation. In this sense, the anxiety they may suffer at missed performances is counterbalanced by the transcendent moments they may experience at concerts they do attend.

*   *   *

This chapter has shown how active concertgoers, particularly avant-jazz fans, collectively identify and express themselves through improvised music. Gregarious yet self-contained, intimate communities like the downtown scene(s) exemplify both an extended family and "a group of separates." Sharing affinities and values, bonded through frequent contact in a series of adopted "club/houses," their understandings of music are empathetic and astute, a mixture of conscious and unconscious responses to individual and communal criteria. The downtown scenesters' restless quest for "blood" or "the perfect set," manifested in the near-constant presence of a core group of fans at avant-jazz events over several decades, is clear evidence that these listeners are both curious and serious.

Chapter 4

PROVIDING A PLACE AND TIME

Jazz Presenters

Jazz presenters play an indispensable role in connecting artists and audiences in the here and now of improvised performances.[1] Those interviewed for this chapter include Mitch(ell) Borden (see Figure 30), former owner/manager and current partner of Smalls and Fat Cat; Frank(o) Christopher (see Figure 8) and Paul Stache, co-owners of Smoke; Marjorie Eliot, founder of Parlor Entertainment; Dale Fitzgerald,[2] former manager/artistic director of the Jazz Gallery; Lorraine Gordon (see Figure 9), owner of the Village Vanguard; Horst Liepolt, former owner of Jazz Centre 44, co-owner and artistic director of Sweet Basil, manager of Lush Life, and a prolific festival and record producer, both in Sydney and Manhattan; "Brother" Bruce Morris, coproprietor of 5C Café & Cultural Center; Gordon Polatnick, former proprietor of EZ's Woodshed; Michael Torsone (see Figure 10), former jazz nightclub manager; and George Wein, promoter, former president of Festival Productions and producer of the Newport, Playboy, Kool, and JVC jazz Festivals, the New Orleans Jazz & Heritage Festival, and others. All of them are or have been full-time professionals whose primary income derived from patrons of their venues and productions and/or contributions from private or corporate sponsors. In contrast to the fans I interviewed, most of whom concentrated their concertgoing activities around avant-jazz venues, the presenters in this chapter represent a more diverse selection of jazz scenes and styles, from Wein's large popular festivals, to Borden's and Gordon's midsized mainstream clubs, to Eliot's and Morris's intimate neighborhood spaces.

Like the inveterate avant-jazz fans, these presenters are active, longtime participants whose daily lives are deeply invested in jazz-making and who are thus well qualified to speak about live performances. As individuals, they manifest multiple identities in jazz communities. Several are skilled musicians: Mitch Borden and Horst Liepolt studied instruments as youngsters (Borden is known for playing violin while tending door at Smalls, entertaining entering patrons with classical music excerpts), Marjorie Eliot is the primary pianist at weekend recitals held in her living room, Michael Torsone gigs as an organist/pianist, and George Wein has made cameo appearances at his annual Newport Jazz Festival, accompanying luminaries like Lester Young on piano. Furthermore, everyone in this group is a jazz fan, some with sizeable record collections and prolific concert attendance. Finally, many have engaged with jazz in various artistic and professional capacities. Horst Liepolt founded and managed a twenty-year jazz festival in Melbourne and produced hundreds of jazz records, several nominated for Grammy awards;[3] he currently paints, exhibits, and curates work treating jazz artists and themes. Dale Fitzgerald established the Jazz Gallery as a combination concert/exhibition space to display paintings, photographs, and other visual art; he studied language and religion in Ghana, holds a PhD in anthropology, and writes and speaks eloquently about jazz. Bruce Morris hosts lecture/demonstration/listening sessions on jazz history in his 5C Café & Cultural Center. Marjorie Eliot brings jazz groups to local schools and nursing homes, conducts theater and singing workshops for aspiring performers, and writes moving poetry and testimonials. Michael Torsone repairs and maintains Hammond organs and Leslie speakers in Manhattan's jazz clubs, performs regularly, and is an active concertgoer: "I'm out every night, if I can." At one time or another, all of these people have not only procured places for jazz but have also acted as musicians, professionals, and/or fans. And, like the other jazz community members represented in this book, all have made the music a central focus of their lives—aesthetically, emotionally, and financially.

FOR LOVE OR MONEY? THE BUSINESS OF LIVE JAZZ

If we think of jazz as a type of art world(s) described by Becker (1982), then presenters form part of a larger web of interactive, interdependent "workers." Jazz venue operators, like dealers who run galleries, are intermediary professionals who specialize in a particular style of music, while jazz producers, like impresarios, marshal the various elements needed to present the music before knowledgeable and receptive audiences. As in other art worlds, jazz venue operators and event producers work in conjunction with critics and other commentators whose explanations and evaluations build the reputation and value of—and ultimately the market for—certain artists and artworks. Although they are anonymous figures to most patrons, presenters must know their audiences well, insuring that the latter get their money's worth based on commonly held standards. The most successful presenters, artistically and financially, are those who listen to (and learn from) the audiences, artists, and others they associate with.[4]

Most jazz presenters get their start in the jazz business as fans. As a boy growing up in a musical household in Berlin, Horst Liepolt heard a 78 rpm LP of Louis Armstrong's *Savoy Blues*, started buying jazz records, and amassed an eight-thousand-volume collection. Moving to Melbourne, Australia, in 1951, he opened Jazz Center 44 (named for the year he "got into jazz"), a members-only listening club featuring bop and trad. He moved to Sydney in 1960, booking bands for The Basement, producing over two hundred records and numerous festivals after thirty years down under. In the sixties and seventies, he annually trekked to New York to hear live jazz and pick up hard-to-find recordings. His long-held dream to immigrate was realized in 1981 when he became a partner in Sweet Basil and ran its music program very successfully from 1981 to 1992. Over seventy years later, Liepolt remains a passionate advocate of traditional, modern, and avant-garde styles: "See, to me, jazz is jazz. If it's jazz, then it's jazz. If it isn't jazz then they can go and *stuff* themselves!

Dale Fitzgerald turned on to jazz at the Newport festival. Fascinated with Manhattan—"I was *all* about New York"—he moved in and got jobs at the legendary Tin Palace[5] and then the Village Vanguard. He was exposed to an eclectic roster of avant-jazz leaning players, thanks to Stanley Crouch, the Tin Palace's booking agent at the time. "The Tin Palace job was not that many hours a week, just enough money to keep me [solvent]," he noted, "but you get to know the staffs of all the other clubs and you get into all of them. So I could go out and hear music every night of the week, and did, three or four different places, for months." He became intrigued with artists like Arthur Blythe, David Murray, Henry Threadgill, and especially Don Pullen, following their gigs: "One thing would lead to another; it was an endless, endless rotation of places to go." The prolific free-access club-hopping that Fitzgerald describes is less feasible today, when ongoing gentrification compounded by a sluggish economy has yoked Manhattan venue operators with dramatically escalating rents and narrow profit margins; door revenues are carefully scrutinized now and even press access is tightly regulated.[6]

Bruce Morris, a fan for over fifty years, went to live jazz five or six nights a week as a young man. He estimates he's seen Miles Davis and John Coltrane over a hundred times each, Thelonious Monk fifty to sixty times, and Eric Dolphy twenty-five to thirty times. "They're the innovators. Monk: I've seen him in *many* different configurations, because after all, as great as he was, he wasn't working a lot. So whenever you got the opportunity to see him, you went to see him—I mean, that was just what you did." Morris calculated these numbers as follows: "Any artist that comes to town, by definition, you're going to see him *twice*: at the beginning of the week, and you're going to try to see him at the end of the week; if you've got more money, maybe in the middle. At that point in their lives, Miles and Coltrane were hitting Philadelphia at least four times a year, maybe five. It's pretty easy to get to a hundred, isn't it? But that's not seeing them a lot; it *sounds* like a lot, when you say 'a hundred,' but we're talking about a fifteen-year span." Why see an artist twice in the same week? "Well," Morris explained, "because what they're doing on Saturday night, even if they did the same stuff on Tuesday night, is going to be different, the approach; it's just different energy. These are jazz musicians: they don't play it with the exact same lick or in the exact same way; that's just not what they do! They're creative about it, alright?—I mean, the *great* ones." He described a series of Ornette Coleman concerts that had varied greatly from night to night and crowd to crowd. Like other active concertgoers described previously, Morris became attuned to artists' musical personalities, discerning details and appreciating nuances that might change from set to set or year to year. Moreover, like hardcore avant-jazz fans, he felt an obligation to be present for these one-of-a-kind events: "That was just what you did."[7]

Not all jazz presenters are avid fans.[8] Horst Liepolt purported that the Village Vanguard's founder, Max Gordon, whom he characterized as an "old bohemian," was more interested in jazz's supposed artistic merit than the music itself: "Max couldn't give a fuck about jazz, basically. He liked the beat poets, the folk shit, and all that. When it didn't work anymore, his agency said, 'Hey, maybe it's time to book some jazz in the joint,' and Max said, 'Yeah, why not?' If jazz came in, well, that was okay. Read his book![9] All of its enthusiasm is [for the period] *before* jazz took over, and then it became a business." To illustrate Gordon's indifference, Liepolt reported that "John Coltrane never said hello to Max; they never spoke one single word to each other!" an observation Gordon himself confirmed: "[Coltrane] was always surrounded by worshippers. I loved his music, but I never said four words to him."[10] Critic Nat Hentoff wrote of Gordon: "He actually stayed with the music he respected and *even sometimes liked* [emphasis added] rather than cash in on current scams."[11] Despite Gordon's apparent ambiguity toward the music, performers and fans alike respected his tenacity and vision, his lifelong preservation of a jazz oasis: "That's one thing he did," Liepolt conceded, "he *kept* to it."

Max Gordon was succeeded after his death in 1989 by his wife Lorraine, who at this writing still runs the Vanguard (with assistance from her daughter Deborah), the oldest continuously operated jazz club in the world. In 2013 she became the first woman to receive the NEA Jazz Masters Award for Jazz Advocacy. Her club has achieved cult status as the holiest of jazz shrines because of the numerous jazz icons that have performed and recorded there over more than eight decades. "[It] is the closest thing we have to the Camelot of jazz rooms," wrote Nat Hentoff; "[It] kept the jazz faith during parched years."[12] "It's sacred ground," confirmed Lorraine Gordon, noting how musicians, fans, and tourists often make a pilgrimage there, descending the stairs during off-hours to take a quick sample of its special vibe: "Some people don't want to come *in*, they just want to look at the place," she groused; "After a while you get historical— *I get hysterical! [laughs]*" In spite of her humor, Gordon is extremely serious about the music: "I always loved jazz. That's a very important part of running a club: you have to love the music or what you're doing. Otherwise *forget it!* It's an artistic business, you know? It's not just manufacturing paper clips or whatever. You have to love the music, and to me that's the key." Unlike her late husband, Gordon seems to be more motivated by the music than its potential profits.

Judging by the rampant turnover of venues, presenting jazz is a difficult business. Over a five-year period beginning September 2002, I compiled a list of over eight hundred and thirty venues and locations that featured jazz in New York City, a great majority of them in Manhattan, many in Brooklyn (over one hundred and forty), some in Queens (over thirty), and a few in the Bronx (about a dozen). In the ensuing decade, at least one hundred and thirty venues either closed or discontinued jazz programming,[13] while more than a hundred clubs and locations either opened or initiated jazz programming.[14] Presenters are often forced to close their businesses—sometimes relocating elsewhere—when leases expire, overheads escalate, and/or programming policies change.

A few examples will illustrate the transient existences of jazz presenters. Mitch Borden founded Smalls in 1993, ran out of money in 2002, was forced to close May 2003, then returned in March 2005 as the interim owner's employee (see Figures 30 and 31). Horst Liepolt was the primary curator of Sweet Basil until it closed in April 2001, then James Browne started Sweet Rhythm on the same site, which ran from October 2002 to October 2009. Thirty years after its initial closing, Earl Spain reopened the historic Minton's Playhouse in May

2006 until he was shut down in August 2010,[15] succeeded by Richard Parsons, who reopened the club once again on October 21, 2013. Suzanne Fiol and Marc Ribot launched the ISSUE Project Room in 2003 on the Lower East Side, moving to Gowanus, Brooklyn, in 2007; the organization won a twenty-year, rent-free lease for a downtown Brooklyn theater in 2008 and, in the wake of Fiol's death in 2009, is now developing the future site into a "permanent home for experimental arts culture."[16] In 2003, Bruce Gallanter moved his Downtown Music Gallery (established in 1991 in Cooper Square) from its second location in the Bowery to a more affordable but less convenient site in Chinatown. Shortly before CBGB's closed in October 2006, drummer Dee Pop transferred his Freestyle Events music series north to Jimmie's 43 Restaurant in the East Village for a couple of years, then south to the Lower East Side's Cake Shop, and later to Local 269. After fifteen years helming the Knitting Factory (seven years in its first location, eight more in the second), Michael Dorf stepped down in 2002; in September 2009, the club was moved to a new downsized location in Williamsburg, Brooklyn. Steve Cannon founded "A Gathering of Tribes" in his house on 3rd Street in the East Village in 1991; he sold the building in 2004 but retained the art gallery/salon/performance space on premises under a ten-year renewable lease. In spite of a prolonged grassroots campaign to save the venue, he was finally forced to relocate to a small apartment nearby in April 2014, when the original occupancy agreement expired.

Not all jazz presenters are entrepreneurs. Marjorie Eliot holds weekly workshops and concerts in her living room at her own expense: admission to Sunday concerts is free, complimentary punch and snacks are served, and donations are left to visitors' discretion. One regular performer observed that many of her visitors don't contribute money and wondered how Eliot covered costs, further speculating that many regulars would stop coming if she instituted a door charge.[17] In 2003, Eliot incurred financial difficulties when her eldest son Michael's medical condition required constant caretaking, placing her in arrears with the rent and prompting an eviction warning from the landlord. In response, Steve Zeitlin, head of City Lore (a nonprofit organization that had inducted her into its hall of fame) organized a modern-day "rent party"[18] for her, publicized in the *New York Times*.[19] The concert drew a large, paying crowd, temporarily resolving Eliot's fiscal predicament, allowing her to stay in "busi ness."

At the other end of the spectrum—on a scale and in a class by himself—is promoter George Wein, the so-called "Godfather of the Jazz Community."[20] Wein's company, Festival Productions (founded in 1969), once produced the largest and most profitable jazz shows anywhere, including the Newport Jazz

Festival (founded in 1954, the country's first and oldest annual jazz festival); New York City's JVC festival (running 1984–2008, a catholic and comprehensive "jazztravaganza" staged in prestigious venues like Carnegie Hall and Lincoln Center); and hundreds of other national and international events per year. "I'm one of the few people making a living in jazz from a profit point of view," he noted in 2003, "and the only reason I do it is I'm very good at holding on to my sponsors." Beginning with the Schlitz Salute to Jazz and Kool Jazz festivals, he was the first and most successful promoter to get corporate sponsorship for jazz events. "All the jazz festivals that I compete with are nonprofit," he said, citing the Monterey and San Francisco festivals plus two or three dozen smaller events affiliated with various schools featuring name musicians. He had to scramble for sponsors when, in response to the economic slump, JVC ended a twenty-five-year stint backing some of his largest festivals. He sold Festival Productions in 2007 (which went out of business less than two years later). He reinstated the Newport festival as a nonprofit in 2012: "I'm working pro bono," he stated; "It has nothing to do with business."[21]

Like an endangered species, jazz struggles to survive in a capitalist marketplace yet thrives in "captivity" via nonprofit protection. How have jazz festivals come to rely almost exclusively on nonprofit support? First, jazz productions—even those featuring name artists—capture only a small fraction of the concertgoing public. George Wein estimated jazz records "only amount to one, or one and a *half*, percent of the market, collectively."[22] Second, the best-selling jazz is so-called smooth jazz, a slippery category that generally refers to jazz-influenced music that incorporates elements of rock and other popular musics while deemphasizing harmonic dissonance, rhythmic ambiguity, and improvisation. Purists don't consider this music "real" jazz. "If you took out the crossover jazz," observed Wein, "the [market share] would [drop], because one jazz hit, or Harry Connick [Jr.] selling a jazz album, or putting a Kenny G in the jazz bins, sells more than 20 percent of the whole jazz market. Take those kinds of artists out of it and *God knows* what the percentage at the bottom [would be]! It's *infinitesimal!*" Even if, as he suggests, the demand for "real" jazz is minute, nonetheless "it's *enough* so that nonprofits can afford to present these artists, because even though you're paying ten or fifteen thousand dollars for pianist Cyrus Chestnut, or whoever, or seventy-five [hundred] to John Zorn, or *whoever* it is, it is still cheaper than looking for a rock group that wants seventy-five, a hundred, a hundred and twenty-five thousand dollars a night—and so they have budgets that can give music to their so-called 'curious listener,' and it can be part of their cultural programs for the year. So it's nonprofit; that's what's keeping it alive right now."

Jazz has sidestepped market competition by becoming, in essence, a ward of the state, fostered by government and corporate philanthropy. Once marginalized, North America's autochthonous art form has become a national emblem embodying essential American values: freedom, integration of diversity, celebration of individuality, and so forth. At the federal and state levels, jazz's considerable cultural capital generates grants, tax shelters, property rights, and other legislation. In the private sector, jazz enjoys sponsorship by companies that want to be associated with its image and by charitable individuals and organizations. But even with this support, jazz business isn't booming, especially for small-scale venues and events, where proprietors and producers must closely monitor markups and sales turnover to turn a profit.

Most club owners rely on door charges and food and drink revenues to sustain solvency, but other jazz presenters obtain nonprofit status and/or secure alternative funding through grants and other outside sources. Marjorie Eliot's arts outreach programs in schools, rest homes, and other community settings are supported by grant monies, though she acknowledged that these are difficult to procure. By converting the Jazz Gallery to nonprofit status, Dale Fitzgerald was able to garner grants from New York State Council on the Arts, New York City Department of Cultural Affairs, American Music Center's Liberty Initiative for New York, and other foundations.[23] The venue also received assistance from Paul Weinstein, a seasoned fan with a long mailing list of well-to-do, jazz-loving associates. "All of his life, Weinstein has been involved with jazz, as financial mentor, as a benefactor, as someone who finds the bread to get the [job done]," declared Fitzgerald, "and he helped get the whole New School program off the ground." Weinstein personally mailed a hundred and seventy letters to friends soliciting funds for a new program called "The Early Set," an evening concert series catering to elderly fans wishing to go to a show and return home at a reasonable hour. Pleading that Fitzgerald was forced to run the Gallery on "a shoestring," Weinstein's letters quickly generated enough cash to float the project. The Gallery couldn't survive without such assistance, Fitzgerald explained, because ticket sales alone weren't meeting overhead costs.[24]

When a new lease increased the Jazz Gallery's rent almost 200 percent, even as several grant sources dried up, pressure to generate revenue intensified. In December 2002, Fitzgerald's emailer to "Jazz Gallerians" cited "harsh financial difficulties" and climbing costs: "On every front, and from clearly established patterns in current economic trends, [for] not-for-profit cultural institutions . . . the word is 'cutbacks'/'defunding'/'sorry we're not interested at this time.'" His communiqué avowed: "[W]e can do but one thing: look to those individual[s] and institutions that have recognized the significance of our enterprise and make clear to them that the future existence of such an undertaking is in their hands."[25] The Gallery held its first benefit concert in June 2004, featuring the donated services of Dr. Lonnie Smith and Roy Hargrove,[26] and has continued to run seasonal benefit events to meet expenses. In 2009, Dale Fitzgerald retired as executive director, succeeded by Deborah Steinglass, who initiated a number of innovative fund-raising approaches, including a pledge drive to fund musicians' use of the building as a practice space during the day.[27] In September 2011, Pat Metheny, one of jazz's highest paid artists, opened his private studio to perform a last-minute fund-raiser to help the Gallery. In December 2012, new zoning regulations coming into effect upon the expiration of Gallery's lease obliged its relocation, after seventeen years in SoHo, to a new space on the fifth floor of a generic office building in the Flatiron district.

In addition to concert halls and clubs, jazz is often experienced in less formal performance spaces. Business models vary, but most of these venues have 501(c)(3) nonprofit status, some with food or liquor licenses, and are funded by a combination of ticket sales, public grants, and private donations. Such venues have idiosyncratic histories, some well worth a book-length study, but a brief survey should suffice to demonstrate their diversity. A Gathering of Tribes and ABC No-Rio are both cultural/community centers—the former (relocated in April 2014 to a small apartment) supported by donations from foundations and individuals, the latter the recipient of several million dollars from various government agencies. The Douglass Street Music Collective and Ibeam Brooklyn are artist-run rehearsal/performance spaces, the latter also used for private lessons. Downtown Music Gallery is a record store by day, a performance space on Sunday evenings. ISSUE Project Room landed a twenty-year, rent-free lease and acquired millions of dollars from public and private institutions. The Stone, a nonprofit owned and underwritten by musician/record producer John Zorn supports itself solely through private donations, benefit concerts, and limited-edition CD sales—with all concert revenues going to performers. University of the Streets is a member-driven, nonprofit community center/vocational school. Because they are independently funded, some with grassroots support, such performance spaces are under different economic constraints than for-profit venues. Most importantly, they are at liberty to present overtly *non*commercial concerts such as avant-jazz and other experimental music and performance art, a boon for curious listeners.

Jazz presenters running their venues as for-profit businesses face a separate, though related, set of challenges. When Mitch Borden closed the original Smalls after a ten-year run, he cited "dwindling patronage, post-9/11, debts, and skyrocketing rent" (starting at $800/month, it rose to $8000/month) as contributing factors.[28] Borden had also been slapped with Fire Department violations, the citywide smoking ban in bars and restaurants (enacted April 2003) didn't help, and tourist traffic had dropped in the wake of the World Trade Center terrorist attack. On the other hand, Borden was notorious for putting music before business. *New York Times* critic Ben Ratliff characterized him as "nearly selfless . . . the opposite of a good business model."[29] The original Smalls ran all night, every night, with a ten-dollar cover and a BYOB drinking policy, becoming a chic underground (literally and figuratively) destination for savvy fans. Musicians regularly slept in several nooks and crannies in the building's bowels and rehearsed there during the day; an unused walk-in freezer furnished with a piano doubled as a practice room/crash space.[30] Borden routinely waived cover charges for musicians he knew: "Once you play here, then you never have to pay again."[31] Unfortunately, although his musician-friendly, the-means-justify-the-ends attitude inspired much loyalty and creativity, it also led to bankruptcy. In late 2006, Spike Wilner, a jazz keyboardist who'd hosted graveyard-shift open jam sessions (2–6 A.M. every night) at the old Smalls, along with Lee Kostrinsky, a musician/poet, bought the building's lease and liquor license from an interim owner who'd tried to convert it to a Brazilian bar. Wilner assumed managerial and booking duties, retaining Borden as a partner, and has since tried to maintain the original club's Bohemian flavor in a fiscally responsible manner.

Like Borden, the Village Vanguard's Lorraine Gordon grants free admission to musicians when the house isn't sold out, putting them in the rear of the club to reserve the best seats for paying customers: "It's not open house, but musicians are welcome guests here, always." The club's iconic reputation guarantees a steady flow of tourist trade, and many established musicians will accept lower fees for the privilege (and pleasure) of playing there. Even so, George Wein characterized the Vanguard as a "mom-and-pop operation," venturing his doubt that Gordon could stay in business "if she wasn't in there every night."

Former nightclub owner Michael Torsone gave a pessimistic overview of the economic challenges inherent to running a jazz venue. "New York City has become completely controlled by a group of entrepreneurs that have raised property prices *beyond belief*," he explained, "to the point that a jazz club, which only seats maybe seventy-five people, cannot survive and do business here: pay rent, insurance, liquor license fees, liquor prices, upkeep of the place, maintenance, employees, health insurance, bartenders, waitresses—whatever. You've got to have seventy-five sitting in a room, for two shows, seven nights a week, and you've got a band of musicians that want to get at *least* thirty or forty dollars an hour for their time—which they *should* get." Club proprietors must attain equilibrium between ticket prices, band fees, and overhead costs. "How do you get people to pay for this without feeling like they're being insulted?" Torsone mused; "The only way you can do it is to have name acts, so people will *pay* enough to see a show, then charge at the door and have a minimum for the tables. You have enough people in New York that are demographically sophisticated enough to want to do that, but the clubs are still not making any money. They *can't* be; it's impossible." Even well-located, tourist magnets like Blue Note in Greenwich Village or Iridium in Times Square are not immune to these constraints. Torsone elaborated: "If you've got a hundred people times twenty-five [dollars/ticket], whaddya got, twenty-five hundred dollars? That's about what it's gonna cost you for a decent jazz act, for a name. So what are you making? You're *hoping* you sell liquor that night, so you can make a profit. If you make three or four hundred, even a thousand dollars a night, how are you going to justify spending a thousand dollars a month for rent? It doesn't make sense."

Most New York City venues presenting jazz are restaurants and/or drinking establishments that primarily depend on food and drink revenues, using jazz to enhance their business. For example, some places offer jazz brunches or advertise "live jazz" without naming the performers. Even venues featuring expensive name artists implement table minimums of $10 or more per person per set, and ticket prices range considerably. In Fall 2011, Blue Note charged $75 per set (not including table minimum and tip) to see smooth jazz artist Kenny G, $65 for Pat Metheny, $45 for David Sanborn (all artists with crossover appeal); $35 for mainstream acts like McCoy Tyner, Gary Burton, and Michel Camilo; down to $15 for relatively unknown artists featured on off-peak nights early in the week. During the same period, Iridium charged $27.50 to $37.50 to $40 for jazz and jazz-rock fusion artists, its ticket prices carefully calculated to strike a balance between supply and demand, affordability and interest. Whether a venue is primarily a restaurant with jazz on the side, or a jazz club serving food, all potential revenue is significant.

Although many large New York clubs and concert halls feature jazz stars, many more small and midsized clubs can't afford name acts. Smoke, a midsized venue located off the beaten tourist-track on the Upper West Side, is run by Frank Christopher and Paul Stache, both avid jazz fans.[32] They have developed an effective booking formula that presents mainstream name artists on Fridays and Saturdays and lesser-known, more affordable artists performing crossover styles (e.g., latin-jazz and jazz-funk) on weeknights. Christopher discussed some of the struggles they face:

We open at five o'clock and run a happy hour; we *have* to, because we have to get income in here any way we can in order to present what we present, because if you want to own a jazz club and make money, you're a fool, because there're easier ways to make money. That [*pointing to the club's high-tech sound system*] could be ripped down, all that equipment could be sold, we could have a pool table over there, and a dartboard over here, and I *trust* that I would make more money, with less headaches. *We* do not run this place to make money. We have, like, a ten percent profit margin. It's ridiculous! We run this place because we like the music, because of the *artistic* end of it.

Jazz is often a loss leader in clubs and restaurants, not a primary source of income. While jazz musicians may consider themselves artists, jazz businesses must view them as commodities.[33] Even clubs charging hefty ticket prices "gotta have some other sources of income, and jazz has gotta be a side venture," argued Michael Torsone. He conjectured that the only way to run a Manhattan jazz club is to own the space: "It's the *only* way. If you make up your mind to go in that business, you're going to have to have enough money to buy the building so it can support itself with the rents. The jazz is going to be a *loss*, a handicap of the whole investment. You can't produce jazz music in an intimate atmosphere in New York City and make money unless the room is actually free. Then you just let the jazz club run, so that the art form can be expressed. Nobody's getting rich off of jazz in New York—*nobody*. They *can't* be."

While some might see presenters as philanthropists, and certainly many take satisfaction knowing that they are "keeping the art form going," they are also business people who have to meet their bottom lines. Nonetheless, their patent enthusiasm for the jazz and their willingness to incur financial obstacles to present it suggests that most are professional amateurs: people whose love of jazz brought them to the business, and not the other way around.

CURATING CREATIVITY: RELATING TO MUSICIANS

Relationships between jazz presenters and performers are a mix of complementary and competitive agendas. Although both parties share the common objective of staging creative music for the public, aesthetic differences, economic issues, and clashing interpersonal chemistry can cause problems. Most conflicts arise because musicians rely on presenters for income and a place to play, while presenters rely on musicians to generate income, leading to all manner of negotiations over fees, hiring, schedules and hours, working conditions, types of music represented, and the like. In spite of these inherent challenges, close cooperation between presenters and performers is critical to jazz's survival and success.

The glut of talented musicians in New York creates a buyer's market, giving jazz bosses an edge over players. "The best [musicians] are the only ones that are gonna get the work, that's what it boils down to, 'cause there's so much frigging competition," noted Michael Torsone; "Nobody's gonna hire a mediocre musician, because they can't pay their bills." When I asked Lorraine Gordon why she decided to book saxophonist Mark Turner, who had formerly appeared in her club as a sideman, as a weeklong headliner, she responded: "[B]ecause I *like* him—because I have to happen to *like* what I'm hearing. And if I see them in the context of the room, and I see the audience reaction and my own reaction, and I say, 'Wow!' or I say, 'Oh, for*get* it!' I have to take a chance too. I don't just book four-star—whatever—'wonder-boys,' or -men, or -women. I don't know; it's complex: it's what I *like*; and what I *feel*." When Melissa Aldana held a release party for her second CD at Smalls (see Figure 35), her first gig there as a leader, emcee/owner Spike Wilner announced over enthusiastic applause at the end of the second set, "We like her, don't we!?" as if he *and* the audience had mutually decided that the young Chilean saxophonist "belonged" there.[34] Sure enough, Aldana's groups were regularly featured at Smalls after that. Word of mouth and critical buzz about upcoming artists provide additional feedback for proprietors, but their most important gauge of an artist's potential is the audience response to that artist.

Knowing that the impact of live jazz doesn't translate well to recordings, presenters usually prefer to see unknown musicians perform before taking a chance on booking them. They do refer to trade publications and other publicity, but slick promo-packs and well-produced CDs cannot convey an act's on-stage charisma, nor indicate its work ethic. For these reasons, Michael Torsone used to insist that musicians come to his club for a daytime audition before hiring them:

> I'd have the bandleader come to me, and [I'd] say, "I wanna hear ya." "Okay, I'll tell you what: I'm playing over here. Can you come and see me?" I said, "No, I can't." He says, "I guarantee you, if you hire me here, I will pack this club and you'll make money. I have a mailing list, I email my people, and wherever I go they follow me. I have a *following.*" "Okay, alright; that's good, but I *still* wanna hear you." And they hand you a CD. I said, "Yeah, [but] I wanna *hear* you. . . . I wanna see what I'm getting, and . . . you're only gonna have to come down here once and show me what you've got. And if you've got it, you're gonna come back, and you're gonna be here.

As a part-time musician who has often sat on the other side of the hiring desk, Torsone understands that musicians have to hustle. As a former club owner, however, he also understands that bandmembers' musical chemistry and on-stage charisma are keys to successful performances and that their professionalism and congeniality are keys to a successful working relationship.

From a business standpoint, experimental music is riskier to present because it attracts a smaller audience. Club owners have to maximize their potential market, notes David Such: "To insure their economic survival, bar owners . . . feel compelled to hire only those artists whose work appeals to the largest section of a particular audience."[35] Some have come under fire from critics and other scene observers for their understandable reluctance to employ cutting-edge artists.[36] In an essay on the late-sixties loft scene in lower Manhattan, Amiri Baraka protested that "whatever specific penchant the owners of these various clubs may show, there seems, quite frankly, no way to get them interested in hiring men like [Ornette] Coleman, [Cecil] Taylor or any of the younger musicians associated with what's been called 'the new thing.'"[37] Baraka chastised club owners for focusing on "names that mean more to columnists and people in the entertainment world, than they do to the serious jazz public," and for simultaneously ignoring the "youngest and most exciting musicians,"[38] a criticism still valid today.

Public jam sessions, which often serve as workshops and networking sites for musicians seeking to (re)integrate themselves into the scene(s), require close cooperation between proprietors and participants.[39] They are generally scheduled on slow nights early in the week or after hours, when patron traffic is slow. Club owners may pay a fee to the house band or host but more likely will provide them with meals and/or well drinks (that is, drinks made with lower-cost liquors), a nominal investment for live entertainment. The house band may be willing to work for minimal wages or tips because sessions occur when they aren't likely to be working elsewhere, and because a regular "gig" lets them practice on the bandstand and network with peers.[40] For the club owner, having a host or house band helps insure that performances meet certain standards, especially if few or no musicians show up to sit in, or if those who do are incompetent; some clubs even screen out prospective jammers.[41] Musicians sitting in may get free admission to the club, but proprietors usually expect them to buy a drink or two; habitual jam session participants who don't spend any money will soon wear out their welcome, even if they play for free. Clubs like Harlem's Lenox Lounge compromised by discounting admission for guest musicians.[42] House musicians recognize that club owners rely on them to draw a crowd that will pay a cover charge and pay for food or drink, preferably all three. Jam session bandleaders, therefore, may be overheard exhorting audiences—"Drink up!" or "Don't forget to tip your bartender/waiter!"—hoping to increase revenue and facilitate goodwill among the proprietor, venue employees, performers, and audience members.

Big-band gigs are another situation in which both club owners and musicians must make some compromises to establish mutually beneficial working conditions.[43] During 2012, clubs like Birdland, Gospel Uptown, Jazz Standard, Smoke, Swing 46, and the Village Vanguard featured big bands once a week. While the club owners cannot afford to pay a large ensemble the same per/member wages as a smaller group (assuming both play for similar clientele), these gigs provide opportunities to fraternize and network, work on technical skills (e.g., reading, blending, and intonation), and learn new music. Furthermore, each "chair" in a big band is relatively replaceable because much of the music is written out in "charts"; if a higher paying or more artistically satisfying job comes along, bandmembers can temporarily "sub out" their spot to someone else with the requisite sight-reading and section-playing skills. Hiring more people usually adds overhead, however, and a number of venues have had to drop large ensembles from their programming.[44] The Charles Mingus Big Band has weathered many such changes: it appeared weekly for over a decade at the Fez under Time Café, then led an itinerant existence for four years in the mideighties, eventually landing a regular Monday night slot at Jazz Standard in 2008. Toshiko Akiyoshi's jazz orchestra enjoyed a residency at Birdland from 1998 until 2002, though her husband and coleader Lou Tabackin later joked that they could never really "afford it."[45] The transience of big-band residencies underscores the difficulty of sustaining equitable working conditions for both venue management and musicians.

Because proprietors and performers view jazz scenes from disparate perspectives, they don't always see eye-to-eye (or hear "ear-to-ear"). Unresolved differences occasionally escalate into confrontations that sabotage future financial transactions and social interactions. A potent example occurred in the midnineties when Knitting Factory owner Michael Dorf fell into a feud with John Lurie, John Zorn, and other downtown musicians, resulting in a mass exodus to Tonic and other venues.[46] Dorf had built his club's reputation on the concertizing of cutting-edge artists, while, for their part, the performers were grateful to have a club/house and laboratory for their dissonant musical experimentation. Despite a long working relationship, the delicate balance was quickly destroyed when musicians became convinced that Dorf was exploiting them. With limited leverage against club owners like Dorf, Zorn used his power of veto (refusal to play) to retaliate; today, as owner of Tzadik records and The Stone, Zorn has amassed considerably more bargaining power via his various ventures as producer, proprietor, publisher, composer, and performer.

Despite such conflicts of interest, examples of mutually beneficial working relationships between presenters and performers abound. During the early days of Smalls, Mitch Borden stayed up all night, slept during the day, and spent many hours hanging out with musicians, leaving little time for his wife and children. He allowed musicians to sleep and rehearse in the building, provided them with high-quality recordings of their gigs, paid fair wages (not high, but equitable considering the circumstances), and looked after musicians' general welfare. I once overheard Borden commiserating with an unidentified musician about a weekly gig that wasn't drawing well. Borden reluctantly suggested canceling it and the musician reluctantly agreed, though both felt that the band had been great. Part of the problem, Borden remarked, was that most of the audience members were other musicians (whom he had let in free), rather than paying customers. Another problem was that the female bandleader, though extremely talented, was not well-known enough to attract other patrons. Concerned for his employee, Borden asked, "Well, what will you *do*, if I don't have that gig for you?" and the musician replied, "Move back to Russia." "Really?" asked Borden, nonplussed, "It's that bad . . . to leave New York?" "It's like everybody; it's not too good," came the reply. When I ventured that most of the musicians whom I'd talked with said that they couldn't make much money from local gigs, Borden retorted: "Unless they're sucking on Smalls! Smalls is like a slaughtered elephant: you gotta cut off the meat and suck the blood." Borden's wry smile underlined the many sacrifices he'd made for musicians and foreshadowed the club's looming bankruptcy.[47]

Several jazz presenters described close ties they'd developed with musicians. Lorraine Gordon considers many musicians who frequent her club—employees and/or guests—as more than business acquaintances: "They don't just *come in and watch*: they come in, they kiss me at the door, they see me or shake my hand, or we hug each other, and they go sit in the back. I know 'em not only as musicians: they're my *friends*! You have a communal feeling for them. You know their wives, in many cases, or children—so you have attachments to the musical family." Horst Liepolt opened Sweet Basil with his new partners over a handshake, insisting: "If I say yes, it can't be just a club. It has to be *more* than that." He wanted to interact with musicians "*not* as a manager, not as an agent, a working relationship, like *friends*, you know?" A German Swede with traces of an Australian accent, Liepolt became intimate with the all-black, politically outspoken Art Ensemble of Chicago through their long-term association at

Sweet Basil: "[We were] very good buddies . . . it was a pretty close relationship. . . . You know, white and black don't really have close relationships . . . they may become friendly, but it's not really a close thing . . . but that was pretty good."[48] For Liepolt, jazz established connections across significant racial and cultural gulfs.

While nonlocal artists passing through on tour will be "fresh" to local fans, as will local artists who play primarily for tourists, locally based artists must apportion their appearances to sustain fans' interest. Presenters therefore try to strike a balance between under- and overexposing an artist.[49] One way is to increase patronage through a steady turnover of acts. "We first started out booking a lot of different acts, everyday, like Smalls did, and a lot of the places," noted Smoke's Frank Christopher: "Like, Tuesday night would be this guitar trio, and then next Tuesday would be another piano trio, or what have you. And we found it was a lot of work to do the booking [and] it was more expensive to entice musicians to play here." Extended bookings work only if the artist is eminent enough to fill (or mostly fill) the venue for the entire run of the booking. Clubs that can afford name acts typically present them for two to five, sometimes six, days in a row, but only once or twice per year. On the other hand, frequent appearances can boost a local act's following, attracting regulars and developing a scene. To maximize their admission sales on any given night of the week, club owners must derive a successful booking schedule that may include recurrent appearances by local artists and occasional appearances by name artists.

Through close personal ties to Nat Adderley, Art Blakey, Paul Bley, Steve Lacy, McCoy Tyner, Sun Ra, the Timeless All-Stars, Cedar Walton, and other front-running artists, Horst Liepolt could consistently feature premium performers at his venue, securing their dates a year or more in advance: "They *knew* that they had two weeks at Sweet Basil in May; they didn't take any other gigs. . . . So I formed those kinds of programming relationships. . . . I was relatively flexible, they were flexible, and it always worked out. So I always had some really good shit going." When Sweet Basil changed ownership, however, the new management wasn't as well-connected as Liepolt, and programming immediately suffered. "When I finished with Sweet Basil, it was a *well*-run, hitting, powerful jazz club; it was more or less full every night of the week—I mean, it was *happening!*" stated Liepolt, noting the change when he left: "Inside six months, all the names didn't play there anymore. . . . They lost them all overnight. . . . The club is only as good, then, [as] what you got happening on the stage." The new establishment, renamed Sweet Rhythm, gradually improved its reputation through relationships with a new circle of musicians but eventually closed in October 2009.

While name artists can take advantage of national and international touring circuitry to find sufficient work, particularly in Asia and Europe during the summer season, lesser-known, locally based artists have to get gigs nearby. Regular local appearances may wear out a musician's welcome but can be successful in heavily touristed venues with high audience turnover. Iridium featured guitarist Les Paul every Monday night from 1996 until he passed in 2009 (Paul had been a fixture at Sweet Basil for a decade before that) and continues to feature the Les Paul Trio on Mondays, now a "ghost band"[50] with a rotating roster of guest guitarists. The long-term success of this weekly gig owes more to Paul's stature as a cultural icon—the inventor and namesake of a classic model of electric guitar—than to his role in the jazz community. Moreover, Sweet Basil and Iridium could capitalize on the steady infusion of tourist traffic because Paul's same old shtick was new to those who hadn't seen him before.[51]

Although Smoke's Frank Christopher and Paul Stache originally believed that more variety would draw more clientele, they soon realized that repeat engagements were a win-win proposition for both management and artists. Christopher remarks: "A steady gig—which is what we do now—is a valuable thing to a musician, as opposed to: 'I play at Smoke Tuesday, two, three times a year.' The cost of paying the band goes down by saying, 'Hey man, you're gonna be here every Tuesday,' because the payment is a little bit for the pocket, a lot for the soul and the mind, and also the opportunity to—'Hey man, if I get a better paying gig, I can always sub that one out.' So it works out good for us and the musicians." For struggling artists, steady low-paying gigs with perks may be better than intermittent high-paying gigs.

Artists sometimes denigrate club owners for their allegedly mercenary attitudes, but club owners could level similar criticism against them. "A lot of musicians have a very high opinion of themselves as far as what they should get," observed Michael Torsone, "because they feel that they've earned it, have a discography, a résumé, and they've been *here*, and *there*, played with this one, that one, they're on records, have some kind of established career, they've spent their whole life studying music, they've got a degree, come from some kind of conservatory, and they have standards that they feel they should get. And some people are very arrogant about it [*imitating an artist*]: 'I'm sorry, but that's what I have to get if you want me to perform.'" Unfortunately, proprietors can't always pay performers what they "deserve." "I can name ten people I can *not* have—who I like—because they're too expensive for me," Lorraine Gordon noted. Many up-and-comers she'd nurtured eventually outgrew her club: "There're many wonderful, great musicians [who] come here to play, but they can get more money somewhere else—and they go; I don't have exclusivity.

But [if] they want to play the Vanguard, if they have any real love of tradition, of standards, or [for] a club that's hung around so long. . . . And if they can't take five bucks less and play in a room that's a really great room, then I say, 'Hey, goodbye.'" When rising artists become unemployable, Gordon restocks her talent pool from the next generation: "[There're] a lot of young wonderful guys coming up. I use them, and they're *all* great."

High overheads and limited seating in New York jazz clubs can create tension between operators and clientele. Smoke's Paul Stache and Frank Christopher complained of musician-fans and others who stand at the back of their club, slow-nursing sodas while enjoying a no-cover-charge set. Some months before my interview with them, while I was conducting fieldwork in their club, loitering in the "musicians' corner," I was suddenly transfixed by Stache's steely gaze that telegraphed a silent question: "Isn't it about time you ordered that second drink?" Later, during our interview, I asked Stache if this psychological warfare had been intentional and he admitted it was. "You can't be taking up that room," Christopher explained; "I know that I could put somebody else there that's gonna spend some money—that's the way we think now. I mean, it's *so* ridiculous: like, when the trumpet player comes in on Sunday and he takes a chair off the floor, I *lose* it! I *lose* it! I'm, like, 'Man! I have drum thrones[52] downstairs.' 'But it doesn't support my back.' 'Well, you know what? I'm sorry.' It sounds petty, but that's thirty bucks, because that's one person who's not gonna come in here because they don't have a seat." Operating a jazz club leaves no room for casual business practices, so what performers may perceive as petty or avaricious behaviors by presenters are in fact mandatory for survival, necessary "evils" to insure that musicians have a place to play.

CULTIVATING CLIENTELE: RELATING TO AUDIENCES

The continuing success of presenter-performer partnerships rests on the shoulders of fans, constituents who "vote" for certain artists and venues with their patronage. Club owners therefore keep close watch on their clientele, knowing that satisfied customers mean repeat business and favorable word-of-mouth publicity. This section considers how jazz presenters think about and relate to the people who attend their shows, the strategies they employ to attract and retain clientele, and some of the issues that may arise between them.

Club owners must ask themselves three basic questions: How do I get people into my club? How do I get them to spend money? And how do I get them to come back again? Fans coming to a club are primarily drawn by the artists who play there but may also be influenced by a club's location, size, atmosphere, affordability, or scheduling. Audience members vary from elderly Dixieland fans at a Sunday brunch, younger "cats" waiting to sit in at a late-night/early-morning jam session, inattentive tourists in a midtown restaurant, or ardent aficionados at an "insider" haunt. Fans who come for the music often pay scant attention to club owners and support staff. "Sixty percent of the audience wouldn't know who the boss of the club was or who the promoter of the concert was, because that doesn't interest them," opined pianist Errol Garner; "All they want to know is if you're there and if you're going to play what they have at home on a record."[53] "Some people seem surprised that the Vanguard *has* an owner. I know what they mean. Half the time I feel as though the place owns me,"[54] wrote Max Gordon of his legendary club, acknowledging that it had taken on a life of its own. Nonetheless, proprietors and patrons are partners in the shared enterprise of live jazz, both responsible for a venue's vitality.

When a venue draws a regular crowd—whether people come for the club itself, the music it features, or both—the crowd's collective energy creates a palpable "vibe" that gives the space a distinctive character. Unfortunately for club owners, this kind of buzz is a bottom-up, fan-driven phenomenon, virtually impossible to engineer. They can, however, *enable* the development of a scene, first by establishing a hospitable environment and then allowing the musical activities to take their course. Neither Max Gordon nor Michael Dorf were renowned for their love of jazz music or musicians, yet both became central figures in two of the most influential scenes in New York City,[55] in part because each recognized the musical currents already in circulation around them and then figured out ways to channel the energy. Scenes associated with the more expensive clubs have a different character than those associated with smaller clubs, primarily because local fans can't afford attending them on a regular basis. The only "regulars" in the highest priced clubs are their staff and the various publicist, critics, and photographers who make frequent appearances in the course of their work.[56] Intimate scenes are possible only at more affordable venues, where repeat customers become familiar faces.

In Manhattan, tourists are a dominant presence in many jazz clubs, the reason why so many jazz proprietors in so contained an area can stay in business. Although it dropped dramatically following the World Trade Center terrorist attack, tourist trade is generally strong year-round, swelling slightly during winter and spring breaks, surging dramatically in summer. Not all tourists going to jazz shows are avid jazz fans, but some are alternative tourists, ready to get off the beaten tourist track for an "authentic" jazz experience in neighborhood bars,[57] and others are serious fans. French, German, Scandinavian, and Japanese fans have a reputation for being extremely knowledgeable about jazz (more so perhaps than their North American counterparts);[58] their appreciation and attentiveness imbues concerts with an aura of dignity and depth. Whatever their inclinations, tourists are a big boon to venue operators because they cycle through the city in steady streams with disposable income designated for entertainment.

In contrast to heavily touristed clubs, small- and midsized venues typically see a slump in club attendance during summer when locals leave town: students and other fans for vacation, musician-fans for work. Many or most of the audience in large jazz clubs are likely to be tourists. "I think if you went in and interviewed the customers," speculated George Wein, "you'd find an *incredible* percentage of them [are] tourists, not only tourists, but tourists from *overseas*, a *huge* amount, maybe thirty, forty, fifty, *sixty* percent of the people, because when people come to New York, it's like going to Madrid and then somebody saying, 'Let's go to a *flamenco* club.' Jazz and New York are symbolic."[59] These concertgoers may be more attracted to the *idea* of jazz—as a symbol of New York, of hipness, and so forth—than to the music itself. If, as Wein claimed, the New York scene is *"relatively* healthy" because of heavy tourist trade at the most prominent venues,[60] then it's ironic that the affluence of these venues depends, in part, on patronage by some of the least devoted fans, those drawn to the iconicity, not the sound, of jazz.[61]

How do club owners deal with clientele who *aren't* jazz fans? To judge from their less-than-fully-attentive behavior, many tourists are dilettantes, not dedicatees, who prefer jazz as a pleasant backdrop for eating, drinking, and conversation. Unlike formal concert halls, jazz venues tolerate talking, but only to a limited extent, as when customers order drinks from circulating waiters during sets. Most prominent clubs air live or prerecorded announcements informing the audience of proper concert etiquette, usually urging that talking during the music be kept to a minimum. The Village Vanguard posts its policy on its website: "We do not serve food. We haven't served food here in 25 years. . . . During performances, QUIET IS ENFORCED. We're a jazz club, not a chat room."[62] "Enforced" translates to a polite comment or meaningful look from proprietor Lorraine Gordon when patrons violate protocol. I have also observed the 5C Café & Cultural Center's "Brother" Bruce Morris and others employ similar tactics. Sometimes fellow fans or even performers will glare at or shush talkative patrons. At a Blue Note concert in July 2013, I noticed the band's pianist repeatedly try to censure a group of talkative tourists sitting close to the stage.

Proprietors don't want to alienate any customer who's paid good money to enjoy a show, so they must accommodate both casual and serious listeners: giving the former latitude to relax and respond without disturbing the latter. At a

Village Vanguard concert in July 2014, the emcee asked the audience to silence their smart-phones and suggested that they switch them off (to eliminate visual distraction by glowing screens and to keep their focus on the music). The audience reacted with an audible silence, so to break the tension the emcee joked that the venue wasn't "a prison camp" and that it was "okay" to talk since the music hadn't started yet. A tween boy, part of a large French-speaking group, continued to look at his smart-phone screen throughout the show—a sign of the times perhaps—but most patrons listened with rapt attention. One of my colleagues, who goes to hundreds of concerts in a professional capacity, often uses his smart-phone during performances, but is careful to keep it out of sight so as not to reveal that he is not paying full attention to the music.

Tensions over talking during performances came to a head one night at the Village Vanguard when Lorraine Gordon reprimanded hiphop artist Q-Tip (aka Kamaal Fareed) for disrupting a show. Fareed is renowned for sampling classic jazz tracks on his recordings with A Tribe Called Quest, and was featured in a *JazzTimes* cover story shortly after the incident occurred. "I think the problem with the jazz community is that it is the most pretentious [music scene] right now," he commented in the article; "Music is ultimately supposed to be something that you enjoy and respond to and move and say, 'Ummph!' But if you say something in the Village Vanguard, the lady who works there will almost chop your head off. She wants to keep jazz locked up in a cage."[63] Gordon took offense, called the magazine, and gave them a piece of her mind: "I said, 'Hey man, if this bugs you, you should [leave]; nobody asked you to stay here. You're not in a cage here.' I was *furious.* I said, 'How *dare* you come here and complain!' [Fareed's] little arrogance really got me angry. That's it. If he comes again, he'll sit down and be quiet. You can talk when there's no music—this is not a prison—but when the music's on: respect it—I say." Then she sent *JazzTimes* a poetic rejoinder, which was published in the "Letters" (to the editor) column the following month:

"The lady who works there"
Is not a square.
If she keeps you quiet
It's 'cause the musicians care.
The audience too want to hear their jazz
Without your hip-hop razz-ma-tazz.
If you like to "ummph" when artists play,
Jazz people say, Well, that's OK.
Kamaal, wake up to reality,
The Vanguard's not the place for hip-hop mentality.

The "cage is not locked,"
And you're free to flee,
But please leave a Q-Tip on your way out!"[64]

Fareed's desire to respond audibly to the music proved incompatible with the Vanguard community's desire to listen actively. Within the venue's walls, Fareed's freedom of speech ended at the downbeat of each new tune.

Although jazz holds artists and audiences to high standards, club owners can't afford to take a superior attitude with ordinary customers. "Most of the people who come in [to a club] don't even know the difference between a trombone and a clarinet, which is understandable—it has nothing to do with it," remarked Horst Liepolt. Instrument names, song forms, and other musical details, he insisted, mean nothing if people don't "get a buzz and enjoy it." "I've seen, over the years, people walking out and saying, 'Oh, man! That was a fantastic show! I *loved* it, and I *really* loved the clarinet player!' when there wasn't a clarinet player in the band. I *never, ever* set 'em straight. If you *do*, you lose 'em; they never come back. They hate jazz, because you make 'em look stupid." He maintained that a live-and-let-learn outlook is the best approach. "The guy who actually comes in with his wife, I ain't gonna make that guy look stupid in front of his date! Let 'm be happy, because he's gonna invite people—and *that's* public relations for jazz, *not* education. *Expose* 'em . . . [then] let *them* pick it up; let *them* discover what it is." To judge by his successful stewardship of one of New York's most critically acclaimed and financially successful clubs, Liepolt's antielitist attitude toward patrons served him well.

To make jazz affordable for their customers, Smoke's management initially featured name artists on weekends for a ten-dollar cover with no drink minimum and lesser-known artists on weeknights with no cover charge. Unfortunately, according to Frank Christopher, "nobody drank; nobody spent any money. So we upped the cover charge a little bit and then increased the drinking a little." When they tried charging entry on weeknights to cover the musicians' fees, Smoke's managers found out that their patrons weren't willing to pay for lesser-known musicians: "We had to figure out all kinds of ways to get people in the door, noted Christopher; "In the beginning we started doing the drink tickets. People would come and we'd tell 'em, 'It's a ten dollar drink minimum,' and we'd literally have to chase 'em around the room. They'd be standing over here [*indicates*] and they'd notice that you were tabbing them, and then they'd move to somewhere else and think you wouldn't recognize them, you know?" Rather than play cat-and-mouse with parsimonious patrons, Smoke's proprietors eventually settled on a policy of no-cover weeknights with a requisite drink minimum, strictly enforced.[65]

An effective way to enhance customer traffic is by offering a variety of entertainment throughout the week, catering to separate sub-scenes on separate nights. Some club owner/fans might prefer to feature mainstream musicians most of the time, but this isn't always realistic. Michael Torsone supplemented his schedule with more popular musical genres: "Wednesday night was blues night; Thursday night I had an open mike, where people would come in, a jam session; Friday night would usually be an R&B-jazz band; Saturday night would usually be a straight-up jazz vocalist, or sometimes we'd have a sax group; [and] then Sunday nights we would have Dixieland and ragtime." Smoke's Paul Stache and Frank Christopher tried a similar tactic when their initial all-jazz booking policy proved unprofitable. "We reassessed what type of music we were gonna play," Christopher recalled, "that would appeal to us artistically, that wouldn't upset us because it wasn't representing the venue, and that would appeal to the jazz crowd—but also would be good introductory jazz music to people who are not really hip to jazz." Smoke's management team eventually hit on a successful weekly format: latin-jazz on Sunday, organ trio and late-night jam sessions on Monday, funk/fusion on Wednesday, and mainstream jazz music on Thursday through Saturday. The menu was strategically eclectic: by hiring "real" jazz artists alongside of "jazz-ish" groups, the managers built Smoke's reputation as a serious jazz venue at the same time as they courted layman listeners. Ironically, the house funk group, composed of jazz musicians, was criticized by other funk musicians as being too jazzy; as if to allay audiences' fears, the band posted a promo flyer in the front window that read: "98% Funk, 2% Jazz!"

Proprietors like Dale Fitzgerald and Deborah Steinglass, former directors of the Jazz Gallery, launched various initiatives to encourage amateur fans, members, and musician-fans to get involved with their venue. Fitzgerald urged "Jazz Gallerians" to become more active attendees through electronic newsletters and a tiered subscription membership program that offers a range of special privileges including free or reduced admission to shows, access to members-only events, "insider visits during artist residencies," and even a "private musician event in your home."[66] Deborah Steinglass allowed musicians to use the venue during off-hours, providing them with free rehearsal space.[67] In 2012, knowing that many New Yorkers would leave town in summer, she tried to boost attendance by granting members free entry to all July and August shows, a bargain for "Solo"-level members who paid a mere $6.28/month, and still a great deal for nonmembers who paid $35 for a two-month pass.

For jazz club owners, the best fans are sometimes the worst customers. Serious fans come to clubs first and foremost to commune with the music; predominantly male, attending alone or in small groups, they are generally more interested in listening than in carrying out romantic maneuvers, enjoying a meal, or catching an alcoholic buzz—though they often "talk shop" with fellow aficionados. More importantly for the proprietor, they are less likely to bring along spouses or casual dates, buy big dinners, or run up bar tabs. "It's very funny," observed Frank Christopher, "because you cannot make money off of the jazz people, so you have to figure out. . . . How do we make it a bar and still make it be a jazz venue?"

Proprietors can augment their constituency by attracting hybrid audiences. "We've mastered the melding of the non-jazz crowd and the jazz crowd," Frank Christopher claimed; "and if we hadn't, we would've been out of business a long time ago." The best way to market jazz clubs to "the non-jazz crowd" is by casting a wide net for potential patrons via eclectic programming—anything that will get them in the door—with the hope that they will eventually develop loyalty to the venue. Smoke's Sunday night latin-jazz group, SYOTOS, proved popular with salsa lovers. "It brings in the least jazz-loving crowd," Christopher explained, "but *that* has gotten people into the club, and people have discovered the club. They say, 'Wow, this place is *cool!*' *That* has introduced non-jazz people to the club, which then in turn introduces them to jazz." Popular, more accessible forms of jazz not only attract the non-jazz crowd, these genres gently inure casual listeners to the dissonance and irregularity of "real" jazz, hopefully arousing their appetites for aurally challenging music.

Frequently featured artists help build brand recognition for a venue, raising patrons' expectations and comfort level. "Having regulars is a *good* system," Michael Torsone maintained; he had used regulars for years at his own club, and praised Smoke for similar programming: "Michael LeDonne's there almost every Tuesday. People *know* if they go down there on a Tuesday night, they're gonna hear one of the best jazz organists in New York." If customers develop loyalty to certain of a venue's featured artists, they may also come out for other acts. Smoke's managers found that people who enjoyed funk on Thursdays or salsa on Sundays might take a chance on Tuesday's jazz organ trio. Frank Christopher compared deepening jazz appreciation to a parallel process in dramaturgy: "My wife *hates* jazz, but she's slowly starting to like it because, you know, it's like theater. You don't start them with Shakespeare, as many people try to do: you start them with Sam Shepard, and *then* you get them to dig Shakespeare; you sort of work them to the more heady stuff." Christopher has seen some of his patrons develop a taste for mainstream jazz: "Start 'em with the mighty-burner: soul-blues organ jazz.[68] . . . And then [they might] come back on a Thursday night; that's more of an electric-fusion kind of jazz. And every so often, people start to make the break, and then you start seeing them here on weekend nights, where it's straight-ahead bebop." "The break" Christopher describes is both physical and metaphorical, a gulf transited as casual fans become curious listeners, primed for "the more heady stuff."

Conflicts between club owners and clientele may arise over a variety of issues. Lorraine Gordon ran into controversy when she hired The Bad Plus, a keyboard trio led by Ethan Iverson that performed in a progressive- and pop-rock–influenced style, covering songs by ABBA, Aphex Twin's, Black Sabbath, Blondie, Gloria Gaynor, Nirvana, and a few standards, along with avant-garde–edged original compositions. Gordon first heard Iverson when he had sat in on a gig with guitarist Kurt Rosenwinkel, liked what she heard, and—after hearing him again in another sideman context—hired his trio as headliners, sparking fervid debates in the jazz community over whether such genre-bending groups were appropriate fare for the Village Vanguard. Gordon explained her decision: "I don't care what [The Bad Plus] means, I like the name. And, he's playing original music; and I've been told by rock groups these songs are *big, big*.[69] Not in my world—in the world of rock groups. I didn't know the difference; I didn't even know those songs. It's just the way he played the music interested me—*that* was it." Many fans, musicians, and critics didn't share her views: "So a controversy came up about Ethan Iverson bringing non-jazz to the Vanguard. It was written up in the mags. I said, 'What are they talking about? He's terrific! The group is terrific!'"[70] Confirming that her instincts were on target, half a year after their eponymous debut was released on an independent jazz label, the group was signed to Columbia, in large part because record executives had been impressed by their June 2002 gig at the Vanguard. Over the ensuing decade they became a top draw at the venue, playing popular New Year's Eve Shows beginning in 2009 that commanded up to $150 per ticket.

Jazz musicians often come to clubs as fans: to watch an admired artist, show support for a friend's gig, and/or network with colleagues. At Smalls, Jazz Gallery, and many other artist-friendly venues it is common to see professional-level musicians in the audience, and often these musician-fans make up a significant proportion of the crowd. Proprietors frequently form close associations and friendships with artists who, in their dual capacity as hired performers and musician-fans, are frequent denizens of a venue. Performing musicians are usually allowed free passes for guests, who are often other musicians, and who may or may not have to pay for drinks. Venue habitués may develop expectations that a manager will provide food and/or drinks, give them free admission on nights they're not performing, or show other forms of favoritism. While Lorraine Gordon and Mitch Borden have been generous toward nonperforming musicians, Frank Christopher sees the other side: "Musicians don't wanna spend the money, which I understand; they're not working. But I'm an artist too. I'm a playwright and I had to get a gig."[71] Christopher's day job as a jazz club owner has only confirmed his attitude that it takes a whole art world to make art: "We'll get musicians through the door and they won't want to pay the drink minimum, the reason being: 'I'm a starving musician.' 'Well, listen: if you're a documentary filmmaker and you watch Channel 13, you should send them some money, so that you have a place to sell your films. If you're a jazz musician, somehow scrape together ten bucks to go into the club, because if the club's gone, where're you gonna play?"

Venue operators occasionally witness what Christopher characterizes as a "push-and-pull" between the jazz and non-jazz patrons. "There's a party of five over there with a hundred and fifty-dollar bar tab, that's hooting and hollering and pissing off the other ten jazz lovers who are having one club soda. The jazz lovers are *so* offended by the people being rude to the musicians that they haven't even considered the fact of the conditioning. They think: 'Oh! Those people are *so* rude!' No! They're not rude: they don't know any better! They've been taught this way." He believes the media has trained people to listen to jazz passively, as background music: "We have to teach them, slowly, and get them to appreciate the music. And you don't do that by turning to them and going, 'Hey, can you *shut* the *fuck* up?'—[be]cause that's what my jazz customers do." Proprietors are caught in the middle of this push-and-pull, their loyalties divided between soda-sipping jazz lovers and "unconditioned" patrons with larger bar tabs.

Relationships between presenters and patrons are only part of larger patterns at play in jazz communities. In the following interview excerpt given by Frank Christopher at Smoke before opening hours, he discusses a number of issues from a club owner's perspective, describing the three-way "tug-of-wars" that can occur between presenters, performers, and patrons when their separate agendas come into conflict:

> Michael LeDonne and Eric Alexander and those guys play here pretty much every Tuesday, for *fucking* peanuts! I like to say, "The musicians play for less than they deserve and more than we can afford." . . . And this is why I call the jazz audience "star fuckers"—and they're fucking it up for themselves. They have to understand that Eric Alexander wasn't always Eric Alexander. I mean, [he] was some kid from Washington State who moved to New York and played saxophone; nobody ever fuckin' heard of him, but he worked his ass off and he got known. And an example is: sometimes musicians don't show up. You can't expect it: there's no cover charge; they don't make very much

money. Tonight they're supposed to play. You know, ten minutes before the gig, any one of the guys in the band—Peter, Eric, Joe Farnsworth—somebody might call them. Cedar Walton might be playing at the Vanguard; he might call Joe Farnsworth and say, "Listen, my drummer didn't show up; I need a drummer." And who's gonna tell Joe, "Fuck you, Joe! You're supposed to stay here and play this gig!" when he's making peanuts and he can go down there and make three times the amount. So, okay, you [the fan] show up at Smoke, Tuesday night: you *expect* to see Joe Farnsworth on the drums [but] he's not here. What? Are you gonna cry? You gonna freak out? They *do*! They *freak* the *fuck* out! [One guy] called me up from his apartment on the East Side on a Wednesday to bitch me out because he took a cab all the way here from his apartment and Eric Alexander wasn't here—on a Tuesday night, for no cover charge—and bitched out my bartender. And this is not just one person; this is a *lot* of people. They'll come and they'll say, "Eric's not here?" "Yeah, no, Eric's not here, but we've got this great young guy, Mike Carne." [He's] another *great saxophone player*, top-notch, very good in his own right. [*Imitating a pompous patron:*] "I'm not gonna waste my ten-dollar drink minimum on some young guy I never heard of!" Okay, [the patron] storms out. Okay, cool! That's the way *you* look at it. Because the way *I* look at it is: I'm giving you the music for free; I'm giving you the opportunity to give me some money so that I can stay afloat [*phone rings*], so that I can operate this business, and for you to support this art form [*phone rings again*], and for you to turn Mike Carne into the next Eric Alexander by checking him out. Excuse me for one second." [*Christopher answers the phone, listens briefly, and replies to the caller:*] "Uh, Eric is *scheduled* to play this evening. . . . Um, you'll have to call back after five o'clock. As far as I know, he's supposed to be here, but you never know. I mean, it's a no-cover-charge night, so . . . um, he's supposed to be here, but don't shoot us if he's not here. So call back later and make double-sure. . . . You're welcome" [*hangs up*].[72]

Christopher describes here a network of partnerships, between presenters and performers, presenters and patrons, and performers and patrons. On the surface these relationships are confrontational, each party vying for representation, but in fact they work together synergistically: Eric Alexander provides music, patrons provide support, and Christopher provides the space. Mike Carne, after all, can only become a name artist if he has a place to play and people to hear him.

Complex community interactions are also evident at the 5C Café & Cultural Center, where curators Bruce Morris and Trudy Silver were embroiled in a seventeen-year legal wrangle with avant-jazz saxophonist Jemeel Moondoc over noise levels and acceptable hours for live performance. In 2000, Moondoc, an upstairs resident of the low-income co-op that houses the venue, secured a petition from the state government that allowed only string instruments at the venue. Overturned in 2004, a new ruling prohibited live music at the venue after 7:00 P.M. weekdays and 9:00 P.M. weekends. In 2007, the café's curators solicited community attendance at an upcoming court hearing via Jim Eigo's publicity machine, attesting in their email that members of the European jazz community were boycotting Moondoc by refusing to hire or play with him "until he fixed what he has done."[73] In 2010, Moondoc and the co-op board tried to evict Morris and Silver, who countersued for alleged damages, winning a $700,000 decision in 2011, only to see it overturned four months later.[74] According to Morris and Silver, the eviction proceedings were motivated by money, not music, because a new lease would allow the board to raise the rent by almost $84,000 per year.[75] A flash point for conflicting economic and artistic agendas, the 5C Café's owners' struggles reveal both deep rifts and strong bonds within a local jazz community.

* * *

This chapter considers the attitudes and activities of venue proprietors and concert producers in the context of their professional endeavors and particularly in their interactions with musicians and fans. Part of the unseen scene, their role in providing a place and time is vital to collective expressions of music. Their perspectives offer insight into the interworkings of jazz communities, revealing not only the inherent tensions with musicians and patrons over conflicting economic and artistic agendas, but also how close communication and cooperation between these parties facilitates mutually satisfactory solutions.

JAZZ JOBBING

Music Professionals

Jazz professionals, like venue operators and concert-going fans, are active participants in the live music scene, insiders who are intimate with the inner workings of jazz communities. As fans, critical listeners, on-task workers, creative artists, and/or co-performers, they engage and understand the music through diverse means. Their observations of and interactions with musicians, club owners, concert promoters, serious fans, transient tourists, professional colleagues, and the others they come in contact with reveal much about collaborative expressions of art in improvised jazz communities.

Jazz professionals are defined here as active denizens of the live music scene that base (or intend to base) a majority of their income on jazz-related activities, ranging from criticism/journalism, publicity/promotion, and merchandising to painting, photography and tour guiding. It's a slippery category because many of them—like other jazz participants—don't separate easily into professionals and amateurs; some are artists in their own right who compose and improvise original works informed and inspired by live jazz. Because this book emphasizes live, face-to-face participation, the people discussed here are all active concertgoers,[1] while less active participants (e.g., people working in the recording industry) are only of peripheral interest.[2] Although a few of them are strongly associated with the avant-jazz scene, most circulate through many different scenes throughout the city, and so are in a position to provide a comparative overview of the jazz community at large. Like the presenters discussed previously, they are workers in the jazz art world, providing crucial services and support for performers, fans, venue operators, and each other. In another sense, these offstage jazz-makers "perform" for their own constituencies of viewers and readers. This chapter examines their attraction for and attention to jazz, their roles as creative improvisers and co-performers, and their relationships with other jazz scene participants.[3]

PROFESSIONALS AS AMATEURS

Hardships are evident in many sectors of the community: the International Association for Jazz Educators folded in March 2009; *JazzTimes* magazine, the flagship of the jazz press, temporarily stopped publication in June (returning two months later); and recording revenues are scant and shrinking steadily. In recent years, the increased use of digital technology and social media allows, even compels, artists to take on publicity, booking, and other functions previously allocated to professionals. Newspapers and magazines, the traditional outlets for jazz journalists, now compete with blogs and other social media written by amateurs or musicians, and the modest pay for such work often has to cover additional expenses (e.g., most clubs charge a minimum per set, even to journalists on assignment). In this climate of bottom-up, DIY business models, even established professionals must cobble together freelance work and day gigs to support their jazz activities. In this section I show how entrepreneurs meet the challenges of doing jazz business, suggesting—as I did in the previous chapter—that their lifestyle is an outgrowth of their ongoing enthusiasm for and commitment to the music.[4]

David Adler writes for several leading jazz magazines, is an accomplished guitarist, and has been a prolific concertgoer, averaging fifteen to twenty shows per month in the early nineties. Even as his articles began to be featured on the cover of *JazzTimes* he supported himself by proofreading for an advertising firm: "I'm trying to eke out an existence here," he half-joked at the time.[5] Currently he lectures in jazz history at the City University of New York.

Downtown Music Gallery proprietor Bruce Gallanter got interested in what he called "progressive music" upon hearing Frank Zappa's *Freak Out!* and reading the album's extensive liner notes, he asserted, "really made me *think*." Later, a jazz history course in college showed him that he'd been "missing out on a lot of things," and he became a "curious listener" with a lifelong passion for experimental improvised music. Soon he was a fixture on the downtown scene, going to three or four shows a week, maintaining the pace for over two decades. In 1975 he started taping shows, amassing a huge archive of live recordings, which he occasionally dubs for friends, hoping someday to self-release them online. Gallanter's diminutive store, now in its third location, becomes a performance space Sunday evenings; musicians and fans crowd between CD bins, many seated on folded chairs. Occasionally, he'll close early or cancel in-store concerts for a "momentous occasion," as when Paul Lytton, Evan Parker, and Alexander Schlippenbach made a rare stateside appearance at Tonic (see Figures 28 and 29). "This," he explained at the time, "is more important."

Writer Gary Giddins, originally from Long Island, caught the jazz "bug" early on: "I went down to New Orleans when I was fifteen and I heard a live band there, and I *loved* it." The future cultural critic was especially enamored of the local jazz community: "I not only loved the music but I loved the fact that the audience—for the first time in my life—was *totally* integrated. I'd never seen that, certainly not in the South, and not even here. I thought that was so hip, just from a social point of view. I thought, 'This is the people I want to be with.' These people are *far, far* advanced of the parochial life/neighborhoods I had come from, where every black person that you saw was a maid. This was a different world." Shortly afterward, he heard a Louis Armstrong record: "*That's* what gave me the bug: when I heard his 1928 recordings.[6] I had thought, before that, that the greatest moment in the history of mankind was Bach's B-minor mass, and Armstrong's records had the same kind of power as that. It completely changed my life, and then I became a complete addict and a fanatic."

In contrast to his peers, who were listening to the Beatles and other rock & roll groups, Giddins virtually ignored pop music, spending his adolescence in frequent pilgrimages to Manhattan to see Miles Davis and John Coltrane at the Village Vanguard. "I started going to clubs when I was fifteen with phony ID. It cost me three bucks to get into the Vanguard, and nurse one drink. One drink, and Long Island Railroad's $1.49 round trip, getting a hamburger—I mean, the whole evening was ten bucks." Vanguard owner Max Gordon related an anecdote about the teenaged Giddins and the notoriously irascible Miles Davis: "One Sunday, Miles, walking off the bandstand at the end of the first set, stopped to rub out his cigarette in the ashtray on Gary's table. 'Here, save it,' he said to Gary; 'someday it's gonna be worth some money.'"[7] Undeterred, Giddins returned to see Davis many more times, estimating that he went to see jazz four to five nights a week as a young man.

Giddins always wanted to be a literary critic, but discovered in journalism a means to combine his joint passions for writing and music. His biweekly *Village Voice* column, "Weather Bird"—named for one of the Louis Armstrong recordings that had given him the bug—ran for nearly three decades. His *Visions in*

Jazz: The First Century is the only work on jazz to receive a major literary award,[8] a clear indication that his art as a wordsmith transcends his chosen milieu. In later years he has written a monthly column for *JazzTimes* and continues to go out regularly but has turned his focus more to longer works and spending time with his family. Countless hours logged in jazz clubs are fodder for his creative process; his passionate testimonials on Ken Burns's PBS series *Jazz* mark him for a fan that hasn't lost his fervor.

Born in Roosevelt, just outside of the city, Gordon Polatnick was "immediately bitten by the jazz bug" upon returning home from the West Coast in 1995.[9] He has a day job as a New York City tour guide, a "night" gig as jazz tour guide, and has been a freelance jazz journalist/historian/photographer on the side. He briefly managed pianist Jean-Michel Pilc, ran EZ's Woodshed/Big Apple Jazz Center (a store/tour office/performance space/café) for two-and-a-half years, and organized the Underground Big Apple Jazz Festival in 2009. Through his website, New York City Jazz Clubs Bible,[10] and his business, Big Apple Jazz Tours,[11] he has championed lesser-known, locally based jazz journeymen and -women,[12] and small, "off-the-beaten-path venues,"[13] many of them in Harlem. On tours like "Greenwich Village Hidden Gems" or "Harlem Juke Joints," Polatnick fulfills his "mission" to "introduc[e] fans to the more authentic and hidden events that occur below the radar of most visitors."[14] His avid attendance at pianist Jean-Michel Pilc's shows led to a temporary gig: "I've been bringing my jazz tours to see these guys [Pilc's trio] for three years," he noted; "My enthusiasm has rubbed off and now Jean-Michel wants me to be his manager."[15] Polatnick's active patronage and promotion of "underground" musicians and clubs has increased their visibility to the general public.

Jim Eigo runs Jazz Promo Services publicity firm, produced "Legends of the Clarinet" for the JVC Jazz Festival, formerly booked artists at Iridium and Cornelia Street Café, owns a prodigious collection of jazz recordings and loft-era[16] paraphernalia, goes to clubs frequently, and plays guitar.[17] His father had been a fan of big bands—especially the playing of Johnny Hodges, Duke Ellington's alto saxophonist—so Eigo heard a lot of Swing Era jazz while growing up. Eigo recalled when a fellow post office employee invited him to listen to a state-of-the-art stereo component system: "He was just this wild man, and he was *heavy* into jazz. He had the first *real* record collection I ever saw [and] he was a *serious, serious* collector. I never forget the *first* record he played for me was *Mingus Mingus Mingus*. He put that on and then, *man*! With those speakers—I *never*—the music just jumped out at me. And that was it: I was bit by the bug."[18] Eigo became a serious collector too, amassing an estimated 55,000 LPs (later sold off) and an extensive archive of loft-era playbills, historical documents, and other jazz arcana.

Record retailer Manny Maris, longtime business partner of Bruce Gallanter at Downtown Music Gallery, is part of a close coterie of avant-jazz fans, fraternizing with many of them through his job. An active concertgoer, he will arrive early to save seats for friends, always up front where the experience is most intense. Once a concert begins, Maris, like his colleagues, becomes deeply attentive, closing his eyes, bowing or bobbing his head in response to musical passages. One night, during a dynamic set by guitarist James "Blood" Ulmer's group at the annual Vision Festival, Maris left his midauditorium seat to sprawl on the floor in front of the stage, where his facial expressions and body language conveyed that he was thoroughly in the thrall of Ulmer's music. "This," he remarked to me, "is what I came for."[19]

Jack Vartoogian is interested in many musical and moving art forms. As staff photographers for the World Music Institute, he and his wife Linda often go to ballet, modern dance, opera, musical theater, jazz, pop music, Indian classical music, flamenco dancers and musicians, and African pop artists—enjoying them all. His photographs reflect a fine sensitivity to the expressive emotionalism of theatrical performances. His images have been featured in the *New York Times*,[20] top jazz periodicals like *DownBeat* and *JazzTimes*, textbooks, and photo portfolios;[21] one (discussed later) hangs among the Village Vanguard's "wall of fame" portraits. In contrast to many professional photographers who leave in the middle of a performance once they have shot the images they need for their assignment, Vartoogian stated that he's also there "to hear and see what's going on," earning himself a reputation for being "the only photographer who stays for the whole show."

These profiles establish their subjects as jazz fans who are interested in the music on its own terms. Occupational demands may conflict with personal tastes, however, and active engagement with jazz—like anything else—may lead to overexposure, saturation, even burnout. David Adler has written hundreds of CD reviews and liner notes, once at a rate of five to eight articles per week, and his inbox is usually inundated with newly released CDs. "When I'm listening to a specific CD and writing a review I give it my undivided attention, and I will say I'm *absolutely focused* on the world of that CD," he noted; "The problem is that, when I'm done with it, I might very well never listen to it again, even if I *like* it." Once, he remembered, he had an impulse to relisten to something that had caught his attention, but couldn't figure out where it was in his vast collection. He believes that saturation has muted his enthusiasm: "This is the problem with high-volume stuff: I do *not* absorb music the way that I used to. I mean, when I was a teenager and I was getting into music I would play an album five hundred times—and *memorize* it! I memorized every single [musical idea] on Mahavishnu Orchestra's first two records; I can sing along with every lick, every line. And one of the things that I really miss is *that*. I find I'm *not* connecting to music in the same way, unless I force myself." He speculated that if someone gave him a random blindfold listening test from his own CD collection, chances are he wouldn't recognize it, even if it was a recording he had "absolutely *loved*." For critics, high-volume concentrated listening can become routine, even monotonous, motivated more by professional obligations than genuine inspiration.

Concerts, too, may lose their immediacy, leading to a sense of oversatiation or detachment. Jack Vartoogian avoids this by varying his diet, switching among dance, classical, jazz, and world music presentations during his work week. "One of the things that's good, for what I do, is that I'm doing a lot of *different* things," he explained; "So it's kind of like when I don't hear the music I love, I love the music I hear—most of the time." On the other hand, David Adler reported feelings of "disconnectedness": "Often, going out and hearing live stuff, I'll find, like if it's the fifth show of the week, or if it's the third time I've been to Cornelia Street Café in a week, I might be tuning out a little bit 'cause I'm getting a little burnt out by the surroundings, and a little bit lulled into kind of a stupor. And are you really connecting with what the artist is trying to say? Maybe not." At such times, a little distance helps him get close again: "If it gets too much like that, I really try to back away a little bit and maybe not go out for a little while, and just try to reconnect with what the music is about, somehow."

Another factor constraining professionals' enjoyment is the need to be on-task for their jobs. A photographer, for example, must attune to visual, not auditory, stimuli in order to fulfill an assignment. "If you look for those emotional moments, they *usually*—not always, but usually—coincide with something special in the music," noted Jack Vartoogian, "but you can't *concentrate* on that." He recalled an occasion when the music temporarily took priority over his work: "With the first note, I knew that it would be something special and beautiful. And so for the first two or three minutes, five minutes, whatever, I just put the camera down—I wanted to hear it. And there was still time to take pictures; if there *hadn't* been time to take pictures then I would've had to take them." Even as he momentarily immersed himself in music, Vartoogian maintained a peripheral awareness of his professional responsibilities.

Though they come to jazz work as fans, many professionals eventually confront the challenges of underpayment, overexposure, boredom, burnout, and/or multitasking. What happens when the music's aesthetic and emotional payoffs are compromised? When jazz is just a job? Some people presumably drop out of the scene because of these and related issues, while those who don't must sustain their enthusiasm in the face of professional constraints. A key factor in the latter's perseverance seems to lie in the improvised spontaneity of the music itself, a constant source of variation within the nightly "routine."

CHANNELING THE MUSE: PROFESSIONALS AS CO-IMPROVISERS

Live jazz can become a conduit for creativity, a muse that inspires and influences artistic activity. Some people respond to the music through inspired co-improvisation: a writer expressing him- or herself in prose or poetry, a visual artist drawing or painting pictures, or a photographer freezing kinetic energy into still images. These individuals create original artworks in the moment of performance, channeling and translating jazz's audio-visual-kinesic stimuli into alternate physical media. More than merely "capturing" musical expressions, they re-create them in their own images, articulating distinctive interpretations and reshapings of the musical event. Their presence in the room becomes part of the pageantry as audiences witness their participatory choreography or peruse their unfolding designs.

A critic listening to and writing about a new recording improvises in much the same way musicians do: transforming his or her musical excitement into words, then emending the spontaneous prose for publication. The buzz generated in such moments stems from immersion in the creative process, and perhaps from the anticipation of the work's reception by an imaginary readership, who will discover and reexperience the author's private performance. Unlike jazz performers, however, authors have lag time to recompose their improvisations before airing them.

During his almost thirty-year stint at the *Village Voice* Gary Giddins produced biweekly articles of substantial length. "It's not easy to find a subject you want to write eighteen hundred words about!" he exclaimed; "there're a lot of records that come out and you say, 'Well, this is fine, but I don't have an essay to say about this.'" Musical inspiration proved to be a *sine qua non* for his creative process: "So part of the motive for what I'm looking for is what stimulates me as a writer, what gets me really excited. I put in a CD and instantly I know, 'Oh man, I could really go to town on this!' There are other things that might be perfectly fine but—you know—*you* write about them, because they don't interest me as a writer." To avoid biasing his impressions, Giddins's assistant loads his multi-CD player every morning to prevent him from peeking at the jewel cases, so he "listens blind" to virgin screenings of new releases and reissues.

In order to sustain enthusiasm for jazz, Giddins has toggled between coverage of the contemporary scene and rereleased recordings over the course of his career. "When I first started writing about jazz in the early seventies, historically that was one of the really bad periods in jazz history," he observed, "but it was thrilling for me because it was one of the great periods for reissues, so it was a great time for me to learn about a lot of relatively obscure musicians, and great ones whose major recordings were just being discovered, even though they were dead for many years. I mean, all of a sudden somebody finds in the vaults Lester Young playing with Charlie Christian—no one knew this existed—or Clifford Brown's last session. So you'd write about that." Giddins's focus switched to current music "when the music started getting really exciting again in '74, -5, -6 with the loft era—that's what consumed me for the next five or six years," reverting back when the loft movement dried up: "And then there'd be another period where every new record that comes in is crap, so you say, 'Well, what reissues are here? Oh! Somebody just put out the entire Sarah Vaughan on EmArcy. Great! I'll write about Sarah.'" In his view, historic recordings may be more newsworthy than new ones: "I can pretty much choose what I want to choose [to write about] and still be current, because jazz is constantly existing on these two planes . . . what's going on right now, and . . . cannibalizing the past."[22]

As with musical improvisation or frequent concertgoing, writers may lose inspiration due to overexposure, burnout, or apathy. Gary Giddins compares his struggles with writer's block to musicians with improviser's block. "As a writer, you find that you use up subjects," he observed; "Dizzy Gillespie said, 'You'd think that, playing all these years, the trumpet would get easier, but it gets harder.' And I said, 'You mean the embouchure?'[23] And he said, 'No, no, no; nothing about the physical; it's that you use up ideas. And you can't keep repeating them, and you've gotta find new stuff.' It's the same thing with *me*. And I was too young then to realize it, but now I think about what he said all the time, because how many pieces am I gonna write about Louis Armstrong?" Even with a constant influx of artists and recordings, writers still need something to spark their imagination. "You're constantly looking for new material but, at the same time, you're looking for material that stimulates you," noted Giddins; "in a sense it's an improvisational mode that you go into as a writer. I mean, every time you sit down to write a sentence you have a hundred thousand possibilities; whatever you choose is an improvisational moment."

In contrast to critics, photographers and some visual artists and poets improvise to *live* music. We've seen how photographer Jack Vartoogian uses music to guide his reflexes to capture a performance's emotional peaks.[24] Visual artists

Jonathan Daniel and Jeff Schlanger (discussed below) intentionally attune their art-making to onstage action, beginning when the music begins, stopping when it stops, with minimal additions or re-touch-ups after the (f)act. All three channel musical (muse-ical) impulses into "re-actions" that accompany, interpret, and expand on the original performance.

When I first met him, Jonathan Daniel (see Figures 20 and 21) was going out two or three nights a week to sketch and paint live jazz performances. Limited to places where he could work unhindered, he concentrated his activities around Smoke, Marjorie Eliot's parlor, the Jazz Gallery, and (before it changed management) Smalls.[25] "I need to focus on an environment for, like, six months—six months to a *year*, really," he explained; "Like Marjorie's: I'll focus on that for a good year before I finish the work I wanna finish. I mean, I've been listening to jazz more than two years, but I've *immersed* myself in this project for about two years. I've only been able to do about two or three places."[26]

He described how he is especially drawn to the physical aspects of sound, mentioning several clubs he wouldn't work in because of poor PA systems, overly loud volume, or other sound production issues. He's especially drawn to the tone (but not necessarily the visible appearance) of the trumpet:

> Trumpet is *it*. I live for that—particularly to draw and paint—listening to the trumpet. There're a lot of bright colors that come out from a trumpet, even when the sounds are saturated, so when I'm thinking of that in terms of color, it's always saturated, it's always a strong sound. Even when the playing is soft there's a strength to it, unlike other instruments. For example, a string instrument like a bass, even an electric bass, will not give you those kinds of sounds. The trumpet, I think, stands apart from pretty much anything else, in terms of that potent color that comes out of it.

I wondered how the sheer physicality of an instrument's sound affected him, and he responded: "It's really hard to describe. I just let the sound come in and make a response without thinking, right on the paper, on the wood. I let the sound inside and make a response of quick reactions." His observations emphasize the kinesthetic dimensions of sound, as if he's *feeling* the "colors" of the music more than hearing them, an intriguing perceptual frame-shift given the visual nature of his craft.

Daniel developed techniques of physical and mental preparation for improvising artwork, originally applied to other subjects, later applied to jazz. He reflected on his artistic process:

> One of the people I learned from has this exercise where he would make me stand up with a piece of paper and a brush and ink on the floor and sort of

hang like this [*demonstrates*]; I bend over and just let my arms hang loose, and he would make me wait 'til my mind was completely clear to make a move. He tried to train me to let the energy flow—my energy flow, or the energy flow all around me—make the marks. So I took that. I did this for years. And then it occurred to me that when I listened to music I could get into that same state where I'm not at all thinking about the marks I'm making on the surface. I'll do an entire picture in a set, on one set/jazz session, and not [stop]. At the end, I really have no idea what—I can't remember even doing it. It's really kinda strange.

Daniel's co-improvisations accompany the musician's improvisations. Part of his preparation is physical (mixing paints, prepping paper, slow breathing, and so forth); part is mental (achieving a "completely clear" state responsive to the "energy flow").

Daniel's artistic modus operandi recalls similar approaches by jazz improvisers and Zen painters, where long periods of conscious preparation culminate in an explosive realization of the artistic impulse, largely subconscious. Musicians tend to emphasize physical and intellectual preparation, methodically mastering specific instrumental techniques and theoretical concepts, allowing them to incubate and then "hatching" them in spontaneous surges, simultaneously recombining and reinterpreting these well-digested musical elements in unpredictable ways.[27] Alto saxophonist Charlie Parker succinctly encapsulated this concept in his famous dictum: "Master your ax, learn the changes—then forget all that shit and just play!"[28] Japanese and Chinese painters schooled in Zen techniques emphasize mental preparation, aiming for a state of emptiness, and then allowing intuition or instinct to guide their artistic improvisations. Ideally, a painting is an effortless extension of the artist's inner mental state, an "artless" artwork.[29] "[T]he artist must fully understand the inner nature of the aesthetic object, its Buddha nature," explains Fredric Lieberman; "[t]echnique, though important, is useless without it; and the actual execution of the art work may be startlingly spontaneous, once the artist has comprehended the essence of his subject."[30] Jazz pianist Kenny Werner contends that all these awarenesses—physical, intellectual, emotional, and even spiritual—must be cultivated for an improvising artist to achieve "effortless mastery."[31]

An artist's mind and body can be envisioned as a conduit or vessel, an instrument for performing jazz. In one sense, artists are active, preparing for music physically and mentally, and then creating it with their hands and minds; but in another sense they are passive, enabled and guided *by* music. As singer Rhiannon writes, "Surrender [but not passivity] is at the core of good improvisation.

Surrender to spirit . . . to the ensemble . . . to the deep self [and] to the energy of the room."[32] For various projects, Jonathan Daniel has deliberately "immersed" himself in certain clubs, and then allowed the "energy flow" to inundate his awareness and inform his actions. "The music puts you in a certain state where you're not thinking like you do in everyday life—when you have to go to the store or cook or—which is a good state to be in. It puts you in that state where you're not thinking." In this condition, his body responds like the resonating box of a stringed instrument, sympathetically transforming and telegraphing musical vibrations into visual images: "The notes, the sounds, come out on the surface [of the paper or canvas] as well." A product of both conscious and subconscious intentions, shaped by specific elements of his immediate environment, Daniel's art bears the stamp of a singular place and time.

Akin to how writers alternate between improvisational flow and self-conscious, self-auditing states, Daniels often revisits his spontaneous pieces: "I will put out a series of drawings—after I work them, say, for a month—by the same [artist/band]. On one side of the room I'll put up drawings by [*sic*] a particular musician or a particular group, and on the other side of the room I'll put up drawings I did of a second one. And actually, I *will* look and do some comparison about how I translated the notes and the marks. So there's a translation going on." He then compares his work on an artist to recorded "translations": "I'll go back and listen to some recordings by the same people who I drew live and try to do some analysis—not detailed analysis, but just sorta sit back and recognize that I made deliberate images, based on the way they sound. That's their fingerprints on the work." Note that Daniel said "drawings *by* a particular musician," a slip-of-the-tongue perhaps, but suggestive of how he shares artistic agency with jazz musicians: both improvise, both try to "forget all that shit and just play," both leave "fingerprints" on their artworks.

Jeff Schlanger's (see Figure 23) approach is very similar to Daniel's, with the significant difference that he works almost exclusively in the dominion of avant-jazz, improvising paintings in a variety of downtown performance spaces[33] and maintaining an active presence on the international festival scene.[34] Schlanger characterizes his practice as "a dance of the hands with wet colors, a human-souled bodily seismograph of the energy, rhythms, and movements in the music."[35] The "dance" is literally a duet because he paints with both hands, *simultaneously*. After a set at the annual Vision Festival, where he serves as the "house" painter, he revealed that each hand has its own personality and way of expressing itself, and that he uses both in order to catch as much of the energy coming off of the stage as possible:[36] "There is way too much coming at us! I wish I had more hands!"[37] His in-the-moment paintings of performances are part of his ongoing "musicWitness®" project, initiated in 1975 when, surrounded by the profusion of creativity marking the height of the loft scene, he was inspired to "get a record down." His media of choice are paint, pottery, and sculpture, the former two (and to some extent the latter) requiring that he work "in time," the way improvisers do, without possibility for substantial editing. His live paintings grace the covers of more than thirty CDs, all recordings of live concerts by prominent avant-jazz musicians such as Billy Bang, Charles Gayle, Julius Hemphill, and William Parker. Gazing at his art, fans can reexperience the musical event in two improvised modalities: the sound of the music and the image of Schlanger's vision. In referring to himself as a "bodily seismograph," a "witness," and a "record-keeper," he reinforces the idea that artists are both passive and active vessels for creative expression.[38]

The artist-professionals profiled provide intriguing examples of how some audience members actively participate in jazz-making. Like sympathetic strings of a sitar, they "resonate" in response to vibrations emanating from the stage and around the room. They are offstage performers, channeling the sonic, visual, and kinesthetic energy of jazz to permeate and prompt their own artistic improvisations.

LISTENING ON THE JOB

While performers must follow and respond to the music of their bandmates, and fans are presumably free to listen as they please, professionals' attention is influenced by job-related contingencies. How does this affect the way they hear and understand music? We've seen that listeners mediate an "act" of music through individual perceptional frames based on musical training, previous experiences, and culturally situated modes of attention and then "re-*act*" to create personalized meanings. A photographer may notice the room lighting, for example, whereas a publicist might informally assess the size and excitement of the crowd. In shared social spaces where collective attention converges on improvised musical events, individual perceptions may diverge radically.

Jazz participants' experiences are affected by the degree and focus of their attention. Audition may fluctuate from inattention, to heightened attention to a particular element or elements, to a more dispersed form of engagement; the focus (or foci) and intensity of concentration hinge on an individual's auditory agenda and capacity, influenced in turn by the music performed (e.g., structured versus open-ended).[39] In his study of free improvisation, for example, David Borgo argues that music lacking overt references and predictability fosters non-directed listening skills.[40] Generally speaking, performers listen to play, while fans and casual listeners listen for "fun," tuning in and out, focusing here and there, as their interests dictate. Like performers, professionals must "decode" musical events, but their task is to translate and reinterpret these sounds to other media (e.g., words, images, or artwork). Like fans, they listen to appreciate, but they must also attend to other elements of the performance gestalt.

Artists Jeff Schlanger and Jonathan Daniel translate jazz into two- and three-dimensional images, concentrating on the visible elements of a performance, though both report that their work is directly inspired by aural elements such as timbre and the kinetic energy of sound. Photographer Jack Vartoogian is particularly aware of stage lighting, sightlines, and other factors affecting his ability to take pictures. "I think jazz, especially, still should be done in a club, primarily. That's where I like it the best. In concert halls you've got much better shooting conditions: the light's usually better [and] if you're really lucky you get a pretty good angle—you don't always. But it's still kinda nice to be able to go and sit in the corner of a club and get the spot and enjoy that." Although he loves Smoke for its state-of-the-art sound system, great acoustics, and cozy ambiance, he notes that the venue's dim lightning makes shooting difficult.

Journalists, critics, and other writers translate jazz performances into text. Many employ a combination of written and mental shorthand to efficiently record their perceptions of the event, needing these to inform their write-ups. Writers need to take note of pertinent information such as performers' names, instruments, set list, solo order, song keys, and rhythmic meters. They must also analyze and interpret the musical and extramusical dimensions of a performance, contextualizing these against prior knowledge. They might recognize that a piece follows the twelve-bar blues form, or that a group has replaced its usual drummer with a substitute who plays more aggressively. The writer's role is always a balancing act because careful listening precludes detailed note-taking, and vice versa.[41]

In his work as a critic, David Adler tackles a variety of projects, including CD reviews, liner notes, features, and concert coverage. For liner notes and CD reviews he can always replay a particular passage for clarification, but live shows are "tougher" because he must rely more on his memory: "If I can, I write down the titles, or at least the progression of the set. If I don't have a title, I'll just write down a few notes to myself just to jog my memory: What kind of experience was it? Was it a fast tune? Was it a slow tune?—that much, just basic information." Like any good reporter, he gets the "facts," but also keeps a nose out for newsworthy material: "If something unusual happens, anything striking, I'll write it down: Did they screw up during one tune? Or was there some kind of a disconnect between the horn players and the rhythm section during one tune maybe? I just jot it down, not to single out flaws, but just to note it if it's worth noting. Like, 'Oh, it sounds as if the band was working something out here; it didn't quite work,' or, 'Oh, the next tune really worked. That meant they were getting the feel.'" He finds he must divide his attention between observation and record-keeping: "It's hard—I never quite know what's enough—but when I take notes at a live show, I'm a minimalist. I see some people [i.e., other critics] writing down a mini-novel when they're out seeing a show—I can't do that." By minimizing data-entry, he maximizes his chances of discovering a "disconnect" or recognizing that something "really worked."

Interestingly, listening strategies may alter to suit the assignment. For his "New York@Night" column in *AllAboutJazz: New York*, Adler wrote informal profiles of his favorite concerts in the previous month, usually covering half a dozen shows. "If something merits it, I can get very detailed," he remarked, "but in the column I don't have to get detailed. I don't *want* to; it can be more of just the impression: 'Wow, this was a great show!' So it's like a journal."[42] On assignment for *DownBeat* or *JazzTimes*, however, he is more meticulous: "*DownBeat* will send me to a show and that's a different deal; I have to take much more complete notes because they want me to fill a whole column space with reflections on one show. They'll give me a certain word count so I'll know what that means and that we're talking about, probably, a song-by-song analysis, where you want to take note of what's happening during each song, in addition to filling out the picture and talking about the context of the show."

Critics with musical training can be more specific in their descriptions of musical elements. "Every reviewer's totally different," Adler noted; "Because I *am* a player, and I have a musical education background, I *do* like to draw on that as much as I can—if it fits, if it feels genuine—because I *can*, but also because that's how I interface with the music too, like, *genuinely*. I'll listen and be, like, 'Oh wow, that was a very weird form that that person wrote in that composition!' . . . I write about whatever reaches me, on whatever level it is: if it's a technical level, or if it's just a pure emotional level." Jazz writers must do more than just describe organized sounds or voice an opinion: they must translate and interpret their understandings of the musical event—*how* or *why* it was good—so that readers can reexperience it.

Communicating to a general readership requires establishing broad contexts for musical performances. Whitney Balliett, longtime critic for *New Yorker* magazine, was an outstanding—and unusual—example of a jazz writer who avoided musical jargon in favor of literary devices (e.g., metaphors, caricature, sensory impressions). Martin Williams, compiler of *The Smithsonian Collection of Classic Jazz* and author of several highly esteemed jazz texts, often described music in detail, particularly in matters of form, but couched his observations in nontechnical terms.[43] David Adler tries to balance both approaches. "Some things I feel free to get much more technical than other things," he noted; "If I hear a piece that has an unusual form I might comment on it and not worry so much if people understand what I mean or not, and I try to say it in such a way that it's not so difficult to understand; even if you don't know *exactly* what I'm talking about you can get the thrust of why I'm saying it and why I think it's important."

Writers often establish contexts for readers through the standard repertoire. For example, George Gershwin's "Summertime" is frequently associated with famous recordings by Billie Holiday (1936), Sidney Bechet (1939), Miles Davis (1958), and John Coltrane (1961).[44] In his review of Joshua Redman's recording of the tune, critic Bill Milkowski—confident that knowledgeable readers would have heard John Coltrane's version with drummer Elvin Jones—wrote that Redman "mimics the tone and intensity of John Coltrane" and that drummer Brian Blade "is obviously and heavily influenced by Elvin Jones"[45] As jazz continues to diversify, however, with many artists focusing on original material, "standards" are not always so standard. Since the seventies, no new songs have been widely canonized, and the original sources of standards—Tin Pan Alley, Broadway shows, Hollywood movies, popular songs, famous jazz composers, television shows—are unfamiliar to younger fans. The generation gap between mainstream jazz and college-age listeners became painfully apparent to Gary Giddins when he picked fifteen versions of "Indiana" for his jazz appreciation class, thinking the song would be a good reference for comparison: "Not *one* kid in the class knew it."[46] Developing musicians still study the classics but increasingly seek inspiration in international folk, popular, and classical musics, or try to connect with peer audiences through contemporary pop music. For example, songs by Björk, Radiohead, and others[47] have been covered by artists such as The Bad Plus and Joshua Redman.[48]

As authoritative commentators, critics stake their reputations on the ability to situate performances within traditional practices. "If there's a tune that I know the title of, but I just can't think of it, then I *must* know the name of that tune; I *have* to. I have to ask [a musician] and get it, because I want to make sure that I'm staying on top of it. I need to clear that up, 'cause you want to convey to the reader that they played x, y, z, or [a] tune that everyone has played." Even veteran writers are occasionally stumped, as when Gary Giddins reviewed a Millennial Territory Orchestra gig in the *Village Voice*, praising the group's "righteous dose of jazz repertory." When slide trumpeter Steven Bernstein replicated Don Byas's tenor sax solo from a Count Basie recording of "Harvard Blues" and then challenged the audience to identify the reference,

Giddins wrote that "the whole class flunked and I was sobbing in shame when the band snapped into Preston Jackson's 'It's Tight Jim,' casually introduced. I had to look that one up."[49] Giddins speculated in the article whether Bernstein actually owned an old 78 rpm recording of the tune or if it had "actually been reissued." Unknown to Giddins, Bernstein had scoured boxloads of obscure tapes in preparation for his gig as the musical director for *Kansas City*, a Robert Altman film featuring music of the Midwestern "territory bands."[50]

In contrast to performing covers of well-known standards, when musicians perform an original composition writers can't compare it to earlier versions. In these situations, David Adler often asks himself, "How harmonically advanced is it? How accessible? Is it accessible? Is it inaccessible? Is it difficult on the first listen?" and perhaps relies on musical analysis or descriptions of his aesthetic impressions to convey his understandings of it. Writers can also establish a context by noting how a new composition differs from previous efforts by the same artist or group, or by comparing a trumpeter's instrumental tone and technical skills to other trumpeters.

Compared to mainstream jazz styles, music from the experimental fringe can be relatively difficult to describe. Ekkehard Jost has characterized free improvisation as "motific chain-association," likening it to James Joyce's stream-of-consciousness compositional technique and to the automatic writings of the surrealists.[51] In record reviews of downtown music, in order to provide detail and context for his curious readers/listeners, Bruce Gallanter may describe extended and/or unconventional playing techniques, use of electronic processing and other timbral manipulations, "in" and "out" (i.e., harmonic and nonharmonic) improvisation, or refer to the professional histories of artists and their assorted collaborators, or to the development and proliferation of esoteric musical sub-genres. The more an artist thinks and plays outside-of-the-box, however, the less meaningful it is to compare him or her with other artists. Paul Zampino, owner/operator of SquidCo, an online retailer of experimental music, partially circumvents this issue by providing short audio clips of purchasable recordings, allowing online shoppers to hear and judge for themselves.

PROFESSIONALS IN THE COMMUNITY

Jazz professionals, like venue operators and concertgoing fans, are active participants in the live music scene, insiders who are intimate with the inner workings of jazz communities. As fans, critical listeners, on-task workers, creative artists, and/or co-performers, they engage and understand the music through diverse means. Their observations of and interactions with musicians, club owners, concert promoters, serious fans, transient tourists, professional colleagues, and the others they come in contact with reveal much about collaborative expressions of art in improvised jazz communities. This section appraises their interactions with jazz musicians, venue operators, and audiences.

How much power (if any) do critics have over the public's perception of an artist? Writers affect an artist's stature and economic viability to the extent that their work influences fans to attend shows or buy recordings. Critics and their editors also decide which artists, recordings, and concerts are worth covering; how much copy to devote to each one; and whether to praise or pan (or both) their music. Bruce Gallanter has written up to ten to twenty CD reviews per month for his online newsletter, which reaches a global subscribership interested in "underground and avant-jazz . . . and the completely uncategorizable."[52] He speculated that plugging a particular recording might increase its sales by five or ten units, but even a glowing review probably wouldn't move more than a hundred copies; his recent favorites, he noticed, tend to sell a bit more, probably because he gives them extra airtime over the in-store sound system, increasing the likelihood that browsing customers will hear them and buy them.[53] The extent to which critics actually help or hinder an artist's career or influence fans' preferences, however, remains an open question.

Gary Giddins, one of the best-known jazz writers, reaches his public through high-profile jazz and general interest organs like *JazzTimes*, *New Yorker*, and critically acclaimed books and videos. "Jazz critics generally have the power to do good," he argued, "but we don't have the power to do evil. I mean, first of all, there's no point in killing a career that doesn't exist. And as for the people that we all universally hate, like Kenny G—I could spend the rest of my life attacking Kenny G; it won't cost him *one* record sale because the people who buy Kenny G don't read me, and they don't go to *All Music Guide*.[54] He cited Arthur Blythe as an example of a lesser-known artist whose CD sales saw a modest spike (confirmed by the record label) as a result of his glowing review, contrasting this with the negligible effect his open criticism of Wynton Marsalis has had on the latter's career.

Relationships between professionals and performers may mature through occupational associations and expanding social networks. "I've developed relationships with a lot of different musicians," David Adler recounted; "I don't know everyone that I write about; I don't necessarily introduce myself to everyone I write about. A lot of it just happens by itself: you're just in the orbit and you get introduced to people." Critics approach musicians after performances to get song titles and composers, musicians' names (with correct spellings), and/or background information. "I'll very often find that I really need to talk to the artist or at least have some way of getting in touch with them," noted Adler; "I'll either go up and get the name of the bandmember or tune, or whatever, or I'll make sure that I have some way of contacting that person—at least—if I can't get to them that night." Musicians (or their publicists) often send writers promotional materials: new recordings, announcements of upcoming gigs, photos, press reviews, and so forth. "Sometimes musicians will get in touch with me and say, 'I know about your column; I thought you'd love to come to the show,'" Adler reported. Critics help artists through favorable publicity, while musicians can reciprocate by enlisting them to compose liner notes for recordings, thereby "enshrining" the writer's words on durable works of art.

Despite their ubiquity, in a certain sense professionals occupy the periphery of jazz scene(s). "I don't often feel like I totally fit into whatever [scene] it is," Jack Vartoogian stated, "but I realize that I go out of my way *not* to, in a way, and I maintain a certain amount of journalistic distance. More and more I think it's important—for what *I* do—*not* to go talk to all these guys, or want to be friends, or see them outside—and even some of the fans too. I mean, I've made a lot of friends doing this." David Adler concurred that close relations can compromise professional neutrality: "It's a pressing matter because, just in the very fact that you're interacting with a lot of musicians all the time means that if you say something really negative about someone, that's someone you might have to interact with at some point and you don't want there to be this tension. You don't want to gain a reputation as someone who's a really negative and unconstructive reviewer." With finite time to handle the glut of solicitations he gets from talented, deserving artists, Adler can't be as supportive as he'd like to be: "Sometimes I just get inundated with stuff and approaches and people wanting me to acknowledge them in print or whatever. At a certain point, there's only so much I can do. I try to at least *respond*, and say, 'I'm sorry, I'm just too busy right now.' I wish I could write about *everything*; I wish there were enough time."

In my own work as a jazz writer,[55] I often deal with artists and publicists. Many of the first paid pieces I wrote were for *AllAboutJazz: New York*, which were then uploaded to *AllAboutJazz*,[56] an anthology website run by a dozen professional staffers but authored by more than eighty unpaid volunteers. I was (and am) regularly asked to review (or consider reviewing) new releases. Without knowing whether I'll get a commission (i.e., paid) for it, or even if I'll like it, I promise to listen to anything they send, but try to make it clear I can't commit to an article.[57] "The more free writing I do," said David Adler, stating the issue succinctly, "the less paid writing I do." Publicists put writers on their mailing lists, sending out new releases by artists in their catalog—sometimes a "hard copy" (CD), but more often a digital file—usually following up with a polite email to see if the writer has listened to it, liked it, and/or has plans to write about it. In assignments for *New York City Jazz Record*, I choose from a list of available recordings selected by the editors,[58] picking those I'm inspired by—or think I'll be. People occasionally write to thank me for a favorable review, to correct a factual error (e.g., a misidentified musician or tune title), or—rarely—to take issue with a frankly critical review, as in the following response from a disgruntled guitarist: "This was an unfair and un-thought-about review. . . . There's plenty of reviews of this record already that say what a jazz review should say."[59] Even when a recording doesn't meet my standards or agree with my tastes, I generally try to accentuate the positive, calling attention to items that may interest curious listeners/readers—a gesture of respect for the artist's effort.

Journalistic autonomy is a complex issue, and writers may change their views as they mature or raise their professional standing. *New York City Jazz Record* editor Laurence Donohue-Greene formerly urged staff writers to return any recording under review should they discover it was not their "cup of tea," indicating that he'd find someone else who wanted to cover it.[60] Ned Goold, a saxophonist I'd reviewed who was familiar with the paper, once wrote me that he'd "never seen a bad review" and asked if that was policy. I replied "no," explaining however that the paper tried to support local artists. He then suggested that this amounted to an "indirect policy," opining that critics are freer to deprecate historical figures because "they aren't worried about running into cats [jazz musicians] when they dismiss things that are obviously inferior," and that "all this pc" [political correctness] surrounding jazz musicians was "just making things worse."[61] On the advent of the paper's tenth anniversary, coeditor Andrey Henkin posted the following communiqué to contributors: "Our mission has always been to support the city's jazz community . . . but as we grow in stature, it behooves us to be less cheerleaders and more thoughtful commentators. So this is a revision of sorts to our positive-only review policy. . . . I'd like to request more considered evaluation of CDs. . . . [I]f there is something wrong with the album, this kind of observation should be included—in as constructive and intelligent means [as] possible."[62] Presumably the paper's change of "policy" came from its increasing clout, or perhaps the editors agreed with Goold that too much "pc" compromises not only the paper and its writers but the artists and even the art form itself.

In contrast to critics, most jazz professionals don't publish their opinions, so their interactions with artists are less scripted. Record retailers Fred Cohen, Bruce Gallanter, and Manny Maris sell artists' recordings and (to a greater or lesser extent) attend their shows, and in turn are supported when these artists patronize their stores. Jeff Schlanger's paintings, featured on album covers, celebrate both his and the musicians' creativity, while Jack Vartoogian's photographs expose both photographer and subject. In all of these cases, both parties benefit from the exchange.

Invariably, the lifestyles of jazz professionals, performers, and fans become inextricably intermingled, as illustrated in the following anecdote. Jack Vartoogian judged a black-and-white photo he'd taken of the late pianist Tommy Flanagan to be one of his best. Knowing that Village Vanguard proprietress Lorraine Gordon was also an avid Flanagan fan, he ordered a 16 × 20-inch print of it, signed it, and gave it to Gordon, who mounted it on the wall behind the club's piano. Although he doesn't usually approach musicians, Vartoogian once introduced himself to Flanagan, mentioning their mutual roots in Detroit and disclosing that he'd taken the photo of Flanagan now hanging in the Vanguard. According to Vartoogian, Flanagan was polite but underwhelmed and then failed to recognize and/or acknowledge him in several subsequent encounters. "Then, at some point, about two and a half years ago, Lorraine took that picture down,"[63] Vartoogian recounted, "and Tommy played the last gig at the Vanguard that he [ever] did; it was just a week or two after 9/11. I really wanted to get down to it, but I didn't, and I knew he hadn't been well. He came in to play, sat down, looked over, and called to Gordon: 'Lorraine, that picture's gone! You gotta put it back!' And the next night it was *back*, and it's been there ever since."[64] Vartoogian was surprised: "That's how you can be *wrong* about your impressions of what somebody is [feeling], how he's reacting to you," he mused; "but clearly, it [the photo] was important to him, and so that pleased me very much." Showing me a digital scan of the original photo, he revealed something even more interesting: a later photo of Flanagan performing in the Vanguard showing the pianist in the foreground, gazing up in a signature gesture that unconsciously replicates his earlier pose in the original photo, which is clearly visible in the background, hanging on the wall just above and beyond his head (see Figure 34). In this image-of-an-image, Vartoogian gazes at his own gaze, just as Flanagan signifies on his own body language.[65]

Jeff Schlanger's perspective on relationships between on- and offstage performers is especially intriguing. His artworks, improvised accompaniments to ephemeral musical expressions, are collaborative co-performances. "One of the things about being around musicians is you *learn* so much," he related; "and one of the things you learn is to really be ready to *deliver*, and to deliver completely; and in order to do that you have to be *very* relaxed. So right there are three incredible things to learn. And, of course, it's practice, to do any of those things. But the more you can learn to really relax in the moment and also, simultaneously, commit to the *whole* of existence during the time you have—it's a form of freedom." He described the extramusical dimensions of such moments: "It does something to the time; it makes the time sacred. It's a *meeting*, in time." Deep listening, he explained, is reciprocal: "For *me*, the audience for the musicWitness®66 project has always been the *musicians*, rather than the audience. I'm part of the audience, there's no question about that, but the audience in terms of the *creative* part of this project—it's the musicians that have picked it up, from the beginning—not *all* of them; not *every* one—every musician's got a different way to see also." Schlanger's perceptions flip the standard script because musicians are now the audience, his art-making a performance for music-makers.

Working in the arena of free (or avant-) jazz, which advocates open-ended, omnidirectional listening,[67] allows Schlanger to experience extremely close cohesion with musicians. "Especially in this kind of music, the connection with the feelings is so direct that the musicians, in general, *do not* make polite chatter at all. If something affects them, you hear about it immediately; if something doesn't affect them, you don't hear *anything*. And that's great too—that's a*nother* form of freedom. So, from the beginning, there have been some musicians, and now many, many, who understand—each in their different individual ways—what is being attempted here." Schlanger gets feedback from performers when mutual connections are made. "There have been many expressions—that have been really encouraging to me—that the nourishment goes around. It becomes a feast that we're having together, a sense of we're all in this *together*; we're all in this business of trying to live creatively and freely and with courage and dignity together, and *share* it. And the sharing is with *everybody*." Schlanger sees creative art as a life-affirming counterbalance to "a culture that is, basically, *totally* materialist, and almost anti-spiritual, at this particular point in history, never *more* so." His observations argue forcibly for the strength and solidarity of the relationships between musicians, himself, and other curious listeners in the avant-jazz scene.

Jazz professionals and venue operators have an inherent conflict of interest: the former need access (preferably free or low-cost) to concert venues in order to work, while the latter run businesses that rely on paying customers to cover costs. We've already seen in the previous chapter how venue operators grapple with admission policies for nonperforming musicians and nonpaying audiences. Former club owner Horst Liepolt summed it up succinctly: "There's only two people who do it: the people who PLAY, and the people who PAY— that's it; everybody else is [along] for a ride." Admission to shows is therefore negotiated with pragmatic compromises. When a periodical covers a concert at a particular club, for example, it publicizes both artist and venue, increasing potential patronage at future events. Venues are therefore usually willing to extend press privileges in anticipation of these benefits to their business, and so critics, photographers, and other press are ordinarily admitted when on assignment, as long as previous arrangements have been made through appropriate channels. "Every club usually has a hired publicist or a contact person who handles the press requests," noted David Adler; "because my 'New York@Night' column is such a regular thing, people just know me at this point. I have my email list, people I've actually gotten to meet and know; you put faces to names and become friendly with these people. I wanted to go to Iridium on Wednesday, so I just dropped Jim Eigo an email on Monday saying, 'Hey Jim, I wanna go on Wednesday.' He's, like, 'Sure, no problem.'" Adler can "zap off five emails on a Monday" and get on all the guest lists he needs to for the week. Critic Russ Musto, a forty-plus-year veteran of the scene, has entrée into many of the most important venues because of ongoing alliances with staff members.[68] As longtime arts correspondent for the *New York Times*, Jack Vartoogian arranged for club admissions by calling the publicist, club, or record company, depending on his assignment. Professionals can also gain access to venues through their connections with performing artists, who are usually allowed to put people on their guest lists.

Jazz professionals face certain issues with venue proprietors, however. For example, the 9/11 terrorist attacks and subsequent recession made club owners more safety- and budget-conscious. "It's getting harder to get into clubs to photograph," Jack Vartoogian reported at the time, "unless you know the right people, or unless you've got an assignment. Everything's tightening up." Prominent periodicals stopped issuing carte blanche press passes to freelancers, and media credentials of any kind became much more difficult to obtain due to security precautions implemented throughout the city.[69] Although it doesn't cost club owners to admit one more person, each chair and barstool represents potential revenue, so prominent clubs with high overheads require all guests to "rent" their spot. One time, when Vartoogian and I were assigned to cover a Brad Mehldau concert at Smoke, proprietor Paul Stache confirmed us for "standing room" only, giving his patrons priority over press, but assured us, "If there is seats u'll get 'em."[70] (We didn't.) "I can get in free," noted David Adler; "but certain places have their minimums—anything at Iridium or Birdland—so I usually have to pay the minimum, ten bucks, buy a drink—it's not totally free." Ironically, the outlay for jazz "jobs" may outweigh the income. "I have to watch that," Adler mused, "because I'm not making a ton of money at this point in my life and, if I go out and pay a whole bunch of minimums in a given month, it adds up—even if I'm not paying a cover, I'm spending too much money."[71]

Other issues arise between jazz professionals and venue operators over on-site working conditions. Some clubs (and sometimes the artists who perform there) impose certain restrictions, while others are relatively lenient. New technologies make it easy to manufacture and market audio and video recordings, artwork, T-shirts, and other knockoff and pirate merchandise, so name artists may resent the appropriation and dispersal of their music, even in the jazz market, where profit margins are relatively meager. These issues impact professionals as well, as in the following incident described by Jack Vartoogian: "I just photographed Pat Metheny at the Beacon [Theatre]. The deal was: 'He's gonna do a half hour solo. You can't photograph that. Then the trio comes out, and you can photograph the first and second songs, and then you have to stop.' Why the first and second songs? I don't know. 'Okay, screw you guys. If that's what you want, that's what I'll *do!*'" Vartoogian's frustration arose because of seemingly arbitrary restrictions that compromised the quality of his work. "All it does is that the chances are the photographs won't be as good, because you've gotta shoot faster. I'll probably end up taking the same amount of pictures—or almost—but they won't be as thoughtful. And I *explain* that, but most of the time nobody cares. They don't change it; those are the rules, at that level of stardom—there're a lot of reasons—and that happens more and more, and it sort of defeats the whole point of it." Metheny's stringent stipulations represent one extreme;[72] generally photographers and other professionals have a lot more leeway, especially in informal venues featuring journeymen jazz musicians.

The presence of photographers or other professionals affects the ambiance of a performance. Jack Vartoogian, conscious that he is a guest of the management, and a representative of his trade, feels doubly obligated to respect his surroundings. Unfortunately, he points out, "a lot of photographers *don't* do that," making it more difficult to convince club owners that he won't disrupt a show: "They *should* be able to trust me. Forget the fact that I've been photographing for thirty years; forget that I've been photographing for the *Times* for fifteen years—a lot of people know me; forget about the fact that, even if they *don't* know me, it's still the *New York Times*; forget about the fact that I've got a long lens and I tell them I'm gonna be far enough away, and—'No, I'm *not* gonna use a flash, of *course* not'—and *all* of these things." Vartoogian takes precautions to minimize his impact: "If you happen to be photographing a performance, you've *really* gotta be careful. And even tonight—where I'm gonna be shooting at Joe's Pub—it's quiet music. I'm gonna take a cover and put it on the camera, a little leather pouch that'll—not eliminate the sound, but it'll reduce it. And it'll make it harder to work, but more importantly, it'll reduce the sound so that people won't have as much reason to fuss at—it'll look like I'm trying to be cooperative, which I *am*." Maintaining good public relations works both ways: when Vartoogian respects performers, presenters, and patrons by keeping a low profile, he's accorded the leeway he needs to do his best work, whereas an irresponsible colleague can put these allowances in jeopardy.

I have encountered similar issues in my own work as a photographer.[73] On one occasion, taking pictures at the Vision Festival, a weeklong, relatively informal avant-jazz event held that year in an old school gymnasium, I was politely advised by Jack Vartoogian (sitting next to me, on assignment) to mute the in-focus beeper on my camera, as it was readily audible to my immediate neighbors. Beep silenced, I moved up front to get closeups, careful not to obscure anyone's sightline, when a man taping the concert told me that the sound of my shutter (far *less* audible) was getting picked up by his highly sensitive microphones, and would I please move further away? Later I noticed several aggressive photographers positioning themselves throughout the room to get their shots, to the point that it became a distraction to the musical presentation, especially when one of them used a flash. Such activity may be tolerated in the relaxed atmosphere of a performance space, but never in formal concert venues. On another occasion, while taking pictures of Dave Douglas's group from a near-front table at the Village Vanguard, despite my efforts to keep a low profile (literally), foregoing a flash (but hefting a protuberant zoom lens), I was politely but firmly censured by an employee who'd been sent over by Lorraine Gordon. After I'd apologized to her post-set, she clarified that photography was okay, but only from the back of the room where it wouldn't detract from the performance.[74]

Critics and photographers are not the only professionals who encounter (or present) obstacles while working in performance spaces. Visual artists who bring an unwieldy assortment of paraphernalia aren't generally welcome in upscale supper clubs and concert halls where space is at a premium, and so will seek out more hospitable venues. Visual artist Jonathan Daniel sought out club owners who'd be receptive to his modus operandi: "I'll deliberately go around and try to find the best location [in the club], the one that I think is best for that moment," he reported; "Some people don't like that. I've almost been kicked out of places, especially when the [drawing] board's rather large. But really, I don't understand why people have a problem with that, because that's what it's all about: it's an unplanned event. So if people start bringing in boards—and as long as they're not knocking over the musicians [*laughs*]—and want to go for it, what's the problem?" He once approached the proprietor of Cleopatra's Needle, explained what he wanted to do and then, in spite of the man's initial resistance, obtained permission to work there. On the first night, Daniel recalled, "I did this elaborate drawing and I gave it to him, [but] he just kicked me out the next time I went after that and wouldn't give me any options. So it was really strange. I figured I was warming up to [*sic*] the guy a little bit, the owner. He was very happy to take my drawing the week before; he was letting me draw there, under certain conditions."

Other proprietors were more hospitable, especially Mitch Borden at the "old" Smalls. "At Smalls, you have free rein," Daniel attested; "They're true jazz enthusiasts. Anything goes there."[75] He had quickly discovered that "assembly-line" venues like Birdland, Blue Note, and Iridium—where drink minimums are strictly enforced and clientele are efficiently ushered in and out between relatively short sets—are not conducive to open-ended sessions or musically inspired artwork. Even a club like the Village Vanguard, with its excellent acoustics and outstanding musicians, is not an ideal workplace for someone like him. "I don't go there too much, more because of time and money," he said, elaborating: "Those sets are pretty short, and fairly expensive. I need to settle into a [flow]. I can be drawing or painting for, like, three minutes, and then if someone comes and bothers me for a minute; that's fine. But the overall evening, I don't like to have a sense that it's time to go after, like, forty-five minutes, or whatever; or, 'It's time to pay for the next set, if you wanna stay.' That puts wrinkles in the experience." Such "wrinkles," he believes, restrict artistic expression: "Again, I'm not a jazz musician, [but] in my opinion, that's not the way to listen to jazz—I mean, from a visual side." Smalls and Smoke, on the other hand, provided an ambiance where he could do his best work. "You don't get that vibe at Smalls, [and] even though Smoke has a short set, you don't get that vibe, really, at Smoke. That's what I like about it: you can settle in, and I can get to work, and I don't feel like it's this business transaction and I'm in and out [and] can't do what I need to do."[76] Daniel has also worked in Marjorie Eliot's Harlem household and the Jazz Gallery—both run on a nonprofit basis and therefore of somewhat independent means; both, he asserted, are "artist-friendly environments."

Certain communities and performance spaces—particularly those associated with avant-jazz and other experimental musics—actively embrace visual artists and other audience participants. During the loft era of the mid-1970s to early 1980s, artists were often allowed and even encouraged to work in a variety of informal venues. Maintaining this tradition, Jeff Schlanger has served as the "house painter" for every annual Vision Festival since its inception in 1996. He prepares for these summer events by setting up equipment in a specially reserved spot at the front of the stage, where his prominent presence as "the musicWitness®" adds a vital element to the spirit of the festivities. After improv-painting each set, he hangs the still-wet painting on the auditorium walls to dry, where event attendees can peruse it along with his other images from earlier performances that evening, comparing what they heard to what he "saw" (see Figures 22 and 23). In contrast to many of the more mainstream jazz businesses, organizations like the Vision Festival welcome artists such as Schlanger for their contributions to the performative pageantry.

From their various vantage points, professionals may understand audiences differently than musicians (who try to communicate and entertain) or venue managers (who sell a service) do. Tour guide Gordon Polatnick associates with jazz fans from other cities, states, and countries who visit New York to check out the scene. "I get people from all over," he reported, "and it's hard to know [where they're] from, but since . . . a lot of people in America . . . get to New York, most of them are from America. Some of them are even from the city and from the surrounding areas, and then internationally it just spreads out." Because his website is in English, his contacts are generally with English speakers—"I do find that British people like jazz quite a bit, so a lot of the emails I get, even if they don't show up here, are from Great Britain."[77]

Polatnick markets his services to so-called alternative tourists and serious fans, offering them adventures in the "hidden" world of jazz. In an advertisement for his 2009 Underground Big Apple Jazz Festival, he wrote: "The New York City jazz scene still thrives in the small inexpensive neighborhood venues. In these clubs, audience members interact—with one another and with the musicians—so there's more community and looseness. You're more comfortable to shout out during a great solo inspiring the musician to greater expression—the give and take that's essential to live jazz. Sets go longer than they're supposed to because nobody's going to stop the roller-coaster in the middle of a great ride. Unscheduled guest musicians stop by and are immediately invited up on stage." In contrast to eminent venues that present name artists in prominent publications, he champions "intimate clubs [with] wonderful musicians deserving wider recognition," where clients can get "an insider's peek into that world which is completely accessible but rarely accessed by the majority of jazz fans."[78] His romantic depiction of journeymen musicians in cozy venues may be part of a strategy to attract clients, but the "give and take" atmosphere he attributes to these less seen scenes is realistic.

Although proactive travelers can consult Polatnick's *New York City Jazz Club Bible*,[79] a comprehensive listing of venues (with photos, thumbnail descriptions, regularly scheduled acts, and recommendations of local musicians), or other sources, out-of-towners often hire him for his up-to-the-minute information and personal touch. Mark Blumberg, then president of the Sydney-based Jazz Action Society, wrote Polatnick: "[T]hank you for last Monday night and the invaluable tips which you gave us. I was a bit suspicious at the outset of our contact as I thought I could find out most or all things from the internet. But, there is, in fact, nothing which surpasses local knowledge. . . . There are venues around town that are tourist traps and there are other venues that involve the real thing presented by real people."[80] "He *really* took advantage of the list and my services," remarked Polatnick of Blumberg; "He saw *everything* he could possibly see in the time he was here, 'cause he came from Australia. He figured, 'This is it; it's now or never.'"

David Adler believes that many tourists come to jazz shows for everything *but* the music itself. "A lot of times, at the expensive clubs, the people there don't even know who's playing," he observed; "People will go *just* to go to the club, because it's in whatever guide their reading, like *Time Out* or *Village Voice*. They might read the listing, or hear word-of-mouth about the club, and they'll go, *not* to check out the band, but just to go to the club. And then they might get exposed to something that they've never heard and that could be great—or they'll talk through the set [*laughs*] and not pay attention."[81] He speculated that most of these patrons are transients: "I think—not based on scientific evidence, or whatever—there's a large tourist contingent there: they're business people, travelers, and then maybe some local people too; and then there's always a percentage of people who are there to hear the act, 'cause Blue Note gets pretty big names for a club of its size." Some patrons, he suggested, only come because it's convenient: "The Iridium is on 51st and Broadway. There're hotels all *over* the place there, so I think . . . they're getting a lot of hotel guests who are right in the area, looking for something to do, and [if] there happens to be a great jazz club that's written up in *Time Out* right down the street, they'll *go* to it. And they don't care who's playing. And they've got money."[82] Adler's remarks confirm George Wein's earlier surmise that most Blue Note or Iridium patrons are relatively apathetic, attracted more to the *idea* of jazz than to the music itself. "I think that's a big factor," Adler asserted, "a *very* big factor."[83]

Based on his long-term experience photographing name acts in pricier venues, Jack Vartoogian speculated that jazz audiences have become more reserved. "Well, people have changed *too*, I think, a little bit," he said, "maybe New Yorkers more than others. It's just not cool to go someplace like [Smoke] and *talk*, unless you're at the back or something. If you're gonna spend whatever it costs to get into a club, if *I* were spending that money—and I'm *not*; I'm going in and *working* essentially—*I* don't wanna hear people talking. I don't wanna hear my *camera* making noise either. That's all bothersome." Whether it's a reflection of changes in the music, people's perceptions of the music, social mores, gentrification, or all of these, the city's changing audiences mirror their time and place.

*   *   *

Whether they participate as attentive listeners, part-time musicians, writers, photographers, publicists, record retailers, and/or tour guides; and whether they identify themselves as fans, artisans, and/or creative artists; the professionals discussed above are some of jazz's most active scenesters, well familiar with the social exchanges and economic practicalities inherent to the music's overlapping and interlocking communities. Their perspectives and commentary begin to fill in some of the inevitable gaps that occur if we confine our understandings of jazz to what musicians play and audiences hear, encouraging a more comprehensive view of what it means to make jazz, both in the moments of performance and in the fulfillment of one's lifestyle.

Figure 1: Musical memorial for Peter Cox (visible in rear-projected image) at Roulette, Mar. 27, 2013. Violinist Jason Kao Hwang, drummer Andrew Drury, and bassist Ken Filiano perform in foreground.

Figure 2: Tenor saxophonist Ras Moshe (with bass clarinetist Matt Lavelle) gazes at a picture of Peter Cox (visible in Figure 1) during a performance at Cox's musical memorial.

Figure 3: Irving and Stephanie Stone in their apartment in the Homecrest neighborhood of Brooklyn. Note copy of *Jazziz* magazine on table with cover story featuring jazz guitarists/married couple Mike and Leni Stern. CD box-sets of Duke Ellington and Charlie Parker are visible on the shelf.

Figure 4: Roberta DeNicola and Richard Berger.

Figure 5: Steve Dalachinsky and Yuko Otomo in their SoHo apartment. Note photographs of jazz musicians on the refrigerator.

Figure 6: Harold Meiselman at Dizzy's in Brooklyn's Park Slope neighborhood.

Figure 7: "Jazz" Judy Balos.

Figure 8: Frank(o) Christopher at his club, Smoke, on the Upper West Side.

Figure 9: Lorraine Gordon in her office at the Village Vanguard.

Figure 10: Michael Torsone.

Figure 11: George Wein in his office at Festival Productions on the Upper West Side.

Figure 12: Bruce Gallanter at the Downtown Music Gallery, then located in the Bowery.

Figure 13: Emmanuel "Manny" Maris outside a restaurant in Alphabet City.

Figure 14: Horst Liepolt holding one of his jazz-inspired paintings at Ward-Nasse Gallery in SoHo.

Figure 15: Fred Cohen at the Jazz Record Center, located on the 8th floor of an unmarked Chelsea office building.

Figure 16: Gary Giddins at his Cooper Square office.

Figure 17: Lujira Cooper at Nizam Fatah's Boerum Hill shop, once an informal hub for the Jazz Associates and other Brooklyn-based jazz musicians.

Figure 18: David Adler at his Upper West Side home/office.

Figure 19: Jack Vartoogian in his Upper West Side office/apartment.

Figure 20: Improv-drawing of trumpet player by Jonathan Daniel.

Figure 21: Jonathan Daniel at his Upper West Side apartment/studio examining his sketch of audience members at a jazz concert at Smalls. A portrait of Louis Armstrong that hangs behind the Smalls stage is visible in the upper-right corner of the drawing. Note other sketches by Daniel from the same series on the wall behind him.

Figure 22: Bassist Harrison Bankhead and tenor saxophonist Fred Anderson performing at Vision Festival VIII, May 22, 2003.

Figure 23: Jeff Schlanger examining his just completed, still wet, improv-painting of Harrison Bankhead and Fred Anderson (visible in Figure 22) after their set at Vision Festival VIII.

Figure 24: Bassist Bob Cunningham and pianist Marjorie Eliot performing in her parlor, Feb. 9, 2003. Eliot's building, just north of Sugar Hill in Harlem, once housed jazz bandleaders Count Basie and Andy Kirk, boxer Joe Louis, and singer/actor Paul Robeson.

Figure 25: Audience at Marjorie Eliot's, including Bessie (center, in black beret, in her usual spot), Bonnie Burgess (to Bessie's left), Barbara Reinfeld (to Burgess's left), Norman (in front of Bessie with gray ponytail), Rhonda (to Norman's left, in fur hat, face averted), Helen White (in far rear corner, face partly obscured by clapping hands), Rachel Kent and Pat Riley Green (both sitting off-camera to the left), and other regulars.

Figure 26: Tour guide Gordon Polatnick (left) with English tourists (left to right): Laurence Gibbs, Jo Gilks, and Jerry Sykes.

Figure 27: Audience for JazzMobile concert at Grant's Tomb July 30, 2003, featuring drummer Winard Harper's group. Note tourist group sitting on steps in front. Most people in the next rows are local Harlemites who have regularly attended the free outdoor summer concert series for over forty years; they brought their own folding chairs.

First row of chairs, left to right: Lucky Blake (baseball cap, white beard); Luther (striped shirt, paper in lap); Billy Brown (with video camera); Victor (dark black pants); MTU (dark cap, mustache); Johnny (dark cap, light shirt); Boz (partially obscured by Johnny); Gerry (glasses, hair tied back). Second row of chairs, left to right: J— (braided hair, hoop earring, name withheld by request); Mickey (fishing-style hat with pouch); Steve (looking to his right, dark cap, glasses). Third row: Ed (far left, wearing tie); Pat (short hair, long earring). Middle background: JazzMobile videographer Hakim (turban); JazzMobile photographer Amun Ankhra (holding zoom lens camera).

Figure 28: Saxophonist Evan Parker and drummer Paul Lytton in concert at Tonic on the Lower East Side, Apr. 20, 2003. Pianist Alexander Schlippenbach, also performing, is not visible.

Figure 29: Audience at Schlippenbach/Parker/Lytton concert (see Figure 28). Foreground: jazz guitarist Amanda Monaco (turned away from camera) with her husband Andrey Henkin, coeditor of the *New York City Jazz Record*. Middle ground (left to right): jazz journalist/DJ Kurt Gottschalk chats with poet Steve Dalachinsky (both standing); jazz author/historian/collector/DJ Cliff Preiss (also standing); avid concertgoer/venue volunteer, Don De Tora (seated, smiling, in far background); Irving and Stephanie (partially obscured) Stone (seated, to the immediate right of Preiss); and Harold Meiselman (seated to Stephanie Stone's left, turning backward). WKCR director/host/historian Ben Young (seated far right, wearing headphones) records the event; late avant-jazz enthusiast/soprano saxophonist Gilles Laheurte (standing behind Young, face obscured) points a camera. Note the many audio, video, and photographic recording devices and the venue's bare brick, "no frills" décor.

Figure 30: Mitch(ell) Borden collecting admission at the "old" Smalls in the West Village, Apr. 2003.

Figure 31: For rent sign in front of Smalls (photo taken three months after Figure 30).

CECIL TAYLOR

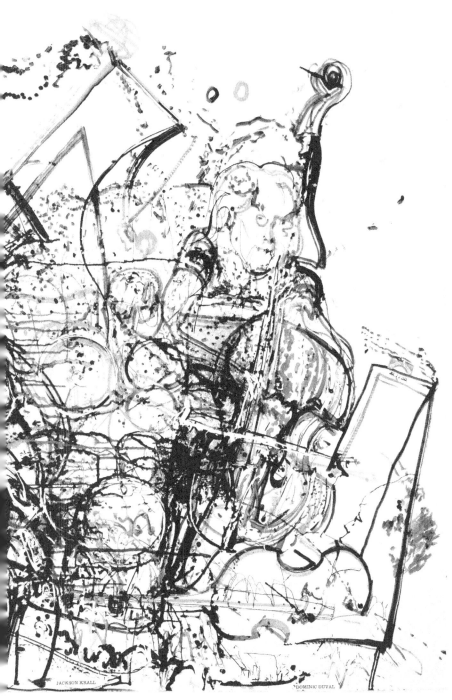

Figure 32: *MC*, improv-painting by Jeff Schlanger of bassist Henry Grimes (in profile, lower right corner) listening to (left to right) pianist Cecil Taylor, drummer Jackson Krall, and bassist Dominic Duval perform at the Leonard Street Knitting Factory on July 13, 2003.

Figure 33: Excerpt from Jeff Schlanger's sketchbook showing Irving and Stephanie Stone waiting for the Cecil Taylor Corona Ensemble to perform at the Houston Street Knitting Factory on Dec. 20, 1989.

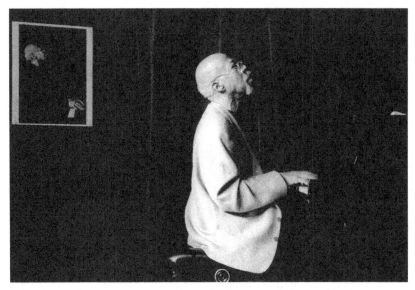

Figure 34: Pianist Tommy Flanagan performing at the Village Vanguard (photo by Jack Vartoogian). Note Vartoogian's earlier photo of Flanagan, in a similar pose, hanging on the wall.

Figure 35: Twenty-three-year-old Chilean tenor saxophonist/bandleader Melissa Aldana performs at her CD release party at Smalls, December 12, 2012, with Italian bassist Joseph Lepore, Cuban drummer Francisco Mela, and California trumpeter Gordon Au. Note photo of Louis "Pops" Armstrong hanging behind the stage and a blanket of Native American design (partially obscured) behind Mela. The mirror over the drumkit gives audiences a bird's-eye view of the drummer; a similar mirror (not visible) is located by the piano. Armstrong seems to peek over Aldana's shoulder, smiling in delight of this new generation of jazz-makers.

Chapter 6

HEAR AND NOW

Collective Improvisation and Spiritual Synergy

In earlier chapters, we considered the many ways that nonmusicians "perform" jazz, alone and with other members of the musical community. This final chapter looks more carefully at communication between musicians and listeners during performances: how performers engage listeners, how audiences express agency, and how both derive deep meanings from reciprocal interactions that culminate in collective improvisations. The focus continues to move through a number of jazz scenes, toggling between the views of musician-performers and that of audience-performers, with special attention given to avant-jazz concertgoers. We'll see how multilateral communication between artists and audiences connects them in a specific space and time, heightening their collective sense of urgency and immediacy, adding depth and dimension to their experiences. As such, it helps explain the participants' deep and ongoing allegiance to live jazz-making.

MAKING CONNECTIONS: ENGAGING AN AUDIENCE

People often use physical metaphors—reaching, touching, moving, and so forth—to describe artistic communication, as if musical sound assumes a material form to do its emotional work. "The only reason for music to exist, for a musician to do it, I think, is to *touch* somebody else with what they do," trumpeter Cecil Bridgewater maintained; "If you don't . . . then what's the point?

If somebody comes into a concert or into a club and they don't feel moved by what you did, then it's—for me—the same thing as going into a dentist's office with a pain in my tooth and leaving with that same pain. They didn't fix it." Being impressive, he contends, is not nearly so important as making an impact: "A musician might go in and display how he knows how to play on this chord or this scale faster than anybody else, but if you don't administer to whatever it is they *need*, if you don't *change* them in some way, then you didn't do your job, I don't care how great you thought you played." Performers can tell if their "message" was received, he explains, from the audience's response: "If somebody doesn't come up to you, or you can't see in their face that they've been changed, that they've enjoyed what you've done, or maybe even be angered by what you did, [if] they come in there feeling a certain way and go out the same way, I guarantee you they will not pay to see you again, 'cause you didn't do what you were supposed to do." A performance's success, then, may be measured by physical manifestations (i.e., facial expressions, body language) of its emotional impact.

Environmental factors, such as where a performance is given and who's listening, influence the way musicians perform. Jam session participants primarily play for each other, seeking inspiration in the musical exchanges. Because such settings tend to forefront the technical and intellectual elements of jazz craftsmanship, soloists sitting in often overplay, cramming ideas into lengthy solos that sound more like practicing in public than emotional revelations. "That happens here in New York: people come in and they want to show their chops [skills], but they're just blowing a lot of noise," noted vocalist Arlee Leonard; "Talk to any bass player or drummer from any jam session in the city and they'll want to nip that muscular stuff in the bud because they're playing behind a tune and *five* sax players all want to get up there and blow twelve choruses. They're not necessarily *saying* something for twelve choruses, but they want to try to show their stuff." Although an adept soloist can create considerable excitement with "muscular stuff," musicians and other listeners quickly weary of tedious "cutting contests" that place a premium on higher, faster, and louder playing. "Chops ain't everything," elaborated Leonard; "sometimes you say more with less. Do you really *need* twelve choruses? Just say what you gotta say and leave some for tomorrow."[1] Technique, then, is only a means to the ultimate end of creating musical artwork of "a unique and expressive character,"[2] something that will move and "change" listeners.

A significant "language barrier" may exist between musicians and lay audiences because the former have invested significant time and energy learning to play with speed, dexterity, complexity, and ingenuity. Although some listeners, especially those with musical training, may get excited by agile craftsmanship and sophisticated musical ideas, general audiences are typically more attuned to an artist's emotional delivery. Aware of the limitations of music-for-musicians, bassist Mike Davis tries to make music "that is more than just complexity, more than just homework . . . that somehow relates a message in a language that you don't need to speak to understand." He finds this quality "missing in a lot of young jazz players. . . . I find they're still concentrating on how well they can play an instrument [so] that I rarely feel like I'm hearing someone tell a story or bare their soul. They're just impressive. But I'm not looking to be impressed; I want to be moved." Likewise, guitarist Tommy Chang feels most gratified when his music engages nonmusicians: "I don't want this stuff to become a pedantic, intellectual head game; I don't want people sitting there dissecting music. I wanna reach people, not *musicians*, not—you know—torpedo-heads." "What makes jazz jazz is often the people who don't know anything about it," explained drummer Billy Higgins, citing the example of bassist Wilbur Ware: [He] used to make everybody shut up. People would be clinking their glasses and so on, but he would start playing, and you'd hear that magic. You could hear a pin drop in the house. To communicate with people, you have to have it born in you."[3] Musicians' music and people's music may address separate audiences, but even the best improvisers must "speak" from their hearts if they are to be widely understood.

In restaurants or on club dates, where people come chiefly to dine or participate in special functions (marriages, bat mitzvahs, corporate events, and so forth), audiences are often preoccupied. Musicians, however, are always acutely aware of the crowd, adjusting their playing to accommodate the social environment. In stark contrast to jam sessions, they may play lower, slower, and softer to enhance the ambiance and allow for table conversations. They will generally eschew dissonant or disruptive music, be sure to include well-known standard songs in their set list, and try to honor guest requests for tunes. "If it's a place where people are eating, you're not the central focus: you're a complement to the central focus, which is the food and the camaraderie," explained Arlee Leonard; "If I *am* doing a gig like that, I tell the club owner ahead of time: 'I'm not gonna come in and try to make it about me if it's not about me.' And I know going in that it's about me adding something to the atmosphere of their overall experience. And that's fine; I don't demand to be seen." On the other hand, she noted, "If what they *are* hearing prompts their attention, without it being demanded, that's always nice." She outlined certain changes she'll make for restaurant crowds: "I probably wouldn't scat as much, or use my range as strongly, or sing with as much power. That's just part of being a journeyman:

it's not necessarily your most artistic time, but you're still able to work on your craft. It's a time when you can explore this space. You can learn and grow in any situation, any setting, if you have that mindset."[4]

In similar playing situations, bassist Bob Cunningham uses familiar melodies as common ground for connecting with disinterested audiences. "On club dates," he said, "I know the people want to hear the melody; they're not interested in a lot of doubling-up and tripling-up on the chords,[5] playing stuff that they don't relate to. And it's not an atmosphere that's conducive for a person to sit and follow that closely. It might be one or two people who'll ease up to the bandstand and listen intently, but for the most part people are conversing, eating, and doing things." Like Leonard, Cunningham is gratified when he can gently draw someone's attention from the other distractions: "I've found that if I play melodies in those kinds of situations, people quiet down, they listen, and maybe at the end of the set come over and say, 'Oh that was so *beau*tiful!'"

Saxophonist Sedric Choukroun regularly plays in restaurants, finding them lucrative, challenging, and occasionally inspiring. "It's harder to concentrate in restaurants," he admits, "so you might be less focused on the music, and so it is going to be less sophisticated or less interesting." Just being on the bandstand, however, is usually enough to inspire him: "You're always trying to do good music. I mean, there might be some musician, kind of worn out, who would go to the gig just to make the money. But music is *so important* to a musician. You can't spoil it; you can't. If you have an opportunity to play, you're gonna do your best, whatever the situation is." Notably, he is most motivated by interactions with fellow musicians and attentive audiences. "I've had a lot of great moments in restaurants playing with great guitar players, and sometimes, the last set, people aren't eating anymore; they're just having a drink, really listening and clapping. It's like a concert, and that's *great* when that happens."

The journeymen jazz musicians cited above share the urge to be creative, even under less-than-ideal circumstances, and aren't fully satisfied until they connect with active listeners. "I can't play to empty tables and chairs," avowed pianist Erroll Garner; "you've got to have somebody to play to. If you come to my house in the afternoon and say, 'Erroll, sit down and play the piano just for kicks,' and you want to play the drums, we jam. You are a public, I am a public, we're playing for each other."[6] At the end of the set of a Village Vanguard concert in July 2014, guitarist Peter Bernstein thanked the audience for coming and remarked: "Without you, we'd just be up here playing for ourselves." Without a public, without others' ears to hear, the music has no place to go.

On the practical side, artists have to consider their viability in the entertainment marketplace. "[Y]ou make your profession jazz because first, you love it, and secondly as a means of livelihood," wrote Dizzy Gillespie; "So if there is no direct communication with the audience for whom you are playing—there goes your living."[7] Communicating with the audience is therefore not just desirable, but indispensable. "[I]t's a three-way thing between the artist, the audience and the club owner," explained vocalist Betty Carter; "The club owner has to make money to keep you working, and you have to please the audience to keep the club owner happy so you can go on working. You can't just cancel the audience. You can't say that just because they don't like you, there's nothing wrong. There's got to be something wrong, and you must find out what it is, why it is that you cannot get to the audience." She stressed that musicians must "cooperate" with club owners: "If you don't want clubs to close, you've got to think about the club owner, the audience and yourself. That's the art of being an artist."[8] Ultimately, everyone's job depends on an artist's ability to "get to" audiences.

For performers, the quality of listening is more important to the musical experience than the number of people present. "Even if there are only one or two people, you want to be able to get to them," attested trumpeter Freddie Hubbard; "otherwise you're just playing for yourself."[9] "There's *always* someone listening," observed Sedric Choukroun, "even in a restaurant—it might be just two tables among thirty—and, especially in New York, you always feel like Wynton Marsalis, or whoever, might be in the restaurant listening to you." "One of my most treasured performance memories," John Zorn wrote in tribute to Irving Stone, "is of a solo concert held at my old apartment on 430 Lafayette Street back in 1976. Three people were present: Kazunori Sugiyama . . . and the Stones. Who could ask for a more perfect audience . . . or a more inspiring one?"[10] All it takes is *one* curious listener to create a "crowd." "It's funny," remarked pianist Ryan Weaver; "In Charlotte [N.C.] there was, literally, one guy, an old man—we called him Mr. Roy—who would go around to all the jazz gigs, to our little Sunday night thing, and hang out, have a drink or two, and leave. And it was, like, 'That's it, our crowd came and left!'"[11] Similarly, avant-jazz fan Peter Cox was referred to in the prologue as a "one-man packed house." Whether it's a casual diner, Wynton Marsalis, or Mr. Roy, the presence of a small but mighty "crowd" is enough to complete the feedback loop, clear evidence that listeners play an active role in collective music making.

In nightclubs and formal concert halls, where patrons pay closer attention to performers, multilateral communication is facilitated. In these settings, artists have more leeway to be creative, but nonetheless must monitor their impact on listeners, though not all artists feel it necessary to court the crowd. Miles Davis infamously refused to announce tunes or bandmembers and often scowled at people. "He turned his back on the audience, ignored them, and insulted them," reported Lorraine Gordon, who saw Davis perform many times at the Village Vanguard when it was still run by her late husband. "So what? He was a great trumpet player. He didn't go to curry favor with the audience—he came to play his music. And he was a little bit skeptical of audiences anyway. So what? People came to *hear* him." Gary Giddins, however, finds fault with young bandleaders who behave aloofly: "They don't talk enough on the bandstand, frequently; [some] of them think it's hip *never* to talk to the audience. It seems to me that it's very important to welcome the audience, and to tell the name of the tune that you're playing, and to introduce the musicians, and to make people feel involved in the set—whereas a lot of guys think they wanna be Miles Davis. Well, Miles could get away with never saying a word because he was *Miles*—you can't do that anymore."[12] Presumably, an artist can afford to be taciturn only if his or her music "speaks" for itself.

At the other extreme are artist-entertainers, many of whom use humor to communicate. Dizzy Gillespie liked to open shows by proclaiming, "I'd like to introduce the men in the band," and then proceed to introduce the bandmembers to each other. Underneath the clownish façade, he was a dedicated artist who did everything, even gags, for a reason. "Comedy is important," he avowed; "As a performer, when you're trying to establish audience control, the best thing is to make them laugh if you can. . . . When you get people relaxed, they're more receptive to what you're trying to get them to do. Sometimes, when you're laying on something over their heads, they'll go along with it if they're relaxed."[13] Gary Giddins illustrated how other artists communicate with comedy: "Sonny Rollins knows how to build a set, and he knows to play tunes that the audience not only is familiar with but doesn't expect, tunes that are so weird for a jazz musician to play that, the first time he plays the theme, everybody starts laughing in pleasure. Clark Terry does it by being funny. He's so funny sometimes people forget how great a musician he is. He'll tell jokes, he'll do vocals—he'll do whatever he has to do to keep the audience in a good mood." Humor, then, proves to be an extremely effective medium for making serious musical statements.

Not all fans appreciate onstage shtick or toadying showmanship. "Some guys ingratiate themselves to the audience. I find that boring," declared Lorraine Gordon, [*imitating an obsequious performer*]: "'Hey! Hey! How are you tonight?' I say, 'Ah, forget it! Just shut up and play. Do your [thing]! The audience is here to see you, man; they came to *listen*. They don't care what you're wearing.'" Like many serious jazz fans, she believes the artful expression of music is entertainment enough. "You are your*self*; an artist is an artist," she observed. "Each one has a different look, a different presentation of this music. Some are very shy. Hey, [saxophonist] Mark Turner can barely talk and announce to the audience. I *tease* him about that, and that's his style. He's a very ingrown, inwardly musician. He doesn't have to get up there and make speeches. Some guys, you say, 'Okay, that's *enough*.' Everyone's personality is different." Because the jazz ethos champions individual expression, audiences often accept an artist's idiosyncratic stage demeanor or lack of showmanship if they like his or her music.

But can music "speak" for itself? Does an artist best please an audience by pleasing him- or herself? The band? The audience? Jazz drummer Art Taylor elicited a variety of responses from well-known musicians.[14] Singer Carmen McRae said she concentrates on herself and the band: "[I]t's a combination of pleasing everybody. If you can start out onstage pleasing each other, 99 percent of the time you please the audience, too. Audiences know who you are, they know what you do and they have come to hear you in person. You only have to do your thing, 'cause that's what they came for."[15] Drummer Kenny Clarke claimed that he plays *only* for the band: "[I]f they're happy, I'm happy. I don't think about the audience, and I never play for myself. I play for the front line and the rhythm section. Period!"[16] In contrast, drummer Max Roach described his orientation as "selfishly unselfish," balancing his own needs with those of his audience,[17] while singer/pianist Nina Simone stated that she adapts her music to fit a particular environment. Like Roach, she juggles selfish and unselfish urges: "At all times I try to play for myself if possible, and I hope that it pleases the audience. I will not do anything for them at the expense of myself. But I try not to please myself at the expense of the audience. I'm really always striving to do both—to have a good time and for the audience to have a ball, too."[18] Although their intended audiences differ, each of these artists is an accomplished communicator.

Musicians may experience tension around the desire to play for themselves (and/or other musicians) and simultaneously connect with the crowd. In an interview with Joshua Redman, Travis Jackson discovered that the saxophonist was annoyed with critic Peter Watrous for writing a concert review that stated that he (Redman) had settled for "hack" musicianship and was "spouting as many rhythm-and-blues phrases as [he] had in [his] vocabulary" in order to pander to the audience. Speaking with Jackson, Redman challenged the assumption that music with popular appeal is therefore "less serious or has less integrity" but acknowledged that people *do* respond to high notes and repetitious patterns. "[T]he problem," he remarked, "[is when] . . . musicians begin to realize that . . . certain techniques elicit certain kinds of audience responses

... sometimes they can start to do those things *purely* for the sake of audience response. And if they begin to do that too much, then it can ... come at the expense of the seriousness of their music or at the expense of them really saying what they want to say ... and I've done it too." Jackson goes on to describe a Redman concert he watched with Watrous, during which a crowd of atypically "young and enthusiastic listeners" whooped and "yeah[ed]" in places, Jackson states, that "neither Watrous nor I felt it ... merited so enthusiastic a response," further noting that "audience members seemed to respond primarily to Redman's playing of high notes, squeals, and repeated phrases." At one point during the concert Jackson observed Redman making pointed eye contact with Watrous, as if in tacit acknowledgment of the latter's criticism. What Jackson reads as Redman's "discomfort" over the situation may have resulted from conflicting desires to communicate with both the less experienced listeners, who seemed to be responding to the more flamboyant aspects of his playing (linked in no small part to his celebrity status), and the more experienced listeners (the band, Jackson, Watrous, and Redman *himself*), who presumably applied very different—even contradictory—aesthetic criteria to his music. In any case, the anecdote clearly establishes the agency of active listeners, experienced or otherwise: the former expecting Redman to be "100 percent genuine"; the latter wanting to establish a bond with him, holding different notions of "genuine." The artist-audience relationship is reciprocal because, as Redman observed, once he's earned *their* trust, they give *him* more license and freedom to play the way he wants to.[19]

There is a tendency, especially in casual settings, for bandleaders to overindulge their sidemen at an audience's expense. "A lot of musicians—especially because the money isn't good—feel an obligation that everybody in the band has to get a solo. Boring! Boring!" protested Gary Giddins, noting that Duke Ellington referred to bass solos as "TV commercials." Giddins disparages the common practice of giving every musician a solo on every tune: "It's okay to do it on one tune, but if you do it on two or three tunes, then the audience feels abused, because you realize [the leader's] not calling the bass solo because he thinks the audience needs to hear a bass solo: he's calling it because the bass soloist is doing him a favor by being on the gig and he feels he needs to do that. Well, good leaders, experienced leaders, don't do that." In formal settings, bandleaders are more likely to choose only one or a few soloists per number, curtailing bass and drum solos to one or two per set so as not to tax the audience's enthusiasm.[20]

In concert halls and other formal venues, clientele come primarily to listen, so performers play to a more attentive audience. Many jazz fans feel, however, that the physical separation between stage and seats and the decorous atmosphere of such spaces preclude intimate interactions between artists and audiences. Upscale nightclubs facilitate rapport between artists and audiences with announcements that remind patrons to silence their cell phones and refrain from talking or picture-taking during sets, but this is undermined somewhat by the frequent circulation of waitstaff to take and deliver orders. Clubs like the Village Vanguard and Blue Note are notable for their "tiptoeing" waiters that quickly and quietly take second-drink orders midset. Less formal venues will tolerate some talking during a performance, while performers in clubs like Harlem's American Legion Post #398, St. Nick's Pub (now closed), and Showman's *expect* audiences to "talk back," spurring them on to greater musical heights. In direct contrast to restaurant gigs, where musicians avoid attracting undue attention, they may have to fight for attention in a noisy club. Whether a particular venue's code of conduct—official or tacit—hews more closely to a concert hall or a party bar, a performer's impact always ultimately depends on his or her ability to communicate with the crowd.

Musicians try to "read" the room. "At each concert, each television show, each performance, I psych out the situation," stated Nina Simone; "Every room is different. The people in it are different, their mood is different, the time of day is different; all that goes through me before I perform. That determines what I'm going to sing and what mood I'm going to try to develop."[21] Bassist William Parker asks himself: "Is there an admission charge to enter? If so, how much is it? Is it a bar that profits from the sale of liquor and attracts a particular clientele? Or is it a trendy coffeehouse decorated with colorful designs and modern paintings that bohemians and businesspeople both like to patronize? What are the size and acoustics of the room? What is the relationship of the stage to where the audience sits?"[22] "I like playing in New York," noted trumpeter Dave Douglas, "because, as skeptical and blasé as New Yorkers can be, I feel like ultimately *I'm* a New Yorker, so people are most likely to get what I'm really playing about. It may not be the same overwhelming ovation I may get in other places, but I just feel like I'm at home." Getting a bead on the venue's "vibe" helps musicians attune their performance for maximum effect. Likewise, a local crowd may be able to "read" a local musician like Douglas more easily.

Several musicians revealed pragmatic strategies for engaging listeners. "My thing was to play songs and treat 'em like the TV people do their shows: see who gets the highest on the applause meter," reported bassist Bob Cunningham; "So, if 'New York, New York' got a great big round of applause, I'd check that off, put a star there." Another surefire way to reach an audience, he noted, is via the groove: when peoples' feet, fingers, or other body parts are in motion, this is incontrovertible evidence that they're being moved, both physically and emotionally.

Many bandleaders plot an itinerary, or narrative arc, for each set. Trumpeter Cecil Bridgewater illustrated a hypothetical program: "Generally, if I have, say, five tunes, the first is something you'd try to grab 'em [with], the second you might ease off a little bit, give 'em something different, the third may be a ballad or a feature for somebody, the next tune you're pushing 'em back up, and then by the last tune of the night you're trying to grab 'em again." The first and last numbers in a set are in "power positions,"[23] so artists tend to fill these slots with high-energy, up-tempo tunes, although ending with an understated ballad can be equally effective. Overly repetitious formats—that is, too many back-to-back numbers in the same key, tonality (e.g., major or minor), rhythmic feel (e.g., swing or latin), or tempo (e.g., ballad, medium, or "up")—can anesthetize an audience. "You gotta be aware of keys," cautions Bridgewater, "'cause if you play three or four songs in the same key it has a dulling effect on the listener, or if you play three or four songs all in a minor key, then you need to play something in a major key to give their ears a little break." At a sound check/rehearsal at the Cutting Room in September 2013, guitarist Charlie Hunter and drummer Scott Amendola ran through a few tricky sections of songs they would play on the gig, but constructed most of the set list in the course of their performance, thus mixing structure and flow. At one point during the concert, brainstorming for the next song to play, Hunter humorously rejected one of Amendola's suggestions, explaining: "It's gotta be a *different* key than the one we just did!"[24] While too much predictability leads to boredom, too much change may confuse and frustrate listeners,[25] so performers try to balance adventurousness and risk-taking with regular references to familiar material.[26]

Flexibility during performance is important, as even a carefully prepared set list might have to be altered to fit the occasion—for example, if a featured soloist is feeling under the weather, or if the crowd's mood requires an on-the-spot adjustment. I once attended a midwinter gig in a drafty, underheated Harlem restaurant where the bandmembers were so cold that the pianist wore fingerless mittens and the drummer dressed in a heavy jacket and knit cap. Singer/bandleader Arlee Leonard responded by calling a series of up-tempo numbers to keep her combo's hands and feet moving quickly, stimulating their bloodflow. At the set's end, she humorously explained her method for warming up the band to the amused audience, making light of the arduous working conditions for everyone's benefit. Cecil Bridgewater noted that many times he'll change things up midset on impulse or by necessity: "We might get through the first or second tune and I decide, 'Well, I don't wanna do a ballad here. Maybe we'll do a Latin tune or something a little different.' There've been times when maybe I followed a long saxophone solo and I may play a very short solo as a contrast to that, so that it balances things. And so I'll change stuff up." The key, he believes, is to find what works for all participants: "You have to be a psychologist or psychiatrist on the bandstand, not only for yourself, but for the musicians on the bandstand, *and* for the audience, because you've gotta make *connections* all the way through."

Choice of repertoire affects an artist's ability to communicate with listeners. For this reason, some performers include only well-known standards in their sets or will cover currently popular tunes that people are likely to know. As we've seen, use of familiar songs allows audience members to create contexts for their listening experience and/or use the melody as a reference point to keep their place in the form during improvised solos.[27] Gary Giddins reported that he was "*very* disappointed" when he took his parents to see Duke Ellington, "because he played all the stuff I've heard him play a million times; it was a very de rigueur set." His parents had a different experience, however: "They were in *heaven*. They *loved* it! And then I realized something very important: Ellington isn't playing this set for *me*; he isn't playing for *critics*, and he isn't playing for musicians—he's playing this set for people like my parents, who pay good hard money, who only come to see him once in awhile, but the next time he's in town, they'll be *back*." In reprising his hits, Ellington consciously tried to connect with certain fans.[28]

While name artists are known for and expected to play their signature songs, performing original material is risky for most musicians. While it may be highly satisfying and stimulating for the musicians to play their own compositions—and also increases their potential income through royalties—these pieces will be unknown and therefore less accessible to most listeners. "I used to do my own stuff down at the Knitting Factory all the *time*, and audiences were *definitely* receptive to it, but it was a different time, and there are fewer and fewer places like that," recounted guitarist Tommy Chang; "I'd like to be optimistic about what people can perceive, and I definitely believe that there's an audience out there that's hip enough to hear shit, and that they wanna hear good stuff." Artists have to consider their circumstances: original material that works for Knitting Factory fans "hip enough to hear shit" may fall on "deaf" ears elsewhere.

Performing avant-jazz is also risky, artistically and economically. As we've seen, experimental improvisation is often hard for casual or uninitiated listeners to appreciate, screening out all but a select group of fans. Lack of appeal to a broader fanbase makes it difficult for artists working in this area to get gigs, as venue operators find it harder to make money on them. Many of these musicians, David Such writes, "find themselves under pressure to alter their style of musical performance in order to fit more acceptable commercial models."[29]

Fortunately, a small but active niche audience for this music, regularly gathering in supportive venues, insures that these artists will be heard and understood.

To connect with audiences, artists must attune to their social environment: Where are they playing? Who are they playing for? What kind of music is most likely to go over? They must be alert to signals from the crowd and remain flexible, open to new ideas if things aren't working, making necessary adjustments to ensure that listeners receive and respond to their musical "messages." Like the spontaneous onstage interactions among musicians, performers must also engage with their audiences, improvising communal musical expressions that will leave lasting emotional impressions.

INTERACTIVE LISTENERS: AUDIENCE AGENCY

For all of their communicative powers and charismatic musical personalities, performers cannot do it alone: they are only one part of a feedback loop[30] that circulates through the entire performance gestalt. "It takes two people to confirm the truth," observed bassist Norris Jones; "One person has to be able to express and the other has to be able to sit and listen."[31] Indeed, artistic "truth" can acquire meaning only through community interactions. "Art by its nature is social," wrote Ralph Ellison; "And while the artist can determine within a certain narrow scope the type of social effect he wishes his art to create, here his will is definitely limited. Once introduced into society, the work of art begins to pulsate with those meanings, emotions, ideas brought to it by its audience and over which the artist has but limited control."[32] What role, then, do listeners play in artistic exchanges? How do they engage and communicate with performers? Can they influence the course of a performance? This section investigates listeners as coagents and co-performers who engender and elaborate collective sociomusical improvisations.[33]

The ephemeral and extemporaneous nature of jazz makes it an ideal catalyst for interactivity between artists and audiences. As a creative process, spontaneously realized, improvisation obliges collaboration between performers and invites audiences to participate as witnesses to unfolding musical events.[34] "[I]mprovisation provides an opportunity to engage with an expansive musical environment during the performance, wherein the nature of the text is open and subject to the energy or 'vibe' of the audience," Dana Reason maintains; "In many cases, this vibe is powerful enough to affect and direct many of the parameters of an improvisation, such as how long to play a particular phrase or motif and whether to play loud or soft, fast or slow."[35] Guitarist Derek Bailey made a similar claim: "The audience for improvisation, good or bad, active or passive, sympathetic or hostile, has a power that no other audience has. It can effect the creation of that which is being witnessed. And perhaps because of that possibility . . . has a degree of intimacy with the music that is not achieved in any other situation."[36] The combination of indeterminacy, transiency, and immediacy inherent to improvised performances creates a unique and fleeting musical moment, a historical "now" never to be repeated, encouraging audiences to attend to and interact with the music.

Audience participation in jazz varies with the venue and style of music, and is mediated by an individual listener's interpretive frame, determined by his or her perceptual skill set, requisite experience, and aesthetic motivations. Formal concerts in large halls attended by casual fans and tourists who sit quietly during the show are very different in character from intimate after-hours jam sessions attended by musician-fans and other insiders. Consider, too, that jazz has a steep learning curve, at least in terms of its musical elements and participatory contexts, and thus "rewards deeper listening."[37] Like flamenco *testigos*[38] and Arabic *sammī'ah*,[39] informed and experienced jazz fans bring important qualities and capabilities to a performance: deep discernment and sensitivity, informed opinions and tastes, aesthetic acuity, and vested enthusiasm. Above all, they create energy in the room, an indispensable force that foments jazz expression.

Audience "energy" is difficult, if not impossible, to characterize or quantify. How to describe the attentiveness of a listener, the quality of a pregnant silence, or the "vibe" in a room? It is nevertheless possible to demonstrate phenomenologically—through eye- and ear-witness accounts—that the atmosphere of a performance space is palpable to participants. "It's hard to describe the energy you get from crowds, from more than one person near you," Jonathan Daniel observed, "If you walk into a particular environment, you just get some vibe. Like, if you walk into a cathedral with a thousand people, you get some kind of feeling that you don't get when you walk into a room, or even that same huge cathedral with, like, two people—the fact that there're all those people there gives off some kind of energy." The quality of the energy, he suggested, depends on the people present, citing Marjorie Eliot's Sunday parlor concerts: "Marjorie's is like a church—or, it *is* church. It's a generous environment and spiritual, I'd say. And that's the vibe you get, maybe 'cause of the type of people that go there." Pianist/composer Ferdinand "Jelly Roll" Morton maintained that performers get "soul" *from* an audience, not the other way around: "Often they surround the band, taking off from its beat and in turn shaping it. As one horn man told us, 'We ain't got no soul—*they* [the dancing crowd] got the soul!'"[40]

David Adler used electricity as a metaphor for audience energy, noting how its presence or absence affects performances. "Some nights the energy is really electric and you can feel the audience really getting into it," he explained; "I was just at Fat Cat last week where this guitarist named Ilya Lustrak was playing and he had Hank Jones in the band on piano, so it was *packed*, and people were lined up, practically up the stairs, waiting to get into the next set. The energy was *incredible* for that show, and there was this incredible spectacle of an eighty-five-year-old pianist and a twenty-something-year-old guitarist making music together. So there are certain rare things like that where there's a lot of electricity in the audience." He noted that room energy varies with the enthusiasm and/or size of a crowd: "There are some nights that people seem kind of indifferent and there's *not* a lot of energy, or/but the five people that are there are there to see that artist and they know that artist and they're really supporting that artist, and so that can be really intense too, sometimes. You never know what's gonna happen between the audience and the artist."[41] Adler's comments confirm my earlier observation that even a small crowd can generate sufficient energy to sustain a successful performance.

How do crowds generate energy? One way is through the expertise and enthusiasm of charismatic individuals, curious listeners with "big ears" who create an atmosphere of seriousness and purpose.[42] Musician-fans, especially prominent ones, can have this effect because they bring an insider's understanding of jazz-making and presumably hold high standards for artistic expression. "*I* notice a lot of *musicians* in the audiences," reported David Adler; "I'm always looking around and seeing faces, like, 'Ah! *So-and-so* is here!' A *lot* of musicians turn out for shows, so that changes the dynamic, too: you've got people who are listening on another level." Interestingly, he claims that musicians are the least vocal respondents: "They are very quiet, respectful listeners and not generally given to loud displays, like, '*Whoo!*' [*laughs*] They aren't gonna be the ones who are calling out and yelling their approval. So in a way it doesn't change *much*, in the way of the *tangible* energy of the room, but it changes the experience of the show, for *me*, to know who's there listening." In other words, jazz artists in the audience don't have to be heard to make their presences felt—to generate a buzz—especially among fellow cognoscenti.

Adler demonstrated how the magnetic presence of accomplished artists in the crowd can heighten the experience for others, citing an incident when bandleader/composer/arranger Maria Schneider and trumpeter Ingrid Jenson sat next to him at a Village Vanguard show:

> I was looking out of the corner of my eye, like, "How's she reacting?" When you're in a show and everyone's mind is being blown, it's *fun* to know that Maria Schneider's mind is being blown, too. And you can *see* it: she's, like,

"Whoa, my God!" They were just freaking out, both having the greatest time listening, and it made it more fun. It would have been just as great if they weren't there, but somehow the fact that they were there was, like: "The heavy musicians are here and everyone's having a great time!" So there can be just an incredible atmosphere of support and excitement.[43]

The presence and positive feedback of distinguished musicians in an audience telegraphs an imprimatur to others present, inspiring the performers and in-the-know fans, lending credibility and clout to the event, making it even more fun.

Avid fans, the so-called "virtuoso listeners" who are aesthetically and spiritually attuned to particular artists and musical styles, can also be magnetic presences at concerts. In the following passage, visual artist Jeff Schlanger depicts the diligence and enthusiasm of free jazz pianist Cecil Taylor's fans:

I have several long sections of sketchbooks that are called "Waiting for Cecil" (see Figure 32). Because in times past, often when Cecil would be billed to play, the hard-core fans would come out from all [over]. People would fly in from Detroit and Chicago, *just* for Cecil, not for anybody else. There's this one guy, Pat Frisco,[44] who comes in from Detroit—he's a *school teacher*, in the public schools! He drops everything and flies to New York for Cecil. But then sometimes Cecil doesn't start playing at the advertised time, and so there're all these avid fans who've really sacrificed to *get* there, and they're waiting for Cecil. And then, meantime, the owner[s] of the venue [are] going out of their *minds*, because they've got a house full of people, and then Cecil isn't there or isn't ready. And I've seen gro*tesque* things going on in these situations on the part of the owners. But the fans are waiting. So I've got pictures of the *whole fanbase*—you know, the hard-core fanbase—waiting for Cecil. And then, of course, Cecil *does* come out, when the time is right and the poetry is right. And Cecil always delivers *more* than *any*body could possibly absorb! [*laughs*] It's always—the feast is *overflowing* with energy and presence, and everybody who's flown in from Detroit *knows* that. So waiting is no big deal for *them*. It's okay. "When Cecil is ready, we're *here*!" [*laughs*]

Schlanger's comments illustrate the fervor and fidelity of Taylor's followers, the lengths to which they will go, literally and figuratively, to provide the pianist with the right "time" and "poetry" to create his music. Note that these energetic fans also inspire Schlanger himself, an improviser working with visual and plastic media, who channels their exuberance by converting it to expressive drawings and paintings.

Audiences also generate energy through cooperation, with each other and with performers. "Music is a séance for me," said Manny Maris; "you have to hold hands and concentrate—even if it's not about holding hands in the audience—but you have to bring that concentration where you clear your mind of everything else for the spirit to arise." This focus, he emphasizes, *has* to be a collective effort: "You can say all the incantations you want, but if you're sitting around the séance table and one person's thinking about how he has to pick up his laundry from the laundromat before they close, and the next one's thinking about how they have to get home and cook, if there's a possibility that the spirit could come out, it ain't gonna happen." If and when listeners are sufficiently synchronized, he asserts, music may manifest metaphysical qualities: "At a performance, you're sitting in the seats facing the stage and you're being quiet, but if your mind isn't also quiet, it ain't gonna happen. You'll hear the notes, you'll say the music was good, you'll hear a great solo, you'll hear a good performance, you can talk about it, but that *extra magic* that was supposed to happen—and that's not a very tangible thing; it's hard to talk about, and it sounds quasi-mystical—but there is something that happens." The "extra magic" Maris emphasizes is a form of spiritual synergy, only possible when audiences coordinate and collaborate—"hold hands"—in shared musical spaces.

Fans express additional agency by communicating with performing artists, using their voices and body language to provide critical feedback and encouragement. "We like to be up front, wherever we go; we wanna be there," noted Richard Berger of himself and his wife Roberta; "We don't wanna be with any of the bullshit in the back: people coming in late, people moving around, people talking. We want to be as close as we can to where the sound's coming from. And when you're doing that, you can't help but have some kind of contact with people: some kind of eye contact or at least an emotional contact." Indeed, many active avant-jazz fans reported that their physical presence inspires artists to greater creativity. "There are a number of musicians who will swear to you, up and down, that they play better if we're in the house," claimed Irving Stone of himself and his wife Stephanie, citing an example: "Dave Douglas once sent a car to take us to Tonic because he wanted us to hear his new band and he said, 'I feel more like playing when you're there!'"[45] Roberta DeNicola made a similar observation: "I've had musicians come over to me after a set and say, 'You always have to sit in the front row when I'm playing. I thought your energy was great, you made it so much better!' Victor Lewis, a drummer—so many different people have come over and said, 'Thank you, you made us feel so good; you made me play better.' So I think they really sense when you're *really* listening." The feedback attentive fans get from musicians is compelling evidence that the former bring something vital to performances. Indeed, in the presence of active, appreciative audiences, music-making becomes, as Alan Lomax put it, "a *source* of energy, rather than a *demand* for it."[46]

Audiences may even generate spiritual energy through conscious meditation, becoming receptive vessels for mediated transcendence. "When [the musicians] go past, when they break from a certain level, and then go out even a little further, I feel it and I open my eyes, and I see it with them," reports Roberta DeNicola; "I see them look over at each other, or one person just laughed because they didn't expect to go that far. And I can't tell you in words how I know that, but I know that and they know I know it, because we all catch each other's eye or something."[47] Margaret Davis Grimes spoke of extramusical communication between similarly attuned artists and audiences:

> You give your soul, and you open yourself completely, and you listen as deeply as you can. And you make it known that you're doing that, which is not a conscious thing—it *should*n't be anyway. There's call and response; there's a response that the musicians receive if you're *really* listening, and really open, and really giving your soul over. You surrender—that's what you do, just as the musicians surrender when they're really playing. That's what it really is. You can practice and rehearse and run riffs and scales and transcribe and do all that stuff. Comes down to it, when the music comes through you, you surrender, if you're really playing, and if you're really listening too.

Interestingly, Davis Grimes's comments characterize deep listening as "a call," a silent act that is nevertheless "heard" and responded to by receptive performers.

The agency of audiences in the avant-jazz community is graphically portrayed in Jeff Schlanger's on-the-spot, in-the-moment paintings, which can contain the drawn image of a human ear somewhere in the composition, often indicating that Irving or Stephanie Stone was in the audience when the painting was made,[48] as well as other images of individual fans. In *Save the Children, Yes,* his painting of a Cecil Taylor concert that appears on the cover of this book, a bespectacled Irving Stone is visible in the lower-right corner of the image, listening attentively. At his studio, Schlanger showed me a picture he had painted of another Cecil Taylor concert that included an image of the recently relocated, revived, and reacclaimed bassist Henry Grimes (see Figure 33):[49]

> And this [*pointing to a figure in his painting*], sitting next to me, was Henry Grimes, who had played with Cecil Taylor thirty years before, and then was gone. And this is the first time that Henry Grimes [had] heard or seen Cecil Taylor in that whole time. He [Grimes, had] just started to play publicly on the East Coast, so this is a historic encounter. Margaret was sitting on the

floor."right in front of Henry. She's in a *lot* of my pictures, and the Stones are in a lot of my pictures, and various other people: Harold, Pete. They're all *part* of it. I usually try to get *some*body [from the audience].[50]

The painting shows Grimes listening intently to Taylor's performance;[51] the others Schlanger mentions are (or were) all active fans. It is noteworthy that he includes them in his compositions, an indication of their ubiquity and impact on avant-jazz scene.

It may seem counterintuitive to suggest that audiences "make" music, but the eye- and ear-witness accounts of avant-jazz fans and other active participants in jazz communities presented in this section provides compelling evidence that the collective act of serious listening generates palpable energy that galvanizes and guides the creative efforts of improvising musicians. Bringing experience, aesthetic acumen, enthusiasm, attentiveness, and personal charisma to the shared spaces of performance, serious listeners express agency through their communication and collaboration with artists and each other. When listeners perform, and performers listen, the imaginary boundary between them dissolves, clearing the way for mutually mediated collective improvisations.

MORE THAN MUSIC: HERITAGE, HEALING, AND "BLOOD"

Jazz people often bring a strong sense of purpose to the music, even as they derive deep meanings from it, embracing it as an integral part of their lifestyle and identity. Jazz's racial, cultural, and artistic legacy, its healing powers, the immediacy and urgency of its improvised moments, even its less tangible numinous dimensions, all contribute to the music's powerful import and impact, its ability to temporarily transcend time and place. This final section considers extramusical and metaphysical aspects of jazz, revealing some of the reasons why people participate, and some of the places it takes them.

Just as musicians are influenced by great performers of the past, fans too may be influenced by their predecessors. Earlier, artist/poet/fan Yuko Otomo expressed her feeling that listening to avant-jazz is "a privilege [to] be shared," but also that the music carries with it a "sense of responsibility . . . to be a *serious* listener."[52] She cited Irving Stone's "obsessive mission" as the embodiment of "that sense of responsibility to be a listener," an example for fellow fans: "That's why I say listening is another form of art, or an art form." She and her husband Steve Dalachinsky will likely be remembered, as the Stones and Peter Cox are, as dedicated practitioners of the art of listening.

For the most devoted participants, jazz is an ongoing commitment, an immersion of time, energy, and self into the music—a way of life.[53] Musicians apply themselves to perfecting their craft and art, and for many intensive practicing (or "woodshedding") becomes an obsessive daily ritual, akin to the practices of meditation or prayer, a means to achieve extramusical meanings through improvisatory exploration. Saxophonists John Coltrane and Sonny Rollins are famous for transforming themselves through dedicated practice. "[Saxophonist] Evan Parker is a tremendous Coltrane fanatic," noted Harold Meiselman, "in terms of his philosophy of seeking to discover some spiritual sense. Like when he goes into these tremendous spiraling, circular-breathing runs, and then through whatever techniques he uses where it sounds like there are three or four different lines going on at the same time coming out of this single instrument. And I don't think he entirely knows what's gonna happen. It's like the improvisation takes on a life of itself. And I think there's a search for spirituality there that was there in Coltrane's improvisation." In trying to reach—and perhaps exceed—the high bar for intellectual, technical, and artistic achievement established by preceding virtuosos, musicians must dedicate hours a day over many years to perfect their craft, and then the rest of their lifetimes to develop a distinctive voice with which to express their art. "Music's not a plaything," avowed pianist McCoy Tyner, succinctly summarizing a jazz musician's mission: "it's AS SERIOUS AS YOUR LIFE!"[54]

Fans have a similar mission, as listeners, to show up (physically and psychically) for the music. "I'd say Roberta and I have averaged going out maybe three or four nights a week, every week for the last twenty years," estimated Richard Berger. "We just started to slow down to three or four," Roberta corrected; "Oh yeah, we're fanatics! We're addicts, babe!"[55] "The music is so alive and real for me," attested Peter Cox; "Jazz to me is like my life—it *is* my life—and without it I would feel less a person, like a dead person. The music has kept me alive and invigorated and I just love it. I mean, I couldn't even envisage a day without listening to jazz in some way, shape, or form."[56] "I didn't really intend to build my life around this music to the extent that I have," claimed Dale Fitzgerald, "but once in it, I've never had a reason to leave, and I can't imagine [it] now. It's a path that takes you all over the world. Wherever you go, you can find jazz people, and where you find one, you'll find others. There are people like me who just, for whatever reason, have tied themselves to this music, and *that's* what they do. And they may or may not be musicians." He had wanted "to do something more than just present the music," envisioning the Jazz Gallery as "an international cultural center where we're making the point that jazz is more than a music, that it's a way of life." In one of his final Facebook entries before he passed from cancer on March 20, 2015, he wrote that founding the venue was not "something that I wanted to do, but rather something that I had to do. This is where the depth of passion will lead you."[57] These long-term fans derive what Travis Jackson describes as a "third register" of meaning from jazz performances, when "participants see an event as a metaphoric expression of a way to negotiate living, as a form of aesthetic 'equipment for living.'"[58] For such fans, jazz is more than a pastime, it's a lifetime.

Many participants have alluded to jazz's healing powers, its ability to provide sustenance and faith in troubled times. Saxophonist Albert Ayler famously titled his final album *Music Is the Healing Force of the Universe*,[59] emphasizing what jazz *does* rather than what it *is*. "It gets me by these days, really," Roberta DeNicola affirmed; "Getting to know these people and digging this music has pulled me through a lot of stuff—jobs ending, the war, losing our whole families and a lot of people to AIDS—and not a lot does that. I remember after 9/11 I'd been to dance, the theater, and so forth. Nothing really pulled me in. But the first time I heard some of the free jazz people after 9/11, I could feel again, and that was good, because you're so in shock, you're just numbed out."[60] Lujira Cooper talked about how the music transports her: "I know [the musicians] are listening to their audience, and just being there takes you to another place. When the music is really good, it's very transforming. Like, if I was listening to Bubba Brooks, it was like an ice cream sundae on a hot summer's day; that's what it did to you. Sometimes I'm listening to other people and it's a storm raging—a quiet storm, but a storm nonetheless. So it keeps your creative energy going." She also spoke of jazz's rejuvenating qualities: "I walked in there [Pumpkins] one night; I was, literally, dead tired. I went to put my stuff on the bar, just dropped everything on the floor, and sat there for about two hours. And by the time I walked out, I felt elevated again; I felt alive. And that's what I feel music is supposed to do: it's supposed to uplift you somewhere."[61] Musicians too get a "lift" when they play: it's not uncommon to see weary-looking elderly artists lumber on stage only to miraculously transform into animated, youthful entertainers. "There were certain much older musicians, and they were really not well," recounted Judy Balos, "but they'd get up on the stage, and all of a sudden—boom!—their tiredness goes away." She surmised that many of them didn't want to get off the stage, because "they love that feeling of aliveness that maybe they didn't get anywhere else at that point in their lives."

For Michael Torsone, jazz provides an antidote to the dearth of spirituality in modern society, feel-good music for feel-bad times: "People are searching for something to fill a void in their lives, okay? And music has always been the thing that has taken people out of the depression and the pain of their life." Certain artists, he observed, have healing powers: "I think that there's a lot of spiritualism, a lot of energy, coming off a person performing music or singing, and if you portray a positive image, a positive energy to uplift someone, you are doing what you were meant to do: returning your gift to make other people get through life with a smile." He cited organist Dr. Lonnie Smith as the epitome of a musical healer:

> If you watch his expressions, he draws you in like a magnet. I promise you, that man will take you out of whatever's bothering you—you will *not* give a fuck. You will have such a good time watching this master at work that you'll forget all the trouble you got: whether your boyfriend or girlfriend is pissing you the fuck off, or you got a landlord that's charging you too much, or whatever, just the things that bother us every day. And it's great to go out to a club and just be taken out of that for awhile.

Comparing Smith to another local organist, Torsone declared, "Dr. Lonnie Smith is a *whole* 'nother ballpark. It's a *visual* as well as musical experience, and it's spiritual, very spiritual—it's about energy."

Roberta DeNicola distinguished between feel-good music and healing music. "I'm a great lover of good regular jazz. When it's good, I think it's fab and it makes me very happy." She defined "straighter" jazz as "softer, more sentimental," that "goes more into my heart," differentiating it from avant-jazz, that "goes into my heart and my mind and my soul." "I feel this is deeper," she elaborated; "I've never said it, but that's my feeling, that there's something more happening here, for me. This [avant-jazz] doesn't always make me happy, but it makes me feel healed inside and whole. Like, if you have a pain or you're afraid of something, I almost feel that it goes through me, that it heals whatever I'm worried about. I don't know, I can't explain it. It's a dimension I have never entered in music before, especially without drugs." For her, avant-jazz is like the proverbial bitter pill, its curative powers more than compensating for any lack of "happy" feelings.

Part of music's healing power lies in its ability to bond artists and audiences together, building mutual empathy through shared experience. Arlee Leonard described herself as a musical healer, or "love missionary," called to "spread love, spread being in touch with one's soul through the medium of music and help people to develop or to find a positive outlook through the medium of music."[62] Beyond catharsis, beyond venting self-pity through "my-man-done-me-wrong-again-songs," she sees music as an avenue for spiritual expression: "I feel like music is such an intense way to touch our emotions, as a music-maker and as a music-receiver. And music can soothe our hurts, inspire us; we can find commonality in it. Somebody else understands what I'm going through or what I've been through and gets solace or comfort from that. And music is just so powerful, and *that's* spiritual in and of itself, whether you believe in a higher power or not." Like many performers, she sees herself as a conduit for external forces: "I personally feel like the possibility is really there for me to be an open channel to have spirit life speak through me in those moments when I'm being part of the universal sound, and that I'm just one small part of many parts of people being tuned to their inner selves, to their inner lives."

Marjorie Eliot has looked to jazz to give her the poise and purpose to carry on in the face of a series of formidable obstacles. When her twenty-eight-year-old son Philip died of a kidney ailment in 1992, she grappled with a bout of extreme depression. On the anniversary of his death, she held a jazz concert to honor and celebrate his memory, continuing this tradition faithfully every Sunday since. When trumpeter Charles McGee, a regular performer in her parlor, contracted a terminal illness, Eliot made him a deathbed promise the show would go on. After financial troubles with her landlord,[63] followed by the loss of her eldest son Michael ("Mikey") to meningitis in 2006, Eliot has drawn spiritual sustenance from both jazz and the embrace of her community, radiating this strength back to her loyal supporters, leading some to describe her as "saintly."[64]

In addition to deep meanings derived from its racial, cultural, and artistic legacies, and from its healing powers, jazz provides some participants with a more direct and personal sense of metaphysical fulfillment or spirituality. This, I suggest, is rooted in the music's spontaneous and ephemeral nature, unfolding and then evaporating before one's very eyes and ears. While much jazz is highly structured, an improviser is generally unaware of his or her next musical move until the instant of its execution. Thus, most of the music is "new," each rendering of a composition unique, each impromptu solo a surprise.[65] This adds an existential dimension to improvisations, a quality of timelessness, an awareness of one's mortality, of life never-to-be-repeated; it compels participants to "be here now,"[66] to fully immerse themselves in the fleeting musical moment as if in meditation or prayer. Many artists and fans can describe instances when a performance acquired a heightened sense of connectedness and urgency, often attributing these transcendental experiences to emotional communication: when an artist "told a story" and when the other musicians and audience members were all part of the "conversation."[67] Manny Maris describes this phenomenon in his recollection of the memorial concert for Irving Stone: "There were heart-stopping moments all day. You wanna talk about the pin-drop, and suspending all consideration, all time, and all thought? That happened *many* times that day, by *all* reports."[68] These deeper experiences of jazz arise when witnessing its creation, being present for history in the making, when a quality of "now-ness" is achieved that obliges full and focused participation from everyone present.

Because music in general and jazz in particular communicates on an abstract level, it opens avenues for the perception and interpretation of extramusical meanings. William James remarked on the connection between abstract symbolism—the creation of meaning without words—and expressions of the divine: "[R]eligion is full of abstract objects which prove to have an equal power [to concrete objects]. . . . [T]he absence of definite sensible images is positively insisted on by the mystical authorities in all religions as the sine qua non of a successful orison, or contemplation of the higher divine truths."[69] Possession states have been associated with instrumental musics like Balinese *barong*, Brazilian *candomblé*, ancient Greek Corybante dances, and southern Italian tarantella,[70] where specific musical forms structure both the passage and *experience* of time. "Being-in-the-world in a musical way can be a particularly powerful mode of lived experience," notes Steven Friedson; "It is a field of action before subject and object, a realm in which the world and our experience of it are given together. . . . Awareness of this immediacy *in its entirety* is precisely what forms the musical tradition of trance," which he argues is "not fixed" but "made up of projected possibilities."[71] While improvised jazz is a framed temporal process, its lack of linguistic signifiers and inherent spontaneity compels participation in the form of active listening, independent constructions of meaning, even ritualized *communitas*, the temporary destructuring of time to create "a relational quality of full unmediated communication, even communion."[72]

In comparison to symbolic languages with clear and consistent grammatical and syntactical logic and linkages, improvised music is less tangible, prescriptive, teleological, or semiotically bound, the very qualities that allow it to "speak to" and express spiritual meanings. "I don't know where I go," said Roberta DeNicola, describing her experiences of listening to live avant-jazz; "I just surrender to it and I feel it go through me, and then I feel, like, stronger. It's not like songs with words, where you see pictures, or Miles Davis, where you might miss an old lover, or it gives you that feeling of "Oh!," or how that kiss was, or something that it reminds you of. It's unique for me; it does something for me that no other music does." "This music *doesn't* remind you of anything," confirmed her husband Richard; "This is not like anything, so there's no memory like, 'Oh, that reminds me of my old lover, or Johnny Hodges, or thinking of what you did when you heard Johnny Mathis's 'Chances Are.' You never *heard* this before! This is so out there, so each moment is unique and new. It's very existential." DeNicola agreed with him: "It's different every time, so you don't reminisce, you're in the moment. That's it! It's so exciting and so intense. How could you wander anywhere? You can't, if you're really open to it. So that's the thrill of it: that it keeps you right in that moment, at that time. How many things really do? Not a lot of them. It *is* very existential." Berger and DeNicola's observations suggest that avant-jazz's relative *lack* of contextual references intensifies its "now-ness," forcing listeners to *develop their own* references, on the spot, to situate and understand their musical experiences.

When jazz is both "now" and "new"—an original expression in and of the moment—it transcends its setting. According to Manny Maris, this is only accomplished when artists "give birth" to music: "Here's what happens: a Tony Williams *Life Time* record comes out and invents jazz-fusion. They didn't know they were making jazz-fusion; they just knew they were making a record 'cause they felt like *that*. There was no precedent for it; there was some sort of movement going on with that record that indicated an audience was a-birthing." Unfortunately, he cautions, much music falls into the "ironic mode," mere imitation of innovation: "Once the category has been established, others are working in the ironic mode, like technicians at Madame Tussauds [wax museum, in Times Square]. They're replicating the outsides perfectly—someone could hear this and that and go, 'Well, they're of a piece'—but in *no way* are they replicating the impulse that made the skin bulge here, and the ear come out here, and the hand have five fingers, or whatever." Spirituality, he argues, arises not from the form but through the *forming* of music: "But *you* can tell. If you're *really* listening, if you're actually awake, you can get a sense of the one that's a wax dummy and the one that was born looking that way without being able to help what it looked like. And the one that was born that way, and represents itself as for what it was born like—there's an energy that happens in the presence of that exhibition, whether it's the playing of the music or whatever, that just does *not* exist [in the ironic mode]—and I'm talking spiritually now." Note that Maris depicts the realization of new musical forms and extramusical experiences as the collective "a-birthing" of artists *and* audiences.

Margaret Davis Grimes expressed a strong preference for what might be called revolutionary—or perhaps reve*lationary*—music: "I *love* old-fashioned jazz—if it's on that same level of prophecy-in-sound and saving the world. And it was then *too*. But I don't want to hear somebody playing it *now*, and try to make it the same, because it's not. It was new and original *then*—now it's not. And I don't want to hear it! [*laughs*]" I asked if a contemporary artist can "prophesize" while playing in a traditional style, but she rejected the idea: "By imitating? No. By doing someone else's thing? No." While many jazz fans share her scepticism toward imitative playing, not as many share her stringent standards for "prophecy-in-sound" or "saving the world."

Some people find divine inspiration or love in jazz, their participation taking the form of religious practice. "I try to play for the Creator, because I believe that's how deep the music is. Music is that deep," asserted pianist Hampton Hawes; "To me music is God, so I play for God."[73] Margaret Davis Grimes described her relationship with avant- or "ecstatic" jazz as a spiritual calling: "I'm listening, working, and worshipping, because the music is a tremendous need in me, my fuel for all the work I'm doing. And it's my *church* too, my mystical life, my inspiration. It's what makes me tick [*laughs*], and groove." Keyboardist Ryan Weaver identified it as the central element in his life: "That's really all I've got going right now: it's just music. It's really the important thing, the only thing that gives my life meaning. And I wonder how other people find meaning in their lives without music. Maybe they do. I'm *sure* they do, but I don't see how! [*laughs*]" Sedric Choukroun believes his deep love for music allows him to communicate with others: "I found people who heard that thing: my love of music. I think they enjoy listening to me because I love it so much, and they love it too, and so we connect." His personal and musical relationship with Marjorie Eliot is based on these shared feelings. "I think the main thing is how both of us love that music. That's why we're so close, 'cause that's the way she is too, even though we might have different tastes when it comes to playing. And to be *in* the music—that's where we felt right away, both of us, that we have that in common. And that's why she trusts me."

Although jazz artists are expected to "speak" with an individual "voice," some believe they must also be selfless, without ego, to make deeper "statements." "I don't think there's any music in the world that's more expressive of personalities than jazz music," argued Michael Torsone; "If you think you're all it, the audience is gonna know it, because it's gonna come out in your playing. If you're a humble person, and you swing your ass off, everybody's gonna love you. That's the way it comes out."[74] "There are so many things to be considered that it becomes a problem just to forget the self to the point where you are able to become totally involved in the music," explained trumpeter Art Farmer; "If you can do that you're no longer the little 'me' and you block out your reactions to the music and the audience. You dedicate yourself to the music and submerge your ego. It's easy to say this, but when you get on the stand and the guy says, 'And now   Art Farmer,' I *am* Art Farmer. And if anything distracts you, you're even more conscious of being Art Farmer." The "truest" music, he concluded, it not personal, but holistic: "[I]f you can react musically to situations, what comes out is going to be more true than if you go out there to react personally. You see, when you forget *yourself*, you get to the point where the music doesn't come from you, it comes through you. You become part of the total experience of 'now.'"[75] "Music don't *belong* to *nobody*," stressed drummer Billy Higgins; "If they could just realize that music doesn't come *from* you, it comes *through* you, and if you don't get the right vibrations, you might kill a little bit of it. You can't take music for granted."[76] Paradoxically, while performers need strong personalities and egos to assert themselves as artistic individuals, they must also have sufficient humility to immerse themselves within their socio-musical environment.

Becoming selfless, or egoless, suggests that musicians are passive vessels, conduits for an external creative—perhaps divine—force that's expressed through their bodies. Dizzy Gillespie claimed that the Creator chooses certain "messengers" to lead the music forward: "I believe [jazz musicians] are the people most 'in tune' with the Universe. . . . How do they come up with things that have never been played before? Where did they get it? They have to have some kind of divine inspiration."[77] The gift of great talent, he wrote, is bestown on certain visionary "runners": "There is no other explanation for the fact that a guy like Charlie Parker had so much talent other than the fact that he was divinely inspired. Other guys practiced just as hard as he did, so why didn't they have it? . . . So, I just go along with, 'God just gives it to you.'"[78] Hampton Hawes described his body as a "tool" for spiritual expression: "I feel that if I play and let everything come out of me, like my body is a tool, if I think deep enough and try to let the truth come out, then I can bring something to the audience. Because if they're thinking deep, the same shit will be coming out of them."[79] Arlee Leonard spoke of "*really* magic moments, where you just hit something so amazing, but you have no idea what just happened. It's *gone*! Those—musical 'orgasms' I'll call them—those times when you're really in the zone, where time and space are just suspended and you're just *in* the sound are really cool. I can think of a couple times—once a long time ago, once kinda recently—where I felt that to a *strong* degree. But I feel it to *a* degree a lot of the time, which is probably one reason I keep doing it! [*laughs*]" These accounts all imply that musicians do not create music by themselves but are receptive vehicles that transmit and translate ambient creative energy.

Musicians often speak of "the zone" or use similar terminology to describe their experiences of channeling, states of flow or trance when music seems to create itself through a constellation of exterior sources. Sedric Choukroun spoke of the interactions between performers and audiences that foster deep concentration:

> The audience makes you play things you'd never think you would play. It's really like a chemistry: it works with the musicians you're playing with, but it works with the audience too. Maybe it puts you in a trance, where you

can connect really deeply to the music, and just connect with everything else, because the audience is there, surrounding you in a way, right in front of you, and reflecting your own music, what you're playing, what the band is playing. So your spirit cannot go somewhere else. And the more the audience is reflecting your music and surrounding you with its attention, the more you forget about yourself and everything which is on your mind, and more and more, and deeper and deeper, you're really just music; you're just playing the music.

Even if an artist's state of concentration is intensely personal, his or her musical expression is public and social, a product of group interdynamics. "That concentration is hard, even impossible, to get just by yourself," Choukroun elaborated; "You can get that with the other musicians, they could accompany you in such a way that you really concentrate on the music, but when the audience does that too, there's no escape. You're in the music, so you'd better play it! So it's chemistry. It makes you play in a different way." His observations emphasize the communal nature of extramusical experiences, the interpersonal "chemistry" that pulls artists and audiences "into" the music.[80]

Transcendental experiences of jazz therefore depend on a confluence of factors, not only an individual artist or group of artists concentrating on and fully immersing themselves in improvised expression but also the collective input of a communal consciousness, the mutual witnessing and "understanding" of extramusical moments by everyone present, manifested through a collaborative web of social synergy. Many avant-jazz participants report they have felt "oneness" among many, a sense that they are part of a greater whole. Although these transformative experiences vary for each individual, many arise from coactive and comediated participation of artists and audiences.

When musicians listen to audiences and audiences perform for musicians, a synergistic feedback loop is created that dissolves the so-called fourth wall that separates actors from audiences and demarcates the theatrical world from "reality." John Cage illustrated this principle with his notorious composition "4:33," in which a pianist pantomimes the ritual presentation of a solo performance, thereby provoking the audience to react with a spontaneous improvisation of grunts, coughs, restless murmurs, and rattling seats. This ambient soundscape, Cage seems to imply, is the "music," but now the traditional roles of performer and "performee" are inverted, negating the distinction between them because everyone in the room is a player.

For spiritual synergy to occur, artists must be completely present: for other performers, for audiences, and for themselves. "To me, a great experience is not by category, it's by *quality*," explained Manny Maris; "So, in seeking out other experiences that would blow me away, I was seeking out something that had as much personality and uniqueness at that moment in time—*in* the moment in time I'm searching for *now*." Like Irving Stone, he used blood as a metaphor for complete and total musical expression:[81] "I need to hear them going for the blood. I need to hear someone doing something because they can't *help* themselves doing it. It's either being themselves or being nothing—there's no in-between. When you find your voice, either by yourself or as a collective of people who have the ability to find their voice, if you can *really* expose that, the energy involved in unlocking that atom is in itself some spiritual force; play-acting at it, *nothing*." Stone held similar criteria: "I want more," he said; "You know, blood, more, whatever. I ain't out there to hear the Modern Jazz Quartet. I heard them, you know? It's nice, it's intelligent, it's worked out, it's pretty—*so*? I'm too old to schlep into the subway to hear something nice. I *have* something nice: a few LPs." Uninterested in technically adept and/or intellectually complex music, Stone stopped going out to hear what he called "Village Vanguard music" (i.e., "sort of post-bebop, fucking with the rhythm a little bit"), looking instead for something he could "feel," or "connect to," or would "knock him out." "Like I said," he summarized; "I'm for blood."[82] The "blood" Maris and Stone seek represents their—and many other avant-jazz fans'—stringent criteria for music that transcends its time and place: something "new" (inherently original) and "now" (absolutely spontaneous).

Audience participation is equally important to spiritual synergy, however, and listeners must be completely present as well. "*All* we have is this moment, right here, right now," Richard Berger pointed out; "I don't know what's gonna happen in the next five minutes, and everything that's happened is gone forever. So I try—it's very hard—but I try to be in the moment, and that [avant-jazz] music is like that: it's very much in the moment, right there." "Be present, and that music makes me presents," quipped Roberta DeNicola; "It's in the mo-ment and real, [it] arrests you, you're a hundred percent present." Matthew Somoroff describes how, during an improvised solo at Local 269, saxophonist Joe McPhee's plain, quiet musical texture "highlight[ed] the audience's *reverent* silence," at the same time as the audience "reciprocat[ed] the concentration of his playing with [its] silences, allowing the space between his phrases to stand out."[83] Yuko Otomo illustrated how some musicians respond to spiritu-ally simpatico listeners: "[Saxophonist] Joe Maneri said that he clearly feels the vibrations from the audience when they play. He said the audience is another instrument—that's how he described it—and in a way I understand what he means, a lot. Because they can play to the air, of course, but they do need some kind of human psychic energy exchange in the space—in the right way—so they can be stimulated and inspired to do more, to *give* more." She spoke of moments when fans collectively reciprocate energy to performers: "Sometimes Irving and Stephanie, even Peter Cox, Steve, and other people here in the same space, we're listening to the *same* music, so-called: we hit the *same* note, like other listeners. We catch the same parts—a 'high spot'—so it's a universal sensitivity. It's more like a strange collective unconsciousness. You *capture* the moment, and when this whole, wholesome giving from the musicians' side happens, it's really amazing. And that's a magic [*sic*]."[84] Like artists, audiences must be receptive to the "new" and the "now," as individuals and as collective listeners.

Spiritual synergy arises when artist-to-artist, artist-to-audience-to-artist, and audience-to-audience communication is synchronized in a dynamic feedback web that amplifies ambient "energy." Yuko Otomo perceives it as a mutual exchange between musicians and listeners: "Every art form is a form of giving your life force, but music, for me, is one of the most giving of arts; [it] is the moment of giving, in full force. Musicians completely give, they *have* to give. There is no bullshit. That's how we *feel* something, because mentally, physically, emotionally, psychologically, spiritually, when musicians give more than a hundred percent, we feel something *true*, for real, [and] we take the same amount." Such holistic experiences have brought her back, again and again, to live jazz. "This feeling, this something true, is *not* a personal thing, it's a real universal thing. That's why I've been really, completely involved, because once you start to see that kind of magic, there's not as much happening in other forms in our everyday lives. Among the so-called human-to-human relationships, music is one of the most impactful, this giving and taking."

Jeff Schlanger also spoke of "gift" exchanges between artists and audiences: "Here is one musician, or a group of musicians, who are sharing the very best of the living energy they have. It's a *gift*, and you can feel that they are taking the fullness of their life and offering it, in the space, in the time—the knowledge that once the sound is over, that's it." His mission as the musicWitness® is to return the gift in the form of handmade images created *as the music takes place*. "It's an attempt to refer to what you can *only* experience by being there, which is this sense of mortality: this is just us with our limited human lives," he explained; "This whole project is an attempt to honor this conscious mortal experience of the audience and a performer's meeting together for something unique and *total*, which gives us *all* courage to go on and live and try to transcend all the limitations and obstacles that ordinary life puts in our way—to express the miracle of existence, with each other—to share a *full* expression of that with each other."[85]

*   *   *

Jazz derives deep meanings from its racial and cultural heritage, its curative capacities, and the spontaneity and originality of its improvised expressions. Moreover, as participants' observations reveal, the music has a numinous dimension, variously referred to here as spirit life, God, divine inspiration, musical orgasms, the zone, chemistry, blood, presents/presence, human psychic energy exchange, collective unconsciousness, high spots, truth, magic, a gift, meetings, and other terms—all alluding to extramusical communication enabled by collaborative interactions within these improvised communities. The realization of these profound intellectual, emotional, aesthetic, and metaphysical "truths" transcends the here/hear and now, the place and time of music-making, to create something more than music: a temporary state of social and spiritual synergy.

EPILOGUE

Making the Changes

To "make the changes" a jazz musician improvises harmonically appropriate melodies over the underlying chord progression of a tune.[1] The phrase is also an apt trope for the New York City jazz lifestyle, a struggle to make and experience meaningful music in spite of significant artistic, economic, and other challenges. The meteoric pace of city life practically demands a spontaneous, flexible approach in order to survive and surmount its incessant changes.

What has changed in the decade-plus since this study began? For one, the city has slowly recovered from the devastating terrorist attacks of September 11, 2001, and tourist trade is up. A sense of loss lingers, however, when New Yorkers catch sight of the Phoenix-like World Trade Center 1, a single silvery exclamation point punctuating the skyline where once there were two. When London was attacked in July 2005, then threatened a year later, Manhattanites had to wonder, will it happen here again? The rupture of the country's housing bubble in 2007–2008 as a result of imprudent practices on Wall Street and the ensuing global financial crisis caused widespread bankruptcy and unemployment, even as New York neighborhoods continued to gentrify, making life less and less affordable for its working-class denizens. As the recession ran its course, jazz entrepreneurs struggled—and continue to struggle—to stay in business. Festival "godfather" George Wein, now a nonagenarian, finally canceled his mammoth twenty-four-year-old Manhattan-based JVC Jazz Festival in 2009, reviving it the following year under a new name and sponsorship; in 2011, he returned to helm the Newport Jazz Festival, reinstating its nonprofit status and working pro bono while struggling to cover overhead costs.[2] *JazzTimes*, the most critically acclaimed trade magazine, went out of and back into business during 2009, the same year that the International Association for Jazz Educators folded for good, although *JazzTimes*, the Jazz Forward Coalition, and the Association for Performing Artists and Presenters collaborated to fill the void with the establishment of the Jazz Connect Conference in January 2013.

File-sharing and music-streaming technologies, along with digital media such as Facebook, artist websites and blogs, YouTube, Myspace, CD Baby, and Twitter have interconnected music, musicians, fans, and industry personnel to a degree never possible before, enabling social/professional networking among niche artists and interest groups worldwide. These developments have spawned innovative bottom-up business models like ArtistShare© or Dave Douglas's Greenleaf Music that bypass music industry machinery, allowing independent artists to market music directly to fans and music professionals, even allowing individual sponsors to invest in upcoming recording projects.

The 2008 election of Barack Obama as the nation's first black president symbolically empowered African American culture, creating a buzz in the jazz community when it was discovered that his iPod contained tracks by John Coltrane, Miles Davis, even Charlie Parker. Poet/activist Amiri Baraka cautioned, however, that "slavery never ended," that African Americans are still second-class citizens, and that Obama's election was a deceptive palliative, not a solution, to persistent class differences in our society.[3]

Change has come for people interviewed for this book. Several have moved away, and a few even moved back again. Irving and Stephanie Stone, Peter Cox, and Dale Fitzgerald passed on; all were celebrated with communal musical tributes. Marjorie Eliot's youngest son, Shaun, who'd been receiving psychiatric care, went missing for over a month in February 2011, eventually turning up safe at a local mental hospital. After two decades, thanks to a "rent party" thrown in her honor[4] and continued support from her extended "family," Eliot's doors are still open on Sunday afternoons, when another son, Rudel, performs in the house band.

Besides the faces, jazz places continue to come and go. From a list of eight hundred and thirty jazz venues compiled between 2002 and 2007, more than a hundred and thirty have closed or discontinued jazz programming, replaced by at least a hundred new ones, mostly in different locations.[5] Jazz at the (New) Lincoln Center opened in the Time Warner high-rise on Columbus Circle in

2004, featuring a nightclub oxymoronically named Dizzy's Club Coca Cola. CBGB's, birthplace of American punk and one of a half-handful of venues to present experimental jazz weekly, closed in 2006.[6] Gordon Polatnick launched EZ's Woodshed March 2006, closing down in June 2008,[7] while Smalls closed and reopened in the same location.[8] After a long grassroots-supported struggle, Steve Cannon was finally forced to evacuate his A Gathering of the Tribes cultural center/performance space for a new location around the corner. After a prolonged search, the Jazz Gallery finally found an affordable new home.[9] The 5C Café & Cultural Center has (so far) resisted gentrification pressures in Alphabet City.[10]

Jazz communities rallied together during crises. When Hurricane Katrina ravaged jazz's birthplace, New Orleans, in 2005, the New York–based Jazz Foundation of America (under the stewardship of Wendy Oxenhorn) came to the rescue, collecting a hundred thousand dollars worth of musical instruments for Louisianans who'd lost theirs—and therefore their livelihoods—to the storm. Numerous fund-raisers were held in and around New York, with local musicians donating their time and talents, while jazz internetworks provided lists of charities where supporters could send clothes, money, and food, resulting in housing and employment for over a thousand needy musicians. When star saxophonist Michael Brecker was diagnosed with MDS (Myelo-Dysplastic Syndrome), a potentially fatal bone disorder requiring a stem cell transplant from a genetically compatible donor, jazz people responded with a donor drive. Unfortunately, no compatible genotype was located and Brecker died of leukemia in January 2007.

And the music itself continues to change. Musicians continue to experiment with novel combinations of jazz with electronica, contemporary classical music, and various global musi-cultures.[11] Artists like Rez Abbassi, Sameer Gupta, Vijay Iyer, Rudresh Mahanthappa, Neel Murgai, and Dan Weiss are adopting and adapting ideas and practices from Indian *Hindustānī* and *Karṇāṭak* musics to develop hybrid musical languages.[12] An ongoing wave of Israeli-born and -trained musicians like Omer Avital and Anat Cohen are introducing Middle Eastern and North African musical traditions like the *maqām* (modal) system and *taqāsīm* (improvisations) into the jazz "mainstream."[13] M-BASE approaches to composition and improvisation propagated by saxophonist Steve Coleman and his colleagues have influenced many musicians. An increasing number of female instrumentalists, young lion*esses*[14] like Melissa Aldana (see Figure 35), Regina Carter, Sharel Cassity, Rebecca Cline, Anat Cohen, Natalie Cressman, Kait Dunton, Tia Fuller, Mary Halvorson, Anne Mette Iversen, Ingrid Jensen,

Grace Kelly, Ingrid Laubrock, Hailey Niswanger, Linda Oh, Iris Ornig, Tineke Postma, Matana Roberts, Ada Rovatti, Bria Skonberg, Esperanza Spaulding, Helen Sung, Erena Terkubo, Camille Thurman, Shirazette Tinnin, and Hiromi Uehara (among others), most of them based in the city, are challenging—and hopefully changing—male domination of jazz.[15]

To adapt to New York's highly variable environment, jazz people do what the musicians have always done: *improvise* over "the changes."

APPENDIX

Interviews

Name:	*Occupation:*[1]	*Date:*
Zach Hexum	tenor saxophonist	9/8/02
Lujira Cooper	columnist/fan	11/11/02
Cecil Bridgewater	trumpeter/educator	11/23/02
Mike Davis	bassist/photographer	12/10/02
Tommy Chang	guitarist	12/30/02
Jerome Covington	guitarist	12/31/02
Rachel Kent[2]	fan/retired	1/11/03
Ryan Weaver	pianist	1/20/03
Michael Torsone	organist/repairman/ tuner/former club owner	1/30/03
Matt Garrison	bassist	2/1/03
Bob Cunningham	bassist	2/2/03
April Matthis	fan/singer/actress	2/9/03
Peter Bernstein	guitarist	2/12/03
Rose Bartu	violinist	2/13/03
Dale Fitzgerald[3]	venue proprietor	2/18/03
Arlee Leonard	vocalist	2/21/03
Marjorie Eliot	pianist/hostess/playwright	3/6/03
Steve Bernstein	trumpeter	3/12/03
Chris Byars	tenor saxophonist/arranger	1/5, 3/16/03
Peter Cox[4]	fan/retired	4/2/03

Richard Berger and	fan	4/9/03
Roberta DeNicola	fan	(same)
John Mosca	trombonist	4/18/03
Jonathan Daniel	painter/graphic artist	4/19/03
Bruce Gallanter	record store owner/fan	4/20/03
Tony Suggs	pianist	4/21–22/03
Jeff Arnal	drummer/ independent producer	4/22/03
Irving and	fan	4/23/03
Stephanie Stone[5]	fan/singer/pianist	(same)
Mitch Borden	club owner/manager	4/24/03
Fred Cohen	record shop owner/ manager	4/25/03
Gordon Polatnick	tour guide/retailer/ café proprietor	4/25/03
w/tour group:		
Lawrence Gibb	tourist (U.K.)	(same)
Jo Gilks	tourist (U.K.)	(same)
Jerry Sykes	tourist (U.K.)	(same)
Margaret Davis Grimes[6]	fan/community activist/ webpage editor	5/4/03
Steve Dalachinsky and	fan/poet	5/7/03
Yuko Otomo	fan/visual artist	(same)
Todd Nicholson	bassist	5/10/03
Franko Christopher	club co-owner/manager/ playwright	7/22/03
Michael Moreno	guitarist	7/22/03
Manny Maris	fan/record retailer	7/23–24/03
Seamus Blake	tenor saxophonist	7/24/03
Bruce Morris	venue proprietor	7/24/03
Horst Liepolt	art gallery salesman/ former club owner	7/25/03
Cecilia Engelhart-Lopez	singer/Festival Productions employee	7/25/03
Kurt Rosenwinkel	guitarist	7/29/03
Harold Meiselman	fan/educator	7/30/03
Jeremy Pelt	trumpeter	8/1/03
Jessica Stone	tenor saxophonist/educator	8/2/03
Tony Jones	tenor saxophonist	(same)
Nick Russo	guitarist	8/4/03
Gary Giddins	author/critic	8/5/03
Sedric Choukroun	tenor saxophonist	1/12, 8/5/03

Brian Smith	bassist	8/5/03
Harold Ousley[7]	tenor saxophonist	8/6/03
Eri Yamamoto	pianist/composer	8/7/03
Roy Campbell Jr.[8]	trumpeter/educator	8/9/03
George Wein	festival producer/ promoter/pianist	10/30/03
Jack Vartoogian	arts photographer	11/23/03
David Adler	critic/writer/educator	11/25/03
Jeff Schlanger	sculptor/painter	12/20/03
Lorraine Gordon	club proprietor	2/18/04
Jim Eigo	publicist	7/28/04
Marilyn Crispell	pianist	9/27/05
Yusef Lateef[9]	multi-reedist/composer	11/21/05
Rudresh Mahanthappa	alto saxophonist	3/11/06
Dave Douglas	trumpeter/composer	8/4/06
Kevin Blancq	trumpeter/educator	12/15/06
Eli Yamin	pianist/composer/educator	12/17/06
Bill McFarlin	IAJE Executive Director[10]	12/18/06
Greg Carroll	IAJE Director of Education	12/18/06
Ralph Alessi	trumpeter/educator/ venue proprietor	3/7/07
Tim McHenry	museum curator/ venue proprietor	4/27/07
Loren Schoenberg	trombonist/writer/ museum curator	4/28/07
Vijay Iyer	pianist/composer	5/10/07
Bill Charlap	pianist	6/7/07
Steve Cannon	venue proprietor	7/5/07
Jim Wintner	museum curator/ venue proprietor	8/31/07
Louie Belogenis	tenor saxophonist	8/31/07
Maria Schneider	composer/arranger	9/30/07
Ted Curson	trumpeter	11/4/07
Charlie Persip	drummer	11/4/07
Michael Marcus	multi-reedist	11/5/07
Benny Golson	saxophonist/composer/ arranger	11/5/07
Roy Haynes	drummer	11/5/07
Harold Mabern	pianist	11/5/07
Dick Griffin	trombonist	11/7/07
Richard Wyands	pianist	11/7/07
Joel Dorn[11]	record producer	11/8/07

Steve Turre	trombonist/shell player	11/07
Dorthaan Kirk	jazz radio deejay/ programmer (WBGO)	11/07
Matt Shipp	pianist	1/26/08
Ben Allison	bassist/composer/ bandleader	4/24/08
Mike Wilpizeski	publicist	6/16/08
Elaine Martone	record producer	6/17/08
Michel Camilo	pianist/composer	6/18/08
George Braith	Braithophonist	12/12/08
Brian Drye	trombonist/teacher/ venue manager	2/27/09
Larry Coryell	guitarist	3/28/09
"Jazz" Judy Balos	fan/retired	8/12/10

NOTES

PROLOGUE

1. All quotes in this and the previous paragraph were overheard at the memorial concert held for Peter Cox at Roulette on Mar. 27, 2013, with the exception of Bruce Gallanter's statement "his appreciation for music . . . was unfaltering," taken from the downtownmusicgallery.com website (accessed July 12, 2013). Thanks to videographer/archivist Susan L. Yung for graciously providing a video excerpt of the event.

INTRODUCTION

1. See Jeffri (2003) for the first comprehensive sociological survey of working jazz musicians.

2. Professionals not included here—but certainly worthy of closer consideration in a future project—include educators, recording industry employees (e.g., sound engineers, producers, record manufacturers, distributors, marketing agents, promoters, A and R wo/men), copyright agency employees, music publishers, entertainment lawyers, deejays, and artist managers and agents.

3. Khun (1962:140) argues that scientific paradigm shifts are achieved through "a whole network of fact and theory," not merely "a series of individual discoveries and inventions."

4. Cf. Berger and Luckmann (1967).

5. Jost (1975:10–11).

6. Panish (1997) argues that white scholars have privileged romanticism, competitive individualism, and ahistorical narratives, while black scholars have emphasized

the interconnectedness of performers and their communities, social backgrounds, and musical traditions.

7. Cf. Such (1993), Fischlin and Heble (2004), Borgo (2005), Isoardi (2006), and Lewis (2008).

8. Small defines *musicking* as "tak[ing] part, in any capacity, in a musical performance, whether by performing, by listening, by rehearsing or practicing, by providing material for performance (what is called composing), or by dancing" (1998:9). An earlier definition occurs in (1988:50).

9. Curtis and Barnes (1989:G-20).

10. Thomas (1979:4), emphasis in original.

11. Becker (1982:34–35, 39). Note that while Becker's work largely ignores audiences, this book's primary focus is on audiences and other nonperforming jazz participants. Furthermore, while Becker emphasizes the division of labor and cooperative functioning of diverse occupations within an art world, arguing that shared understandings of the art's value give it its social resonance, I am less concerned with commercial transactions between jazz world participants, particularly in discussion of amateur fans, and more inclined to recognize highly diverse and/or discrepant forms of self-expression and understandings of musical meaning, as well as a high degree of autonomy and even anonymity among participants—all of which, I argue, may yet be subsumed within the collective identity of a particular scene. Even in acknowledging such disparity and *disunity* in the community, like Becker I hold that the quality and intensity of an art form is filtered, amplified, and evaluated through the united efforts of its supporters.

12. See Turner (1969) and Bauman (1977).

13. See Leonard (1987), Small (1987), Salamone (1988), Jackson (2003, 2012), and Currie (2009) for examples.

14. See Jackson (2012) for a discussion of Bell's (1992) concept of "ritualization" in the context of jazz performances.

15. Jackson's reflexive fieldwork (2012:187–204) is an important step in this direction, particularly in its detailed descriptions of audience reactions (his own and others') to live musical events. In departure from Jackson's work, I frame the audience *as* performers, and therefore agents in ritualization processes. Somoroff's (2014) thesis on the Lower East Side (LES) avant-jazz scene goes even further, containing detailed ethnography and analysis of fans and other scenesters' private and public listening practices. See also n. 58, this chapter.

16. Turner defines *communitas* as a spontaneous and temporary destructuring of time; it "has something 'magical' about it . . . the feeling of endless power" (1969:139). Cf. Ch. 6, n. 72.

17. For studies of religious and metaphysical aspects of music, see Rouget (1985), Friedson (1996), Sylvan (2002), and Bohlman et al. (2006); for studies connecting jazz to ethnic religious practices, see Keil (1966), Ellison (1964), Murray (1976), Leonard (1987), Saul (2003), Muller (2011), and Jackson (2012). Like Leonard, my interest in the supersensual dimensions of jazz is more practical than philosophical, so my evidence for such phenomena is based on the subjective experiences of individual participants.

18. Papenbrok (1985) argues that flamenco *aficionados* (connoisseurs) and other active participants create an empathetic environment at *juergas* (impromptu jam sessions) and *reuniones* to facilitate altered states of ecstasy and *duende* (spirit) possession. Similarly, Hecht (1968:178–80) describes how *testigos* (participating witnesses) arouse flamenco performers to purer expression. See also Pohren (1999:167, 2005:288) and Schreiner (1990:67).

19. Qureshi (1995) illustrates how South Indian *qawwali* audiences respond to musical sounds with rule-governed patterns of interplay that lead to shared meanings and spiritual ecstasy.

20. Racy (2003: 129–33) describes ecstatic feedback loops between Arab *sammī'ah* (sophisticated/initiated listeners) and *ṭarab* musicians that bring performances to *ibdā'* (a higher plateau of creativity).

21. Duranti (1986) describes oral storytelling events in which the audience participates as coauthors.

22. See Baraka (1963, 1991), Murray (1976), Baker (1984), Powell (1989), Floyd (1991, 1995), Wilson (1992), and Jackson (2012).

23. In this book, transcribed excerpts from taped interviews are identified in the text by the name of the interviewee. The date of the interview and an indication of the person's occupation(s) can be found in the Appendix. Italics used in transcriptions of taped interviews indicate when the speaker stressed certain words or syllables.

24. Travis Jackson (2012) cautions against conflating jazz's racial and cultural histories. Advocating the "blues aesthetic" as a central evaluative and interpretative framework for the music, he lists the following criteria: "the importance of having an individual voice; developing the ability to balance and play with a number of different musical parameters in performance; understanding the cultural foundations of the music; being able oneself to 'bring something to the music'; creating music that is 'open enough' to allow other musicians to bring something despite or because of what has been provided structurally or contextually; and being open for transcendence to 'the next level' of performance, the spiritual level" (110). Most of these skills—individual sound, the notion of balance, blues feeling, and "bringing something"—he argues, are predicated on understanding the music's cultural foundations, its African American "performative sensibilities" (116–19). Thus, musicians who are "socialized in communities that transmit values similar to those that have nurtured some of the most influential musicians have an advantage over others—including other African Americans—who have not" (118). Access to the spiritual level, he suggests, is fostered through elder black "masters" who teach younger apprentices to tap, in the words of his informant, saxophonist Antonio Hart, "some of that spirit, some of that fire, of what the music is really about" (118).

25. See Wilmer (1977), Vincent (1995), and Panish (1997).

26. Gillespie and Fraser (1979:252). Note that protecting one's signature sound is not always racially motivated. Early New Orleans trumpeter Freddie Keppard reputedly covered his right hand with a handkerchief to keep other musicians (many of them black) from copying his fingerings.

27. Leonard is of mixed (black and white) parentage.

28. See Dance (1994), Pellegrinelli (2000, 2001), and Hentoff (2001).

29. See Sidran (1981), Otis (1993), and Taylor (1993).

30. Lomax (1973:120). In this context, Bechet is comparing two black subpopulations in New Orleans during the 1910s and 1920s. "Negroes" refers to the darker-skinned blacks formerly clustered in uptown neighborhoods, while "Creoles" indicates lighter-skinned (due to mixed French or Spanish ancestry) downtown blacks who had more access to social privileges and economic opportunities (cf. Herskovits 1941, Stearns 1956). Peretti (1992:60) contends that colorism persisted between New Orleans blacks and Creoles who relocated to Chicago during the 1920s and 1930s.

31. Otis (1993:113). The son of Greek immigrants, Otis identified himself as "'black' by persuasion" (see Garofalo 1997:109).

32. Wilson, quoted in Jackson (2012:118).

33. Other neighborhood jazz venues active in 2014 included The Cotton Club, 449 LA Scat, Ginny's Supper Club, Harlem Tavern, The Jazz Spot, Londel's Restaurant, Paris Blues, Marjorie Eliot's Parlor Entertainment, Minton's Playhouse, New Amsterdam Musical Association, Shrine, and the United House of Prayer for All People.

34. See Ch. 1: "Creating Contexts. See also Ch. 5: "Channeling the Muse: Professionals as Co-improvisers" and "Professionals in the Community."

35. Gillespie and Fraser (1979:139). Minton's Playhouse hosted after-hours jam sessions that allegedly spawned bebop. Thelonious Monk's tunes were (and are) notoriously difficult to play for the uninitiated; trumpeters Roy Eldridge and Dizzy Gillespie were both renowned for their virtuosity. Gillespie's words suggest that he respected fellow trumpeter Carisi for having the chops to cope with Monk's compositions and hold his own onstage with the trumpet titans mentioned. Cutting contests at Minton's and other bop clubs like (Clark) Monroe's Uptown House quickly weeded out outsiders, musical and otherwise (cf. Ellison 1964:207–8, Baraka 1967:21–24).

36. Cf. n. 24, this chapter; see also Fabre and O'Meally (1994) and Ramsey (2003).

37. Many of the prominent New York and European avant-jazz artists listed in this chapter are white. During 2004–2005, women artists active on the avant-jazz scene include Susan Alcorn, Geri Allen, Jane Ira Bloom, Ellen Christi, Leena Conquest, Sylvie Courvoisier, Marilyn Crispell, Connie Crothers, Kris Davis, Shayna Dulberger, Kali Z. Fasteau, Xu Fengxia, Satoko Fuji, Gamin, Mary Halvorson, Susie Ibarra, Terry Jenoure, Jessica Jones, Kyoko Kitamura, Ingrid Laubrock, Joëlle Léandre, Miya Masaoka, Myra Melford, Nicole Mitchell, Patricia Nicholson-Parker, Pauline Oliveros, Jessica Pavone, Matana Roberts, Angelica Sanchez, Jen Shyu, Catherine Sikora, Samita Sinha, Mazz Swift, Fay Victor, Nioka Workman, Eri Yamamoto, and Saco Yasuma. Somoroff (2014:14, 204–205) makes a similar assessment of the relative prominence of women on the (Lower East Side) avant-jazz scene.

38. The concert was held Sept. 12, 2013.

39. See Ch. 6, n. 49.

40. Excerpted lyrics from "Bid 'Em In," by Oscar Brown Jr., from the album *Sin & Soul* (Columbia: CL 1577, 1960).

41. Roberts's statements in this paragraph are from a documentary clip, *NewMusicBox Matana Roberts: Creative Defiance* (Jan. 4, 2013, pub. Feb. 1, 2013); www.youtube.com/watch?v=XXI5pXB0_Ac (accessed Sept. 15, 2013).

42. See Ellison (1964:221–32) and DeVeaux (1997:26).

43. The St. John Will-I-Am Coltrane African Orthodox Church has been active in San Francisco since 1971, enduring several name and venue changes. For a period, twice-weekly extended services were held in Santa Cruz, Calif. Coltrane's likeness appears in church paintings, his words are quoted, his music performed during services.

44. Referring to the following: Louis Armstrong, Lester Willis Young, Edward Kennedy Ellington, Charles Parker Jr., John Birks Gillespie, Billie Holiday (née Eleanora Fagan), and John William Coltrane, respectively. Other common nicknames include Bean (Coleman Randolph Hawkins), Django (Jean Baptiste Reinhardt), Papa Jo (Jonathan David Samuel Jones), Monk (Thelonious Sphere Monk), Klook (Liaqat Ali Salaam, né Kenneth Spearman Clarke), Miles (Miles Dewey Davis III), Sonny (Theodore Walter Rollins), Cannonball (Julian Edwin Adderley), Philly Joe (Joseph Rudolph Jones), Jug (Eugene Ammons), Lockjaw (Edward Davis), Brownie (Clifford Brown), and Sassy (Sarah Lois Vaughan).

45. Ch. 4, n. 50.

46. See Ch. 4: "For Love or Money? The Business of Live Jazz."

47. See Berliner (1994:120–45) on how musicians imitate, assimilate, and (hopefully) expand on their musical influences. See Solis (2008:70–72) and Jackson (2012:110–12) on the importance of developing a personal "sound" or "voice." Solis (2008: 81–107, 135–36) discusses how musicians bring their own voice to interpretations of Thelonious Monk's music.

48. Solis (2008:104–5).

49. Bailey (1992).

50. Jeffri (2003) estimates that 15.6–20 percent of jazz performers are females. For articles and scholarship addressing women's and gender-based issues in jazz, see Dahl (1984, 2000), Davis (1998), Dyson (2003), Enstice and Stockhouse (2004), Griffin (2001), Handy (1998), Heble and Siddall (2000), Hentoff (2001), Miller and Jensen (1996), Monson (1995), Muller and Benjamin (2011), Oliveros (2004), Orgren (1989), Pellegrinelli (2000, 2001), Placksin (1992), Rustin and Tucker (2008), Tucker (2000, 2004, 2008), and Waterman (2008).

51. For articles and scholarship addressing queer sexuality in jazz, see Clifford (2007), Davis (1986, 2001, 2002), Gavin (2001), Hajdu (1996), Middlebrook (1998), Milkowski (2001), Mockus (2007), Robinson (1994), Smith (2004), Tucker (2008), and Wilmer (1989).

52. In interviews for this book, I avoided direct questions about possibly sensitive issues such as sexuality, racism, personal income, political or religious orientation, drug use, criminal activity, and so forth, unless someone broached the subject him- or herself.

53. From September 2002 to August 2006, I compiled a list of over 830 venues that presented jazz on a regular or semiregular basis, located throughout the five boroughs,

the great majority of them in Manhattan, followed by Brooklyn. Restaurants and other venues that featured live jazz but didn't advertise were not included in this tally (see Ch. 4, nn. 13–14).

54. Appadurai (1993) coined the terms *ethno-*, *media-*, *techno-*, *finance-*, and *ideo-scape* to describe five dimensions of global cultural flow.

55. I tallied over 640 Manhattan venues advertising live jazz between September 2002 and September 2007, divided by 23 square miles (from the 2010 U. S. Census Bureau survey) to get 28 clubs/square mile. Note this approximate figure doesn't include nonadvertising venues or private performances spaces such as function halls or hotel meeting rooms.

56. During the principal period of research for this book (Sept. 2002–Sept. 2014), "neighborhood" venues with active community participation included 5C Café & Cultural Center, ABC No-Rio, A Gathering of Tribes, Barbès, Downtown Music Gallery, Marjorie Eliot's parlor, EZ's Woodshed, Freddie's Backroom, I-Beam Studios, Pumpkins, St. Nick's Pub, St. Peter's Church, Showman's Lounge, Sistas' Place, Smalls, Smoke, Tea Room, University of the Streets, and Zinc Bar, among others.

57. "Downtown" literally refers to the Lower Manhattan lofts and performances spaces (below 20th St.) where the music was originally performed.

58. For studies of downtown music, see Barzel (2000, 2002, 2005, 2012), Borgo (2005), Currie (2009), Gann (1997, 2005, 2006), Greenland (2007b), Heller (2005, 2011, 2012), Lewis (2004), Nicholls (1998), and Somoroff (2014). Somoroff's thesis on the listening practices of musicians and fans in the Lower East Side avant-jazz community is a close companion to this book. In 2009–2010, he interviewed some of the same people I had first met in 2002–2003, including Richard Berger, Steve Dalachinsky, Roberta DeNicola (Somoroff uses her married name, Berger), Bruce Gallanter, Yuko Otomo, and Jeff Schlanger. He also spoke with a number of scenesters who don't fall easily into the musician/fan dichotomy, including volunteers at performance venues, a record label owner/manager, a photographer, a poet/part-time writer, and a professor/critic. While both of our studies look at listeners' personal experiences of music, his is more focused on the musical text and its historical valences, while I'm most interested in listening agendas and how these are affected by changing social environments and modes of participation. Both of us frame listening as a performance, and we're both interested in the "social construction of aural experience" (p. 28), the influence of collecting, and the religiosity of listening experiences. Our studies differ in scope, narrative style, and rhetoric, however. For example, Somoroff doesn't include the proprietor of Local 269 bar (one of his principal ethnographic sites) in his definition of "jazz scene participants" (p. 91), whereas I've devoted an entire chapter to venue proprietors.

59. After flourishing throughout the 1970s in lower Manhattan lofts and performance spaces, the downtown scene subsequently became associated with specific venues such as the Knitting Factory, and then Tonic, and during the period of research for this book (Sept. 2002–Sept. 2014) was featured at ABC-No Rio, Brecht Forum, Douglass Street Music Collective, Downtown Music Gallery, Ibeam, ISSUE Project Room, Le Poisson Rouge, Local 269, Roulette, and The Stone.

60. I use the term *precomposition* to indicate something that is composed before it's performed, rather than *as* it's performed, in an attempt to avoid the false dichotomy between composition and improvisation.

61. Many, but not all, avant-jazz fans enjoy record-listening as well. Note that fans from scenes located away from large urban areas such as New York City, Los Angeles, or Chicago have relatively less access to live jazz, such that recorded media may be a more frequent (and perhaps more meaningful) form of participation. See also Prouty (2012a:44) on the importance of record-listening in the formation and maintenance of nonlocalized jazz communities.

62. Avant-jazz fan Stephanie Stone told *New York Times* jazz journalist Ben Ratliff (2003b) that she and her late husband Irving attended 4–6 shows a *week* at the old Knitting Factory from 1987–1997—approximately 2,000–3,000 shows in a decade! Both Irving and Stephanie remained active concertgoers until the ends of their lives, despite critical health problems (diabetes and cancer, respectively).

63. See DeVeaux (1999).

64. A colleague of mine reported that he'd seen Judy Balos for years at various jazz concerts without knowing who she was. Balos herself reported that she often saw a man known as "Big Al" at MOMA's Summergarden shows and at JazzMobile shows, both free events held during the summer season. Similarly, I often recognize the faces (but not always the names) of certain club owners, photographers, and other jazz professionals when I attend concerts.

CHAPTER 1. LISTENING TO JAZZ

1. For research by cognitive psychologists on the "hardwired" dimensions of musical perception, see Deutsch (1982); Holbrook and Huber (1983); Lerdahl and Jackendoff (1983); Sloboda (1985); Dowling and Harwood (1986); Bregman (1990); Krumhansl (1990); Narmour (1990); Cross and Deliège (1993); Blowers and Bacon-Shone (1994); Levitin and Menon (2003); Grahn and Brett (2007); Patel (2008); Hallam, Cross, and Thaut (2009); Juslin and Sloboda (2010); and Cross (2011).

2. For example, listeners may hear a 6/8 rhythm as two slow pulses, as three or four medium pulses, or as six or twelve fast pulses. In his African Music and Dance Ensembles at U.C. Berkeley, C. K. Ladzekpo teaches students to count aloud twelve different evenly spaced rhythmic subdivisions while simultaneously stepping a four-beat quarter-note tactus and clapping a two-bar $^6/_8$ bell pattern. Additional superimpositions to those listed above are generated by permutating beat placements. For example, a three-over-four pattern can be played/heard in four different ways by shifting the entire pattern forward or backward by eighth-notes. Similarly, a six-over-four pattern can be superimposed in two different ways: as downbeats or upbeats (offbeats).

3. For example, consider a chord voiced A-C-E-G bottom to top. In a given musical context, some might hear and/or analyze this as an A minor seventh chord, others as a C major sixth chord in third inversion—to cite two possibilities.

4. See Nattiez (1990) and Smith (1988). Turino (1999, 2008:5–16) uses Charles Peirce's (1931–1935, 1958) "dicent signs" to show how people derive personal meanings from music.

5. See Seeger (1977:16–30, 102–132) for discussion of the "linguocentric predicament."

6. Kivy (1997, 2002) restricts the definition of meaning to the linguistic sense of reference (i.e., designating something) and predication (i.e., attributing properties to something), thus implying that the question of whether music is meaningful or meaningless is in itself meaningless because it can neither refer nor predicate. See also Patel (2008:304).

7. Semiologist Jean-Jacques Nattiez (1990) argues that musical meaning is not linguistically rooted but based on signification (i.e., its association with something other than itself), subject to change based on active perceptions under specific circumstances. His theory derives from Ferdinand de Saussure's (1959) binary distinction between a sign's *signified* (a real entity) and *signifier* (a representation of or reference to that entity), with the additional complication, introduced by Charles S. Peirce (1931–1935), that the *signifier* can itself function as a separate sign, or *interpretant*, leading to a potentially infinite chain, or web, of *interpretants*. Following Molino (1975, 1990), Nattiez also proposes a tripartite structure of *poietic, neutral,* and *esthetic* analyses, corresponding to the creation/composition of a work, its immanent material trace, and its perception and reception. In this book, I address the meanings of jazz at Nattiez's *neutral* level, with its consequent effects on the *esthetic* level. My goal, however, is not to interrogate the philosophical underpinnings of musical meanings, but rather to note how the formation, maintenance, and revision of musical meanings are situated in individuals' specific circumstances.

8. Turino (1999, 2014) uses Charles Peirce's (1931–1935, 1958) concept of *dicent index* (a sign linked by a cause-and-effect relationship to the object/event it stands for) to illustrate how musical experiences acquire authenticity and foster individual and group identities.

9. Turino (2008:42) argues that "'body language' and movement styles are often . . . perceived, however vaguely, as being directly affected by the inner moods and the nature of the person in question. . . . [T]hey operate directly and do not require symbolic assessment; thus they remain lower in focal awareness and function as 'natural' or authentic signs of the people and situation in question." Analogously, when jazz fans watch the facial grimaces and hear the timbral alterations (growls, squeals, and so forth) of improvising instrumentalists—or, conversely, when performers watch the physical responses of listeners (tapping feet, bobbing heads)—these symbolic gestures may be "read" at a relatively unfiltered, subliminal level, assumed to be directly connected to and affected by each participant's cultural positioning and state of mind. Peirce/Turino's formulation thus provides a useful conceptual tool to explain why some of jazz's (and other musics') most important performative criteria—authenticity, soulfulness, charisma, originality—are so difficult to articulate and explicate.

10. Compared with twelve-tone equal-temperament intervals, a "blue third" is sharper than a minor third but flatter than a major third—often in *motion* between them, as when performers of blues-inflected music "bend" the blue pitches up and/or down.

11. At slower tempos, jazz drummers typically play swing rhythms with continuous eighth-notes on the ride cymbal or hi-hat, slightly delaying the second beat of each eighth-

note pair to approach or approximate the third beat of an eighth-note triplet; at faster tempos, the beats begin to even out, with little or no delay between them.

12. Prögler (1995) attempted to measure and quantify Keil's (1966, 1987) theory of "participatory discrepancies" in jazz rhythm sections by comparing the bassist's "walking" quarter-notes with the drummer's ridetaps (swing eighth-note rhythms played on the ride cymbal), observing variances across and within rhythm sections. See also Butterfield (2010a,b, 2011).

13. Borgo (2005:89–121) uses computer-generated fractal correlation dimensions and correlograms, coupled with more conventional interpretive moves, to analyze recorded excerpts from solo and group free-improvisations. Although provocative, the diagrams are less illuminating than the recorded examples.

14. Many jazz musicians transcribe improvised solos from recordings and transpose melodic sequences and harmonic patterns to twelve different keys on their instruments, internalizing this vocabulary for later use in spontaneous musical "conversations" (cf. Berliner, 1994:95–119). This type of practicing allows them to identify rhythms, melodies, harmonies, timbral manipulations, and so forth.

15. As a trained guitarist/pianist/singer and professional critic, it's almost impossible for me to listen to music (recorded or live) without noting its tonality and rhythmic grouping (if any), its melodic contours and overall form, and the number and types of instruments playing. As a record reviewer, I sometimes must distinguish between an alto saxophone played in its lower register and a tenor saxophone played in its higher register (not always an easy task), so I often do this reflexively. When listening to and/or watching another guitarist, I automatically notice left-hand techniques (e.g., hammer-ons, pull-offs, slides, bends), right-hand techniques (e.g., rasquedos, tremolo or sweep picking, fingerpicking), the type of guitar (e.g., solid-body electric, nylon-string acoustic), the use of electronic sound-processing equipment (e.g., echo/delay, chorus/flang, overdrive/distortion), and other guitar-specific details. Listening to singers, I'm always conscious of their vocal register, particularly when they transition between chest voice and head voice/falsetto.

16. M-Base (Macro-Basic Array of Structured Extemporizations) concepts are principally associated with alto saxophonist/composer Steve Coleman and his artistic colleagues.

17. For example, a sixteen-beat phrase, traditionally subdivided symmetrically, could be composed/performed as a nonsymmetric cyclic accent pattern (e.g., 2 + 3 + 2 + 2 + 3 + 2 + 2, felt as a combination of seven long and short pulses).

18. See Giddens (1984, 1993).

19. See Nettl (1974).

20. Cf. Tirro (1967:313–34) and Williams (1967).

21. Similarly, in North Indian *Hindustānī* music, listeners demonstrate their ability to monitor the progress of the *tāla* (rhythmic cycle) by performing claps and waves.

22. See Jackson (2003:60–64, 2012:45–50) for detailed discussion of the "governing structure" of ritual jazz performances.

23. In various interviews, Sonny Rollins and Stan Getz acknowledged that they idolized and initially emulated the playing of Hawkins and Young, respectively.

24. Ellison (1964:175).

25. Whitney Balliett (1959) first described jazz as "the sound of surprise."

26. Andrey Henkin, pers. comm.

27. Louis Armstrong originally used this term to refer to the immediate physical state of his lips (his embouchure), which affected his ability to hit high notes, but it's now used more broadly to indicate technical facility (i.e., speed, precision, range, and volume of sound production; ability to play difficult passages without error; and so forth).

28. When I attended the University of North Texas, I occasionally heard big-band musicians joking that the school's culture seemed preoccupied with playing "higher, faster, louder." Fellow students used the adjective "burning" to describe performances that exemplified these qualities.

29. Brackett (2008).

30. See *Art Attack!* ed. Margaret Davis Grimes, "the newsletter for & about liberation musicians in NYC." www.jazznewyork.org (accessed Aug. 22, 2013).

31. See also Maris's comments in Ch. 6: "More than Music: Heritage, Healing and "Blood."

32. Several versions of this quotation are in wide circulation. One variant, more in keeping with Ellington's urbane personality, is more politic: "There are two kinds of music. Good music—and the *other* kind." Dance (2000:3) cites Ellington saying: "Music is music, and that's it. If it sounds good, it's good music, and it depends on who's listening *how* good it sounds!" Similar statements have been attributed to Louis Armstrong, Dizzy Gillespie, and Richard Strauss. Ellington objected to people labeling his music "jazz," instead referring to his favorite music(ians) as "beyond category."

33. Ornette Coleman and Cecil Taylor were/are important progenitors of free and avant-garde jazz; Louis Armstrong was a pioneer of the original New Orleans (or traditional) jazz and later sang popular songs; Fletcher Henderson was an early innovator of big-band (aka swing) jazz; Ellington's long career encompassed big-band music, sacred suites, and various forms of "African American classical music."

34. Davis released seminal recordings associated with each movement: *The Birth of the Cool* (cool); *Kind of Blue* (modal); *In a Silent Way* and *Bitches Brew* (jazz-rock fusion); and *Miles Ahead, Porgy & Bess*, and *Sketches of Spain* (Third Stream). Davis's second classic quintet (with Wayne Shorter, Herbie Hancock, Ron Carter, and Tony Williams), featured on the albums *E.S.P., Miles Smiles, Sorcerer, Nefertiti, Miles in the Sky*, and *Filles de Kilimanjaro*, developed new rhythmic and harmonic concepts and a high level of group interactivity.

35. A short, incomplete list of such artists might include Peter Apfelbaum, Steven Bernstein, Jim Black, Brian Blade, Dave Binney, Jane Ira Bloom, Don Byron, Uri Caine, Gerald Cleaver, Dave Douglas, Bill Frisell, Ben Goldberg, John Hollenbeck, Vijay Iyer, Dana Leong, Tony Malaby, Andy Milne, Jason Moran, Paul Motian, Jean-Michel Pilc, Dafnis Prieto, Chris Speed, Dan Weiss, and Eri Yamamoto.

36. Held at Dizzy's Club Coca-Cola, Oct. 6, 2009.

37. Both of the Stones have since passed away: Irving on June 18, 2003 (shortly after our interview) at age 80, and Stephanie on Apr. 11, 2014, at age 93. See Chs. 2, 3, 7, for discussion of their important roles in the downtown community.

38. See Meyer (1961:14, 118).

39. See Kernfeld (1988a:562, 1988b:322).

40. Gioia (1988:118–19) suggests that jazz's rich content and radical unpredictability increase the likelihood that uninitiated listeners will be overwhelmed by its variety and lack of patent references.

CHAPTER 2. DEVELOPING "BIG EARS"

1. See Becker (1982), Lopes (2002), and Martin (2005). Martin defines "creation of a jazz work" more broadly to include both physical artifacts and symbolic representations.

2. Small (1988, 1998). See also Introduction, n. 8.

3. See Anderson (1983) and Appadurai (1993). Prouty (2012a) and Moehn (2013) problematize the idea of a "jazz community" in scholarly discourse.

4. See Prouty (2012a,b).

5. See Jackson (2012:51–69) on spatiality and jazz. His monograph shares many themes with this study (though his primary research was conducted a decade earlier); see especially Ch. 4, which provides an overview of New York City jazz in the 1990s, including some discussion of audiences, performance venues, and critics; in Ch. 6, which frames jazz as a ritualized form of social action; and elsewhere in its attention to community interactions. In contrast to Jackson, whose primary protagonists are jazz musicians, this book gives more weight to the perspectives and activities of "nonperforming" performers.

6. See Bennett and Peterson (2004:2).

7. See Straw (1991).

8. Riesman (1950) challenged Adorno and other Frankfort School theorists who characterized popular music fans as passive listener/consumers, arguing that certain "minority" groups actively seek out and find meaning in alternative musical styles. This idea was later embraced by Birmingham School of Cultural Studies scholars such as Stuart Hall (1973), whose influential encoding/decoding model proposes that network television viewers, instead of responding to mass media in ways its creators intend, rather reinterpret these messages on their own terms. See also Hall and Jefferson (1976) and Hebdige (1979).

9. For ethnographies depicting the self-constituting nature of local music scenes, see Cohen (1991), Shank (1994), Mitchell (1996), and Spring (2004).

10. See Kirshenblatt-Gimblett (2000).

11. See Slobin (1993), Kruse (1993), Bennett (2000), Weinstein (2000), and Hodkinson (2002).

12. Kruse (2009) updates her initial research on these scenes, conducted just before the explosion of digital file-sharing in the mid-1980s, where she considers the impact of the internet on these same local scenes.

13. Finnegan (1989:325).

14. In Greenland (2010a), I investigate various ways new media has impacted jazz communities, particularly in the emergence of bottom-up business models for record production and distribution.

15. See Kibby (2000); Harris (2000); Bennett (2002); Lee and Peterson (2004); Wallach (2008); Wallach, Berger, and Greene (2011); Prouty (2012a,b); and Burkhalter (2013).

16. That is, social networks on the internet.

17. Cf. Adorno (1941), Frith and Goodwin (1990), and Cavicchi (1998:7, 60). Hills (2002) gives an insightful overview of critical theory in fan studies.

18. Notable exceptions in jazz studies are Burland and Pitts (2010, 2014) and Brand et al. (2012).

19. For theories of audience agency, see Cruz and Lewis (1994), Brooker and Jermyn (2003), Gray (2007), and Meizel (2011). Although musicians can jam together via Skype and other interfaces, the inevitable signal delay imposed by digital technology makes simultaneous communication—and therefore any meaningful participatory discrepancies—impossible (cf. Ch. 1: "Hearing the "Facts" and n. 12). If future technological innovations shorten this temporal gap, it might permit "expressive micro-timing" (see Iyer, 1998) and "instantaneous" audience feedback across digital interfaces—i.e., a closer approximation of face-to-face musical communication in cyberspace.

20. See Adams and Sardiello (2000); Berger (1999); Cavicchi (1998); Crafts, Cavicchi, and Keil (1993); Cohen (1993); Finnegan (1989); Gilbert (1999); Hanna (1983); Negus (1996); Shank (1994); and Small (1998).

21. Cf. Giddens theory of "structuration" (1979, 1984).

22. For demographic overviews of jazz fans, see Peterson et al. (2000), McIntyre (2001), Jeffri (2003), Ostrower (2005), Riley and Laing (2006), National Endowment for the Arts (2009, 2013), Maitland (2009), Nicholson et al. (2009), and Heimlich (2011). Heimlich isolates three predominant (but not exclusive) modes of individual engagement: internalization (emotional responses or using music to create mental images or stories), externalization (feeling connected to musicians or socializing with other audience members), and intellectualization (critical/analytical responses). DeVeaux (1995, 1999); Warner (2010); and Farnbauch, Brown, and Yoshitomi (2011) provide syntheses and evaluations of demographic studies. The latter study compiles surveys based in several urban areas to report a number of "high level findings" about jazz audiences: they are relatively diverse; their musical tastes are socially transmitted, often through word of mouth; concert attendance is largely artist-driven; and concertgoers strongly prefer informal settings where they can feel close to the artists. Such quantitative data may help arts organizations market jazz more effectively but can't answer the more interesting questions of how and *why* people commune to listen to jazz.

23. See Ch. 1, n. 30.

24. See www.downtownmusic.net (accessed Aug. 4, 2015).

25. Several notable studies have classified fan behavior: Adorno (1941) segregated pop music masses into body-oriented (dancers) or emotion-oriented (sentimental journeyers); Riesman (1950) divided teen rock'n'rollers into star-seeking, cultists-of-personality ("outer-directed") or critical outsider-aficionados ("inner-directed"); Vermorel (1989) catalogued period-specific dance-mania's; and Levine (1988) described hysteria and commercialization surrounding European opera singers and virtuoso musicians.

26. Cavicchi (1998:95).

27. See Crafts, Cavicchi, and Keil (1993).

28. Information on fans in this book is based on formal interviews with Judy Balos, Richard Berger, Lujira Cooper, Peter Cox, Steve Dalachinsky, Roberta DeNicola, Margaret Davis Grimes, Bruce Gallanter, Lawrence Gibb, Jo Gilks, Rachel Kent, Manny Maris, April Matthis, Harold Meiselman, Yuko Otomo, Irving and Stephanie Stone, and Jerry Sykes, and on informal conversations with other active concertgoers (including music professionals and venue proprietors). There are three married couples in this group: Berger/DeNicola, Dalachinsky/Otomo, and the Stones (both now deceased). Gibb, Gilks, and Sykes, all from England, graciously allowed me to tape their commentary during a jazz tour guided by Gordon Polatnick.

29. This observation is supported by several people I spoke with, including journalist David Adler, Jim Eigo (former Iridium publicist), and writer Gary Giddins, who stated: "Jazz clubs now cater primarily to tourists. When tourists come to New York, jazz clubs are on the 'Things to Do in New York.' . . . So if you go to the [Village] Vanguard on almost any night of the week, a large percent of the people will be either Germans or Japanese—tourists" (interview, Aug. 2003).

30. To identify active members of the numerous cliques and micro-scenes within the greater New York area I looked for people to act as "seeds" by pointing me to others, thereby initiating chains-of-referral, an informal variant of Douglas Heckathorn's (1997, 2002) respondent-driven sampling technique. Besides fans, I also solicited club owners, bar staff, ticket-takers, and other jazz jobbers in various venues and performance spaces to identify the "regulars."

31. For example, most have listened to and can appreciate traditional jazz, swing-era jazz, and modern mainstream jazz, though a few of them are not big fans of free jazz, and many would probably be turned off by smooth jazz.

32. I interviewed the following core members of the avant-jazz community: Berger and DeNicola, Cox, Dalachinsky and Otomo, Davis, Gallanter, Maris, Meiselman, and the Stones. Of these, only Gallanter and Maris make a living from jazz (in record retailing). Although Balos goes to many avant-jazz concerts, she doesn't prioritize them to the extent that these other fans do. Note also that even the most hard-core avant-jazz fans regularly go out to other kinds of music.

33. Jeffri (2003, V.III:5) estimated the racial distribution of New York City jazz musicians based on Respondent Driven Sampling (see Heckathorn and Jeffri 2001), reporting 55 percent white, 33 percent black, 3 percent Hispanic or Latino, and 1 percent Asian respondents; the gender distribution was 74 percent male and 26 percent female. In comparison, as part of the same study (2003, V. II:78), a survey of members of the American Federation of Musicians (AFM) reported 71 percent white, 17 percent black, 2 percent Hispanic or Latino, 1 percent Asian respondents, 85 percent male and 15 percent female.

34. As I write this, over a dozen years after my initial interviews with active fans, I frequently see many of them at shows (except Peter Cox and Irving and Stephanie Stone,

who have since passed). For example, at least six went to see Hermeto Pascoal (a Brazilian jazz artist *not* generally associated with the avant-jazz scene) on Aug. 6, 2010, and at least seven attended the memorial celebration for Peter Cox on Mar. 27, 2013. See also n. 35, this chapter.

35. On July 25, 2014, I bumped into Richard Berger, one of the most active attendees on the avant-jazz scene, at a Nickel Creek (a progressive bluegrass band) concert at Prospect Park Bandshell in Brooklyn, where we chatted about, among other things, Bob Dylan's *Blood on the Tracks* album. Berger praised it highly and claimed that it (the vinyl record) got played at least once a week in his home. I also noticed that Berger's attentive listening and physical and emotional responses to Nickel Creek's music did not seem to differ significantly from his listening and responses to avant-jazz concert music. It therefore makes little sense to pigeonhole someone like Berger as an "avant-jazz fan." A more appropriate description spontaneously popped out of my mouth as I was getting acquainted with one of his friends who'd also come to the event: "Richard's a 'music person.'" Cf. Somoroff's (2014:351–54) conversation with Berger about Neil Young's album *After the Goldrush*.

36. On his website (www.bigapplejazz.com/testimonials; accessed Aug. 6, 2015), tour guide Gordon Polatnick states that he's been "bitten by the jazz bug." Cf. statements by Gary Giddins, Gordon Polatnick, and Jim Eigo in Ch. 5: "Professionals as Amateurs."

37. Liepolt dates the incident 1944; the recording was made in 1925.

38. "Diz" and "Bird" refer to John Birks Gillespie and Charles Parker Jr., respectively.

39. Newark, New Jersey's WBGO is the only all-jazz radio station in the New York City area. Several avant-jazz fans singled out director/deejay/archivist Ben Young at Columbia University's WKCR as an important influence on their listening.

40. Flatbush's Pumpkins, now defunct, formerly featured live jazz seven nights a week; Jazz 966 is a concert program hosted by the Fort Greene Senior Citizens Council.

41. WBGO programs primarily jazz. See also note 39, this chapter.

42. The two slogans are taken from each company's webpage. Amazon hopes that you will like (and buy) items that other people who like what you like bought. Pandora pays analysts to rate recordings along a number of parameters, similar to Alan Lomax's cantometrics system, creating thereby a standard by which to judge the similarity of any two recordings. Similar new commercial releases and rereleases are threaded into your personalized station's playlist, tracks that you may not have heard before but will hopefully like (and buy).

43. See Prouty (2012a).

44. Several people consulted for this book—Fred Cohen, Steve Dalachinsky, Bruce Gallanter, Manny Maris, and Gordon Polatnick—are or were record retailers.

45. See Sidran (1981:66–67).

46. Mosaic savvied that releasing all of their box-sets as limited editions increased the likelihood they'll become collector's items through planned scarcity and thereby retain their financial value. Buyers may be more likely to justify such purchases as "investments."

47. Cf. Gary Giddins's commentary in finding inspiration in reissued recordings and how jazz "constantly cannibaliz[es] its past" in Ch. 5: "Channeling the Muse: Professionals as Co-improvisers."

48. Lincoln Center Tower Records (the last of five in Manhattan) closed Dec. 26, 2006; the Union Square Virgin Megastore (the last of its kind) closed June 14, 2009; J&R Music World closed Apr, 9, 2014.

49. In conversations with Gallanter's former employee Mikey Jones, at that time a youthful adult, I was always struck by the depth of his knowledge about and experience with experimental musics.

50. One fan reported that he often sought the advice of a former employee of Tower Records who had worked in the jazz section for many years and could often give him good suggestions based on his preferences.

51. Pers. comm., Sept. 26, 2014.

52. One of former record retailer Manny Maris's pet jokes goes something like this [*imitating a customer*]: "Hey man, I don't buy this stuff to *listen* to it, I just *collect* it!"

53. *Luminescence* (AUM Fidelity: AUM025), featuring saxophonist Daniel Carter and acoustic bassist Reuben Radding, was recorded shortly after the World Trade Center terrorist attacks.

54. Stone may have meant that wear and tear from needle scratches lowers a record's value on the collectors' market (he had sold much of his collection to what he described as extremely finicky Japanese collectors); more likely he meant that each usage of a record incurs some loss of audio fidelity, gradually lowering the quality of subsequent listening experiences.

55. See n. 38, this chapter.

56. This phrase was coined by jazz critic Ira Gitler (1958) to describe John Coltrane's playing.

57. Meiselman was referring to an internet thread discussing Evan Parker posted on "Speakeasy," a members' forum formerly hosted by JazzCorner.com (www.jazzcorner.com; accessed Aug. 6, 2015).

58. I didn't ask Meiselman if he'd posted these observations, but presumably his insights about Parker could be conveyed to counterparts in cyber communities, influencing them to grow "bigger" ears.

59. Duke Ellington ironically stated in his memoir: "Some people *enjoy* [emphasis added] listening to jazz because somebody told them that they should" (1973:413). And one might ask: Did Stone's friend like Ellington because Artie Shaw told him he should?

60. Located in a basement at the corner of Bleecker and Morton Sts., Studio Henry featured downtown music from 1976–1984.

61. Gallanter told versions of this story at memorials for Peter Cox and Stephanie Stone, and posted another version, available at http://www.sonicyouth.com/gossip/showthread.php?t=105719 (accessed July 24, 2014).

62. Pauline Oliveros's conception of "deep listening" (a term she coined) is simultaneously focused and open/global/receptive (see Baker 2003).

63. Following Constantijn Koopman (2005:88), Prouty (2012a:44) characterizes record-listening experiences as "holistic" when they establish both cognitive and emotional connections for the listener.

64. "Misfortune" is in quotes because Cooper gave it an ironic inflection.

65. Daniel was still going to see Chris Byars's octet when the interview was given.

66. Note that "Caravan" (by Edward Kennedy "Duke" Ellington, Juan Tizol and Irving Mills), "A Night in Tunisia" (by John Birks "Dizzy" Gillespie, and Frank Paparelli), and "Sophisticated Lady" (by Edward Kennedy "Duke" Ellington, Irving Mills, and Mitchell Parish) are all strongly associated with the artists that composed them (Ellington and Gillespie), whereas other standards like "Autumn Leaves" (by Joseph Kosma and Jacques Prévert), "All the Things You Are" (by Jerome Kern and Oscar Hammerstein II) or "Summertime" (by George and Ira Gershwin and DuBose Heyward) are less directly affiliated with a particular jazz artist and/or recording.

67. Racy (2003:40) describes the *sammi'ah* as "a minority within the *tarab* public . . . from different social backgrounds . . . some amateur performers, [who], in terms of their common interest and comparable levels of musical initiation . . . can be viewed as an in-group, somewhat like members of a Sufi order, or brotherhood . . . believed to have a special talent for listening, a gift that has been developed through musical exposure and proper polish." See also Shannon (2003).

68. Hecht (1968:177) describes a flamenco *cabal* as someone who is more eminent than an aficionado (enthusiast), who holds traditional values but "is not a rigid dogmatist closed to innovations," and who has "a unique sensibility, a rich psyche, and an unusual integrity."

69. See Ch. 6 for further discussion.

70. Mueller (2013) argues that record-listeners *ascribe* the quality of liveness to live concert recordings.

71. See Somoroff (2014:61) on avant-jazz fans' preference for live musical experiences.

72. "Out" specifically means outside the key area, but more generally implies an experimental aesthetic, i.e., outside the norm. Cf. Such (1993) and Solis (2008:160–61).

73. Monk's now legendary five-month engagement at the Five Spot, beginning July 18, 1957, is considered a pivotal moment in John Coltrane's career because he'd recently kicked heroin addiction, was making important artistic advances under Monk's mentorship, and was undergoing a spiritual awakening. Monk was notoriously underexposed and underappreciated during his lifetime. In hindsight, Stone's instinct to attend as many of those shows as possible suggests that he had a nose for the jazz action.

74. See Sudnow (1978).

75. Bailey is now deceased.

76. According to Telarc International records publicist Mike Wilpizeski (interview, June 2008) and many musicians I spoke with, CD sales at concerts (where the artist can sign it) have become an increasingly important source of revenue for jazz musicians.

77. Indicating Miles Davis, Wynton Marsalis, Charlie Parker, and John Coltrane, respectively. Marsalis has been a controversial figure in the jazz community, but he's known and respected enough to be referred to by his first name.

78. I have approached people like Sonny Rollins, George Benson, and Wynton Marsalis, enjoying brief informal conversations with them during breaks in shows. On the other hand, when I was assigned a cover story on Pat Metheny for the *New York City Jazz Record*, I was not permitted to speak with him in person or by phone; at his agent's request, I emailed Metheny a list of questions, and then quoted his written responses in the article. See Greenland (2010b).

79. "Us" includes Richard Berger, her husband.

80. Unnamed fans reported by Harold Meiselman (interview, July 2003); Lacy passed on June 4, 2004.

81. Cox was referring to trumpeter Roy Campbell Jr.

82. See earlier discussion of dicent signs in Ch. 1: "Hearing the "Facts" and nn. 8–9.

83. Gordon (1980:104).

84. Conversation reported by Harold Meiselman, (interview, July 2003); Stone often used "motherfucker" affectionately.

85. There is no "music itself," of course, but the phrase signifies an enthusiast's desire to experience music with as few "outside" distractions as possible, whatever those might be.

86. Zorn and Gallanter's statements are from the liner notes of *Irving Stone Memorial Concert* (Tzadik TZ 7611-12, 2004).

87. Ratliff (2003b).

88. Many performances from the concert are available on the Tzadik CD (see n. 86, this chapter). See also Manny Maris's comments in Ch. 6: "More than Music: Heritage, Healing, and "Blood.""

89. Stone is depicted in the lower right-hand corner of the painting on the cover of this book.

90. Campbell was another well-beloved figure on the downtown scene who'd died the month before.

91. The loft era, lasting from the early seventies to the mideighties, peaking around 1976, was a free jazz scene based around musician-owned and -operated performance spaces in the Bowery, East Village, SoHo, and warehouse districts of lower Manhattan. Relatively underdocumented, discussion of the loft era is available in Litweiler (1984), Such (1993), Heller (2005, 2011, 2012), and Currie (2009).

92. Most people (including his wife Stephanie) referred to Irving Stone simply as "Stone." In identifying excerpts from their joint interview I use their first names to indicate which of the two Stones is speaking.

93. Note that here and elsewhere, interview excerpts refer to Irving and Stephanie Stone and Peter Cox in the present tense because they were still alive when the interview was given.

94. The statement attributed to Haden is as reported by Irving Stone.

95. See Ch. 1: "Sounds of Surprise."

96. Earlier during the interview Meiselman had remarked: "I don't think you really want to say, 'Oh yeah, I've heard it before,' because that means it didn't do something *new* for you; it didn't take you somewhere where you hadn't been before. That's what Irving [Stone] would say: he'd say, 'What I'm looking for from a performance is I want the musicians to take me somewhere where I haven't *been*.'"

CHAPTER 3. MAKING THE SCENE

1. Pers. comm.

2. "We" includes Richard's wife Roberta; also mentioned are Abby London-Crawford, Peter Cox, and Kurt Gottschalk. Steve the Postman (Spitzmiller) is elsewhere referred to as Postman Steve or Mailman Steve. Somoroff (2014:194) refers to him as "Steve the Mailman."

3. "The Stones" are Irving and Stephanie; Larry Isacson worked as the jazz/classic buyer/manager at the Lincoln Center Tower Records outlet before it closed; Kurt Gottschalk is an author/journalist/deejay/musician/fan. See n. 2, this chapter.

4. J. D. is an unidentified female; "Richard and Roberta" are Berger and DeNicola.

5. Cf. Introduction: "Roots and Shoots."

6. Tonic is now defunct.

7. Somoroff (2014:148); cf. Schütz (1976).

8. See Berger's comments about Cox in the Prologue.

9. Somoroff (2014:194).

10. "Irving" is Irving Stone; "We've" includes Yuko Otomo, Dalachinsky's wife.

11. Pers. comm., names withheld.

12. Pumpkins and Fatah's store are now defunct.

13. Rachel Kent and April Matthis (both interviewed for this book) have attended countless concerts at Marjorie's house; other active attendees include Bessie, Gertrude, Marvin, Pat, and Ray (I didn't learn their last names).

14. Russ Musto's Village Jazz Shop and Gordon Polatnick's Big Apple Jazz/EZ's Woodshed, both defunct, are two former examples.

15. After many years working with Gallanter, Manny Maris is now (semi-)retired.

16. See Kassel (2014).

17. The Knitting Factory moved to its second location at 74 Leonard St. in TriBeCa in Nov. 1994, significantly altering its musical format; CBGB's ran into financial difficulties, forcing the management to cancel Freestyle Events and eventually close the entire venue in Oct. 2006; drummer Dee Pop, curator of the Sunday night Freestyle Events series, moved his base of operations to Jimmy's 43 (43 E. 7th St., also in the East Village), continuing there until mid-2008.

18. See Somoroff's (2014) discussion of volunteer curators/doorkeepers at Brecht Forum's *Neues Kabarett* concert series and the informal barter system used by avant-jazz record collectors (pp. 216–17).

19. The original Knitting Factory, later referred to as the "Old Knit," was located at 46 E. Houston St. in (what is now known as) Nolita.

20. In Somoroff (2014:135), Yuko Otomo and Steve Dalachinsky problematize the idea of the avant-jazz scene having a single "home" by citing other contemporaneous venues that hosted the music.

21. Mirkin (2000).

22. Lurie (2000).

23. Dorf (2000).

24. Zorn's statement is as reported by Stone.

25. Although he is virtually unknown to the general public, Shepp played an important role in the development of avant-garde jazz.

26. Cf. Dalachinsky's similar comment in this section.

27. See Somoroff's (2014) discussion of avant-jazz activity at Local 269, The Stone, Brecht Forum, Bowery Poetry Club, and the "old" Roulette.

28. See www.downtownmusic.net (accessed Aug 4. 2015).

29. Avant-jazz alto saxophonist Patrick Brennan described it as "the only game in town" (in Somoroff 2014:16).

30. Lyrics from "What Is Hip?" by S. Kupka, E. Castillo, and D. Garibaldi, from *Tower of Power* (Warner Bros.: BS-2681, LP, May 11, 1973).

31. "Keiserens nye Klæder" (orig. Danish title), by Hans Christian Andersen, Apr., 1837.

32. Bourdieu (1984) argues that fans "play" by the tacit rules of their culture to cultivate skill, knowledge, and distinction, but his depiction of competitive and calculative struggle for cultural capital has limited valence in niche fan communities with strong affinities for marginalized music, although here social cachet may be accorded to so-called outsider-ness.

33. Portions of this material have previously appeared in Greenland (2004).

34. For example, Dannen (1991) argues that fans, not corporations, create hit songs, though record companies can squelch potential hits through lack of media exposure.

35. "Talent Deserving Wider Recognition" is part of *DownBeat* magazine's annual poll, calling readership attention to up-and-coming singers, instrumentalists, and groups. While conducting research for this book, two consultants, Jeremy Pelt and Kurt Rosenwinkel, won in their categories.

36. See Ch. 1: "Creating Contexts."

37. From the CD *Modern Cool* (Premonition: 1998).

38. Bennett and Peterson (2004:3). The authors cite Chaney (1996) as their source for the idea of fluid and interchangeable identities.

39. Ch. 2: "Listening In" and n. 42.

40. See Ch. 2, n. 72.

41. *The Penguin Guide to Jazz on CD*, 7th ed. (Cook and Morton 2004).

42. See chapter 2 note 56.

43. In *Look* magazine, Aug. 10, 1954. Ellington had a very idiosyncratic approach to composition and arranging. For example, on his famous recording of "Mood Indigo" the low-pitched trombone plays the highest harmony, while the high-pitched clarinet plays the lowest harmony, giving the arrangement a distinctive timbre.

44. See Grossman and Farrell (1956).

45. In early New Orleans jazz (and its 1940s revival by white musicians, Dixieland), clarinet players filled in the tessitural gap between the high-pitched melody of the trumpet and the low-pitched guide-tone lines of the trombone with fast-moving arpeggios, obbligatos, and melodic filigree, complementing and contrasting with the brass parts.

46. Ch. 2, n. 84.

47. Among the musicians I mentioned were Clifford Brown, Miles Davis, Hank Mobley, and Wes Montgomery, mostly hard-bop stylists.

48. Cf. Davis's comments in Ch. 6: "More than Music: Heritage, Healing, and "Blood."

49. "We" includes Yuko Otomo, Dalachinsky's wife; "Irving" is Irving Stone.

50. Cf. Introduction: "Jazz in New York and New York in Jazz" and nn. 57–58. Although "uptown" originally referred to contemporary classical composers associated with Lincoln Center, jazz people use the uptown and downtown labels to distinguish between mainstream and experimental styles and their associated venues.

51. Once, when I invited an avid avant-jazz fan to a "mainstream" jazz (i.e., *not* avant-jazz) concert, he laughed and shook his head derisively, indicating that that would be a waste of his time.

52. All quotes come from the liner notes of *Irving Stone Memorial Concert* (Tzadik 7611-12, 2004). Eigo is a publicist, Gallanter a record-store owner, and Morris a guitarist. See also Harold Meiselman's statement in Ch. 2: "Listening Out."

53. Liner notes, *Irving Stone Memorial Concert.*

54. "They" includes Stephanie Stone; Monk is Thelonious Monk.

55. Liner notes, *Irving Stone Memorial Concert.*

56. Somoroff (2014:222–23) discusses the same phenomenon, also using Dalachinsky and Yuko Otomo as principal consultants, though his narrative emphasizes the obsessive/addictive aspects of the behaviors and neither he nor Dalachinsky use the term.

57. See Introduction, n. 53, and Ch. 4, nn. 13–14.

58. For example, publications such as *Hot House Jazz, Jazz Inside, New York City Jazz Record, New York Press, New York Times, Village Voice, Time Out: New York*; and websites such as Gotham Jazz (www.gothamjazz.com), Big Apple Jazz (www.bigapplejazz.com), and NYC Jazz Report (www.nycjazzreport.com) (all accessed Aug. 5, 2015).

59. The Downtown Music Gallery has since moved from the Bowery to Chinatown; CBGB's has closed.

60. See n. 19 this chapter. The Cooler (now defunct) was located at 416 W. 14th St. in the meatpacking district, about thirty blocks (or 1.5 miles) away.

61. Bruce is Bruce Gallanter; see also n. 2, this chapter.

62. Barbara Burch (in Somoroff 2014:252).

63. "Wow, Steve..." is Dalachinsky's recollection of the statement. "Do the table" refers to his volunteer gig selling artists' recordings at the annual Vision Festival.

64. The old Knitting Factory often presented simultaneous shows upstairs in the main performance space and downstairs in the "Old Office." Quoting interviews given by Dalachinsky and Otomo six or seven years after the conversations reported here, Somoroff (2014) notes that Dalachinsky is *still* going through the mental machinations of "divided nights." See n. 56, this chapter.

CHAPTER 4. PROVIDING A PLACE AND TIME

1. Terms like *proprietor, manager, club owner, promoter, impresario, curator,* etc., are often imprecise. For example, most jazz "club owners" are actually *business* owners—i.e.,

they own the lease, but not the deed, to the buildings they use—while many others are employees of landlords and leaseholders.

2. Fitzgerald passed away Mar. 20, 2015.

3. *Art Blakey & the Jazz Messengers Live at Sweet Basil* (GNP Crescendo: GNPS-2182, 1985) and *Bud and Bird: Gil Evans & the Monday Night Orchestra Live at Sweet Basil* (Electric Bird: CDJ 671, 1987).

4. Cf. Becker's discussion of art dealers and impresarios (1982:108–29). Becker's model, which emphasizes top-down, "public education" of artistic values to the masses can't account for how audiences, particularly in micro-scenes, discover their own values, then "teach" them to the culture industries. Cf. discussion (pp. 99–100) of Irving Stone and other fans' influence on proprietor Michael Dorf.

5. The Tin Palace, located at 325 Bowery (on the Northeast corner of 2nd St.) in the East Village was opened in 1970 by writer/poet/jazz fan Paul Pines, and was later sold to Jack Sherlock; it presented jazz for most of the 1970s. Free/avant-garde jazz (aka "new music") artists were featured on Sundays. Its name came from ceiling tin that covered the exterior wall to mask a fissure on the building's side. The Tin Palace succeeded another legendary club, Slug's, located nearby at 242 E. 3rd St. (between Aves. B and C), the only other underground/alternative jazz club in the area during that period. Slug's, opened in the early 1960s, began presenting jazz in 1965 (featuring Sun Ra's Arkestra on Mondays) until it closed in 1972, shortly after trumpeter Lee Morgan was murdered there by his common-law wife on Feb. 19, 1972.

6. Russ Musto, a veteran concertgoer who made many connections through his Village Jazz Shop, stated that he knows so many people on the scene that he can usually "just walk in" to shows he wants to see (pers. comm.), but this is unusual.

7. "Town" refers to Philadelphia, where Morris grew up.

8. Cf. Ch. 3: "Musical Chairs: In Search of a Club/house."

9. Gordon (1980).

10. In Balliett (2002:721).

11. Gordon (1980:2).

12. Ibid.

13. Since September 2002, the following venues and locations have closed or discontinued jazz programming: 107 West, American Museum of Natural History, Andiamo, Archer's, Arci's Place, Au Bar, Aurum, Awash Ethiopian Restaurant, Baby Jupiter, Bacchus Room, Baggot Inn, Baton Rouge, b.p.m., Cachaça, Café Creole, Café Largo, Cajun, Il Campanello Ristorante, Carpo's Café, Caviarteria, CBGB's, Center for Improvisational Music, Chez Suzette, Churrascaria Plantation, City Hall Restaurant, Clemente's, C-Note, The Cooler, Copland's Restaurant, Cucina Stagionale, The Cutting Room, Danny's Skylight Room, Deanna's, Decade, De Marco's, The Den, Detour, Don Hill's, Downtime, Duffie's Place, Elixir Smart Bar, EZ's Woodshed, Fez under Time Café, Le Figaro, Fuzion on A, Gishen Café, GoWasabi, Greatest Bar on Earth, Green Room, Guggenheim Museum, Harlem Grill, Hideaway, Hughes House in Harlem, InHouse, Internet Café, Izzy Bar, Jack Rose, Java-n-Jazz, Le Jazz Au Bar, Jesse's Place, Jezebel, Jazz on the Park, Jimmy's Uptown, Judi's,

Justin's, K'av'eh'az, Knitting Factory (Manhattan), Kolonaki Café, Lansky Lounge, Leisure Time Bowling Center, Lima's Taste, The Loft at Quilty's, Louis, Luci's, M & S Front Line, Le Madeleine, Malcom Shabazz Harlem Market & Mosque, Marie's Jazz Bar & Performance Center, Meow Mix, Metronome Jazz Lounge, Minton's, Night & Day, Orbit, Perk's, Phoenix Room, Pod, Po'k Knockers, Porter's, La Prima Donna, Psychic Café, Pumpkins, Il Punto Ristorante, Puppet's Jazz Bar, Red Blazer Hideaway, Redeye Grill, Revival, Riverdale Gardens, River Room, Robin's Nest, Sage Theater, St. Nick's Pub, Sam's, Satalla, Scottie's Lounge, Screening Room, Le Singe Vert, Smith's, Soul Café, Sugar Hill Bistro, Sugar Shack Café, Summit Restaurant, Sweet Basil, Sweet Rhythm, Table XII, Tar Bar, Times Square Brewery, Times Square Grill, Tito Puente's, Tobacco Road, Tonic, Torch, A Touch of Dee, Tower Records (Lincoln Center and East Village), Twenty-Two West, Urban Jem Guest House, Virgin Megastores (Times and Union Squares), Wells' Restaurant, Wilson's Grill & Bar, Windows over Harlem Supper Club, Zip Code, and Zipper Room. Note that neither this list nor the one in n. 14 should be considered up-to-date and/or all-inclusive!

14. Since September 2002, the following venues and locations have opened or initiated jazz programming: 101 Park Avenue, 718 Restaurant, 92YTriBeCa, Alor Café, American Folk Art Museum, Antibes Bistro, Apple Store (Upper West Side), Ardesia Wine Bar, Bar on Fifth, Bassline, Battery Park Plaza, Benoit, Bflat, Big Eyed Blues, Bill's Place, Blackbird's, Bocca, Bohemian Hall & Beer Garden, Branded Saloon, Brooklyn Bridge Park, Brooklyn Lyceum, Burger Bar, Café Orwell, Café Vivaldi, Casaville, Chez Lola, Citigroup Center Plaza, C J Cullens Tavern, Club A Steakhouse, Coco 66, Comix Lounge, Complete Music Studio, Crescent & Vine, Crooked Knife, Damrosch Park, Doma, Domaine Wine Bar, Douglass Street Music Collective, Drom, Duane Park, "For My Sweet" Garden & Event Space, Fort Greene Park, Goodbye Blue Monday, Gospel Uptown, Le Grande Dakar, Henry's, Ibeam, Ibiza Lounge, Jack, Jackie Robinson Park, Joe G's, Kellari Taverna, Knitting Factory (Brooklyn), Korzo, Koze Lounge, Lincoln Center Plaza, Local 269, Louis Armstrong House, Machavelle Sportsbar & Lounge, Marcus Garvey Park, Medgar Evers College, Miles' Café, Moldy Fig, Music Hall of Williamsburg, Nino's Tuscany, North Square Lounge, Notaro, Ocean's 8 at Brownstone Billiards, PeaceLove Café, Le Pescadeux, Le Poisson Rouge, Pomme Café, Rappa Experience, Rhythm Splash, Royale, Rustik Tavern, SEEDS, Shrine, Sintir, Solo Kitchen Bar, Sora Lella, Spike Hill, Sprig, The Stone, Sucre Coffee & Jazz Lounge, Sycamore, Tamboril, Tea Lounge, Temple M, Terraza 7, Thalia Café, Tian, Tomi Jazz, Tutuma Social Club, Village Trattoria, Vino di Vino Wine Bar, Waltz-Astoria, Zeb's, Zip Code, and ZoraSpace.

15. The original Minton's, the reputed "birthplace" of bebop, was open from 1938–1974; Chapter 4, "For Love or Money? The Business of Live Jazz."

16. See www.issueprojectroom.org/about/ (accessed July 5, 2015).

17. Pers. comm.

18. Rent parties, an informal Harlem institution, were often held for the very same reason: to prevent eviction. They usually featured "bathtub gin" and stride piano "cutting contests." See James Weldon Johnson (1927) for an evocative description of such events.

19. Barry (2003); the event took place on Sunday, Nov. 2, 2003.

20. Wein reported he had received a humorous, informal award proclaiming him "God-father of the Jazz Community" (interview, Oct., 2003); born Oct. 3, 1925, he was seventy-eight at the time. Wein was named a Jazz Master by the National Endowment for the Arts in 2005.

21. See Kassell (2011). Started as a nonprofit, the Newport Jazz Festival obtained corporate sponsorship in the seventies.

22. RIAA's *Consumer Profile* indicates sales of jazz recordings accounted for 3.4 percent of the total market in 2002, dropping to 1.8 percent in 2005 and 1.1 percent in 2008.

23. In summer 2001, the Jazz Gallery listed the following sponsors on their website: Rockefeller Brothers Fund, Jerome Foundation, Greenwall Foundation, New York Community Trust, Meet the Composer, Aaron Copland Foundation for Music, New York State Council on the Arts, New York City Department of Culture, and National Endowment for the Arts (see www.jazzgallery.org; accessed Aug. 19, 2001).

24. Fitzgerald provided me with a copy of Weinstein's letter.

25. Email dated Dec. 18, 2002. During his tenure as executive director, Fitzgerald wrote regular emailers to "Jazz Gallerians" who joined the list; those who had paid an annual membership fee were entitled to discount admission, invitations to special events, and other perks (see www.jazzgallery.org; accessed Dec. 18, 2002).

26. Trumpeter Hargrove, one of the biggest "stars" of his generation (early 1990s), initially rented the Gallery as a rehearsal space in 1992 and hired Fitzgerald, his road manager, to take care of various financial matters; three years later it opened as an artistic venue.

27. The Kickstarter Campaign to raise funds for "The Woodshed at The Jazz Gallery" began in July 2011, with the goal, according to Steinglass's newsletter dated July 11, 2011, of providing "750 free rehearsal hours to musicians annually."

28. Fishbein (2003).

29. Ratliff (2003a).

30. Kurt Rosenwinkel, pers. comm.

31. The conversation took place at the entrance to Smalls during business hours, while Borden was simultaneously minding the door. I noticed that he was letting a lot of musicians in for free and asked him why.

32. Christopher and Stache met while bartending at Augie's, a jazz club preceding Smoke on the same site.

33. See Such (1993:76).

34. At the time the concert was held (Dec. 6, 2012), twenty-three-year-old Aldana had been on the scene for three years, so she was a relative "newcomer" by New York standards. The following year, on Sept. 16, 2013, she won the prestigious Thelonious Monk International Jazz Saxophone Competition, the first woman ever to do so, a strong confirmation that Wilner and the audience could recognize exceptional talent when they heard it.

35. Such (1993:76–77).

36. Note that critics themselves have come under fire for not covering these very same musicians.

37. "New York Loft and Coffee Shop Jazz," in *Black Music* (Baraka 1967:94).

38. Ibid., p. 93. See "Apple Cores #1" (ibid., pp. 113–20) for more of Baraka's views on NYC club owners.

39. Cameron (1954) contains insightful discussion of jam sessions, though his psychological profiling of jazz musicians as deviants is dated and problematic.

40. In my early days in the city, around 2002–2003, I often saw jam session participants passing out business cards, hoping someone would call them for a gig. If a newcomer sitting in sounded especially good, other participants would often approach them after the number and ask for their contact information, knowing that they might need to "fill a chair" on an upcoming gig.

41. Mike Davis, pers. comm.

42. In June 2012, the Lenox Lounge's lease expired, raising the rent from $10,000 to $20,000 per month, forcing business owner Al Hirt (who had run it since 1988) to vacate the space.

43. Stewart (2007) provides a detailed overview of the city's contemporary big-band scene.

44. Clubs that canceled big-band programming during the last decade include Cotton Club, Fez under Time Café, Iridium, and Sweet Rhythm, among others.

45. Pers. comm., June 2, 2009.

46. See discussion in Ch. 3: "Musical Chairs."

47. Information in this paragraph is drawn from an interview with Borden (Apr. 2003) and several informal conversations. Cf. previous section on the early days of Smalls and its ensuing financial struggles. One time when I was assigned to cover a show at Smalls, Borden asked me to relinquish my seat near the front to a paying patron, implying perhaps that the press, too, are "sucking off Smalls."

48. Born in Germany of Swedish parents, Liepolt lived over thirty years in Australia before moving to New York City.

49. Guitarist Peter Bernstein, paraphrased in Jackson (2012:105), calls this balance "a form of planned scarcity."

50. Ghost bands, usually big bands named for their deceased leader, continue the legacy by playing the same music (or in the same style). Examples include: The Duke Ellington Legacy Big Band, the [Charles] Mingus Big Band, and the Valery Ponomarev "Our Father Who Art Blakey" Big Band (an Art Blakey tribute band).

51. I previously argued this point—in the context of cruise-ship musicians—in Greenland (2002).

52. That is, drummers' stools.

53. In Taylor (1977:93); the late Garner was a "star" in his day, recording one of jazz's all-time best-selling albums, *Concert by the Sea* (Columbia CL 883, 1955).

54. Gordon (1980:10).

55. See, however, Irving Stone's derisive comments about "Village Vanguard music" in Ch. 6: "More than Music: Heritage, Healing, and 'Blood.'"

56. This claim is based on conversations with journalist David Adler, publicist Jim Eigo, photographer Jack Vartoogian, and my own observations as a jazz journalist/photographer.

57. See Grazian (2003, 2004) on how "authentic" blues is manufactured and sold to tourists and fans in Chicago blues clubs.

58. I have often heard musicians who tour overseas stereotype foreign audiences, especially those listed here, as more knowledgeable and appreciative than U.S. audiences (pers. comm.). See also "Europe: Its Role in Jazz" on saxophonist Dave Liebman's website: www.daveliebman.com/Feature_Articles/europe.htm (accessed July 8, 2012).

59. Compare Wein's assessment of tourist traffic in major clubs with that of Gary Giddins (Ch. 2, n. 29) and David Adler (Ch. 5: "Professionals in the Community").

60. Wein's actual statement was: "New York has a relatively healthy jazz scene. I say 'relatively': the Blue Note, Birdland, the Village Vanguard."

61. Cf. Ch. 3: "What Is Hip? Social Determinants of Taste."

62. From the "Info" submenu on the Village Vanguard website: www.villagevanguard.com/html/information.html (accessed July 8, 2012).

63. Murph (2002:37).

64. "Letters," in *JazzTimes* 32(4):22 (May 2002). Used by permission.

65. See previous section on Paul Stache's use of psychological warfare tactics.

66. Information about the Jazz Gallery's membership policies and other programs comes from the "Membership" menu of its homepage (jazzgallery.org/; accessed July 7, 2011).

67. See n. 27 this chapter.

68. In addition to its relatively accessible, R&B-based style, Christopher noted that organ-trio jazz is effective in mixed crowds because the organ can be played loudly enough to drown out talkative patrons.

69. The group's cover songs during this period included ABBA's "Knowing Me, Knowing You," Aphex Twin's "Flim," Black Sabbath's "Iron Man," Blondie's "Heart of Glass," Gloria Gaynor's "I Will Survive," and "Nirvana's "Smells Like Teen Spirit" (cf. Adler 2005).

70. *The Bad Plus* was released Aug. 2001 on Fresh Sound/New Talent; their sophomore album, *These Are the Vistas*, was released Feb. 2003 on Columbia.

71. Christopher uses Smoke as a theater workshop and has presented his most recent plays there (as readings, special events, or limited runs), including *A Fly in the Fridge* (coauthored) in 2010, and *Flutter By* and *Beyond Blue Light* in 2012 (the latter inspired by Miles Davis's record *Kinda Blue*).

72. The house band consisted of Mike LeDonne (organ), Eric Alexander (tenor sax), Peter Bernstein (guitar), and Joe Farnsworth (drums).

73. Quotes and information in this paragraph come from: "5C Café Needs Your Help," an email posted Jan. 8th, 2007 through Jim Eigo's Jazz Promo Services.

74. See Brown (2012).

75. The extant lease was only $500/year; see Millett (2010).

CHAPTER 5. JAZZ JOBBING

1. My primary consultants for this chapter were Dave Adler, Fred Cohen, Jonathan Daniel, Jim Eigo, Bruce Gallanter, Gary Giddins, Emanuel "Manny" Maris, Gordon Polatnick, Jeff Schlanger, and Jack Vartoogian. Further information was derived from informal conversations with and observations of other professional participants.

2. Jackson (2012:92–99) gives a sketch of the jazz recording industry.

3. I previously investigated the role of jazz professionals in Greenland (2006d, 2013).

4. Daniel Cavicchi defines fans as people who "live a lifestyle based on musical activity" (1998:95). See also Ch. 4: "For Love or Money? The Business of Live Jazz."

5. In a similar vein, I once overheard two jazz critics commiserating at a table next to mine at Iridium, one stating he'd sought psychiatric help because of job-related issues.

6. The most famous of these are *West End Blues* and *Weatherbird*, both with Earl "Fatha" Hines on piano.

7. Gordon (1980:99).

8. The National Book Critics Circle Award for Criticism (1997).

9. See "Quick Notes of Praise" on Polatnick's website: www.bigapplejazz.com/testimonials .html (accessed July 14, 2012).

10. See www.bigapplejazz.com/nycjazzclubs.html (accessed July 14, 2012).

11. See www.bigapplejazz.com (accessed July 14, 2012).

12. Some of the players Polatnick features on his tours include Ron Affif, Greg Bandy, Andrew Bemkey, Walter Blanding, Sedric Choukroun, Seleno Clark, Chip Crawford, Marjorie Eliot, Charles Eubanks, Kathy Farmer, Joel Forrester, Tia Fuller, John Funkhouser, "Captain" Keith Gamble, Patience Higgins, Danny Mixon, Jean-Michel Pilc, Rob Ross, Brandon Sanders, Bill Saxton, Arthur Sterling, JC Stylles, Matt Wilson, Eric Wyatt, and Eri Yamamoto.

13. Polatnick's website states: "We specialize in bringing intimate groups of music fans to off-the-beaten-path venues." (see www.bigapplejazz.com/bebopping.html#about; accessed July 14, 2012). Some of the neighborhood venues he has promoted include 5C Café, American Legion Post #398, Anyway Café, Arthur's Tavern, Bar Next Door, Bill's Place, Creole, Ear Inn, Fat Cat, Garage, Harlem Tap, Kitano, Lenox Lounge, Londel's, Minton's Playhouse, Mo Bay, Parlor Entertainment, Perks, St. Nick's Pub, Showman's, Shrine, Smalls, Smoke, Temple M, and Zinc Bar.

14. The "Greenwich Village Hidden Gems" tour has been discontinued; "mission" and the quote that follows is from: "[Gordon Polatnick's] mission, as he puts it, is 'to reinvigorate the jazz scene . . . by introducing fans to the more authentic and hidden events that occur below the radar of most visitors'" (in *U.S.A. Today*, Sept. 2, 2003).

15. Pers. comm., email, Sept. 15, 2003.

16. See Ch. 2, n. 91.

17. During our interview, Eigo drolly suggested that, like himself, many if not most people in the jazz business are frustrated musicians.

18. The actual title of Charles Mingus's record (Impulse!: AS-54, 1963) was *Mingus Mingus Mingus Mingus Mingus*.

19. Pers. comm., Vision Festival IX, May 24, 2004. These statements reflect Maris's activity in the early 2000s; he seems to have reduced his concertgoing somewhat over the following decade.

20. After seventeen-plus years with the *Times*, Vartoogian resigned over issues of photographic copyrights; his work is still occasionally featured in the publication.

21. See *How to Look at Dance* (Terry, Vartoogian, and Vartoogian 1982), *Afropop: An Illustrated Guide to Contemporary African Music* (Barlow, Eyre, and Vartoogian 1995), *The Living World of Dance: Artistry in Motion* (Vartoogian, Vartoogian, and Garey 1997), and *World Music: A Global Journey* (Miller and Shahriari 2012).

22. Giddins is probably referring to *The Complete Sarah Vaughan on Mercury*, successively released in 1985–1987 in four box-sets.

23. *Embouchure* refers to the physical posture of the mouth while playing an instrument.

24. See previous section.

25. See Ch. 4, "For Love or Money?" on Smalls's changing management and policies.

26. Daniel's statements reflect his activities around the time of our interview. I refer to him here and later in the past tense because he has not been visibly active on the scene in recent years and I have not been in contact with him.

27. See Sudnow (1978), Sloboda (1989), Nachmanovich (1990), and Berliner (1994) for descriptions of how musicians utilize incubation followed by spontaneous action.

28. This legendary attribution, firmly established in jazz folklore, circulates in several variants (e.g., Bailey 1976:1).

29. See Siren (2005:101) and Maritain (1953). For general information on Zen Buddhism's influence on creative arts, see Brinker (1996) and Suzuki (1970). Okamoto (1996) and Ryukyu (2001) describe prescriptive techniques specific to the realization of *Sumi-e* ("black ink") painting.

30. From Section II, para. 4 of Lieberman's undated publication, "Zen Buddhism and Its Relationship to Elements of Eastern and Western Arts." *University of California, Santa Cruz*; from Lieberman's home page: http://artsites.ucsc.edu/faculty/lieberman/zen.html (accessed July 21, 2012).

31. Werner (1996).

32. Rhiannon (2013:127).

33. Schlanger has improv-painted at Abrons Art Center, A Gathering of Tribes, Ali's Alley, The Alternative Museum, Angel Orensanz Arts Center, The Brook, CBGB's Gallery, Clemente Solo Velez Cultural Center, Cornelia St. Café, Drom, Environ, Greenwich House, The Knitting Factory (at both the Houston St. and Leonard St. locations), Kraine, Ladies' Fort, Learning Alliance, Leonard Nimoy Thalia @ Symphony Space, Local 259, Lush Life, Merkin Hall, Miller Theatre, New Music Café, Public Theater, Roulette, St. Nicholas of Myra Church, St. Patrick's Youth Center, St. Peter's Church, Slug's, The Stone,

Studio Infinity, Studio Rivbea, Studio WIS, El Taller Latinoamericano, Tin Palace, Town Hall, the Village Vanguard, and Visiones.

34. International festivals he's participated in include AIM Toronto and the Guelph Jazz Festival in Canada, the Tampere Jazz Happening in Finland, Son's d'Hiver in Paris, and InterPlay! in Berlin.

35. Rubolino (2000:3).

36. Pers. comm.

37. Donohue-Greene (2004:2).

38. See Donohue-Greene (2008) and Somoroff (2014:20, 150–58) for more on Schlanger's art and ethos.

39. Barthes (1991) proposes three modes of listening: "alert" (in expectation of desired cues), "deciphering" (to interpret certain known signs), and "modern" (intersubjective); Truax (1986) advocates parallel formulations: "background" listening (nonengaged), "listening-in-readiness" (for familiar and identifiable cues), and "listening-in-search" (to construct meaning from *un*familiar sounds). In contrast, Oliveros's concept of "deep listening," defined as simultaneous focused *and* open/global/receptive attention, consolidates various modes and levels of attention (cf. Ch. 2, n. 62).

40. Borgo (2005:26–30).

41. Bendix (2000) notes the cognitive and emotional dissonance that scholars experience in maintaining an artificial critical distance in their discourse about music for which they feel close emotional affinity.

42. In former years, Adler wrote this column single-handedly; it is now written by four separate writers (including myself), each covering two shows per month, thus allowing more attention and copy space to each reported performance.

43. See Gennari (2006:186–97) on Balliett's and Williams's writing styles; Gennari's book contains an excellent overview and insightful discussion of jazz's most prominent and influential critics.

44. See discography for citations. Other well-known versions were recorded by Louis Armstrong and Ella Fitzgerald; Coleman Hawkins; Duke Ellington; Joni Mitchell and Herbie Hancock; Lambert, Hendricks & Ross; Charlie Parker; and Sonny Rollins.

45. Milkowski (1999). Redman's recording of "Summertime" is from *Timeless Tales for Changing Times* (Warner Bros 9362-47052-2, 1998).

46. "Indiana" was composed by J. Hanley and B. MacDonald.

47. Other pop groups with songs covered by jazz artists include The Beatles, Beck, Coldplay, Bob Dylan, Jimi Hendrix, Michael Jackson, Nirvana, Prince, Paul Simon, Steely Dan, Sting, and Stevie Wonder.

48. Other jazz artists that have covered pop songs include Don Bradon, Uri Caine, Dave Douglas, Bill Frisell, Robert Glasper, Herbie Hancock, Charlie Hunter, Vijay Iyer, Geoff Keezer, Medeski Martin & Wood, Brad Mehldau, Millennial Territory Orchestra, Jason Moran, Greg Osby, Sexmob, and Curtis Stigers.

49. Giddins (2003:99).

50. See Murray (1976), Murray and Basie (1985), Love (1997), Dahl (2000), and Daniels (2002) for more information on the Midwest territory bands. Bernstein later formed a group called Millennial Territory Orchestra in tribute to the music of these bands.

51. Jost (1975:50).

52. In an interview in Apr. 2003, Gallanter reported that his email list had twenty-four hundred subscribers; the figure is certainly higher now. The Downtown Music Gallery website, www.downtownmusic.com (accessed July 22, 2012), describes the music it carries as: "Underground and Avant Jazz, Art Rock/Pop, Contemporary Classical and the Completely UnCategorizable."

53. Another interpretation is that his tastes align well with those of his clientele—i.e., that there is popular consensus within the avant-jazz scene that certain recent releases are noticeably "better."

54. Giddins is probably referring to *All Music Guide to Jazz*, 4th ed. (Bogdanov, Woodstra, and Erlewine 2002). Hard copies of the guide have since been supplanted by the online version: www.AllMusic.com (accessed Aug. 6, 2015).

55. Since June 2004, I have published jazz articles in *Signal to Noise, AllAboutJazz: New York, Journal of the Society for Ethnomusicology, Jazz.com, New York City Jazz Record*, ABC-CLIO's *Music in American Life* (Edmondson 2013), and *The Grove Dictionary of American Music, 2nd ed.* (Hiroshi Garrett 2013), averaging two to three pieces per month.

56. *AllAboutJazz* (www.allaboutjazz.com; accessed Aug. 6, 2015) is edited by Michael Ricci.

57. At this writing (Apr. 3, 2015), I just received a second email from an artist who'd previously requested permission to send me a CD, mailed one out, and then followed up by asking if I'd received it and when I would be reviewing it. I responded that, in accepting his offer to send the CD, I hadn't committed to writing a review of it; I assured him I'd give it a careful listen and apologized for the misunderstanding.

58. Recordings to be reviewed in *New York City Jazz Record* (formerly known as *AllAboutJazz: New York*) are screened by founders and coeditors Laurence Donohue-Greene and Andrey Henkin. Their decisions are partly based on aesthetic criteria (i.e., what kinds of artists and music—both recorded and live—"should" get reviewed in the paper) and partly on other issues, such as the availability of recordings, local appearances by artists under review, and topicality (i.e., commemorating a recently deceased musician; per. comm.). Because their revenue derives from advertisements placed by local concert venues and other jazz-related businesses, it's in their interest to foster the paper's reputation as a supporter of the local jazz communities. Indeed, the webpage (www.nycjazzrecord.com; accessed Aug. 6, 2015, Chapter 4) describes it as "the city's only homegrown jazz gazette."

59. Pers. comm., name withheld.

60. Laurence Donohue-Greene, pers. comm.

61. From email exchange with Ned Goold, May 2007. "AAJ" refers to the paper's original name (see n. 58, this chapter).

62. Andrey Henkin, email to *New York City Jazz Record* staff, Nov. 17, 2011.

63. When I repeated this anecdote to Lorraine Gordon, she didn't remember taking it down, but speculated that she may have been cleaning or rearranging things at the time.

64. Although Vartoogian wasn't at the show, three witnesses independently confirmed the anecdote.

65. Cf. Ruesch and Bateson's (2008) "metacommunication" (or communication *about* communication), Goffman's (1974) frames-within-frames, and Gates's (1988) use of "signifyin(g)."

66. See pp. 122, 167, 182–83 in re Schlanger's musicWitness® project.

67. See n. 39, this chapter.

68. Pers. comm. See Ch. 4, n. 6.

69. In August, 2015 (as I write this), over a decade after the World Trade Center terrorist attacks, it's not uncommon to see SWAT teams and mandatory bag-check stations, or to hear public service announcements urging people to report unattended bags (possible bombs), in the New York City subway system and other vulnerable public areas like Times Square or the New York Stock Exchange.

70. Email to *AllAboutJazz: New York* editor Laurence Donohue-Greene dated Aug. 3, 2009. Cf. Frank Christopher's comments in Ch. 4, "Curating Creativity: Relating to Musicians."

71. See discussion in "Professionals as Amateurs," this chapter.

72. See Ch. 2, n. 78.

73. Since April 2004, I have occasionally published jazz photographs in *Signal to Noise*, *AllAboutJazz: New York*, and *New York City Jazz Record*.

74. The Vision Festival took place in late May 2004; the Dave Douglas concert was May 15, 2006.

75. Daniel's statements reflect the free-for-all atmosphere of the earlier incarnation of Smalls, which has been altered under new ownership and management policies, though Mitch Borden is still an active presence there. Compare Smalls's policy with Smoke's (see Ch. 4, "Curating Creativity").

76. This observation stands in contrast to Smoke proprietor Frank Christopher's comments in Ch. 4 and may reflect an earlier period (circa 2000–2002) when the venue's attendance policy was more lenient.

77. Note that Polatnick's English website may be less attractive to French, German, Japanese, and Scandinavian jazz fans because of language barriers (see Ch. 4: "Cultivating Clientele: Relating to Audiences" and n. 58).

78. See www.bigapplejazz.com/about_big_apple_jazz_fest.htm (accessed July 12, 2012): see also Ch. 1: "Sounds of Surprise."

79. See n. 10, this chapter.

80. Posted on the "Big Apple Jazz Tour References" section of Polatnick's website, www.bigapplejazz.com/testimonials (accessed Aug. 4, 2004).

81. See Ch. 4 for discussion of how club owners handle talkative tourists.

82. 51st St. and Broadway is in the Times Square neighborhood of Manhattan.

83. Adler's final remark is excerpted from the following exchange: DA: "And they don't care who's playing. And they've got money." TG: "So it's more like the—I mean, this is just

my take on it—the *idea* of jazz: 'Oh, let's go see some *jazz!*'" DA: "Right. Oh, definitely! I think that's *big*; I think that's a big factor, a *very* big factor."

CHAPTER 6. HEAR AND NOW

1. Leonard's comments are from an interview given Feb. 21, 2003.

2. Becker (1982:272) uses this phrase to differentiate "art" from "craft."

3. Wilmer (1970:62–63).

4. Scatting, or scat singing, is vocal improvisation employing nonsense syllables.

5. Cunningham might have been referring to double-timing, defined as playing twice the speed of the underlying pulse (i.e., playing sixteenth notes and sixteenth-note triplets instead of eighth notes), or he might have meant the outlining of additional harmonies within the improvised melodies, akin to the way John Coltrane created "sheets of sound" (Ch. 2, n. 56), or a similar technique sometimes referred to as "harmonic backpeddling."

6. Taylor (1993:95).

7. Gillespie and Fraser (1979:483).

8. Ibid. (279–80).

9. See Taylor (1993:198–99).

10. Liner notes, *Irving Stone Memorial Concert* (Tzadik: TZ7611-2, 2004); Tzadik is Zorn's record label; Sugiyama is Zorn's friend and business partner; "the Stones" are Irving and his wife Stephanie. Ratliff (2003b) reports that Zorn's Lafayette St. apartment was called the Theater of Musical Optics.

11. Weaver moved back to the Charlotte area after a brief stay in New York.

12. See also Ch. 2: "Listening Out," and Ch. 5: "Professionals as Amateurs."

13. Gillespie and Fraser (1979:304).

14. Taylor (1993).

15. Ibid. (136).

16. Ibid (192).

17. Ibid. (111).

18. Ibid. (157).

19. Quotes and paraphrases in this paragraph are from Jackson (2012:189–90).

20. I have personally observed many, many jazz sets, even in some of the more prominent clubs, that follow a strict solo order for *every single* selection: after a statement of the head (or main melody) there are sequential solos by the frontline (horns) and then piano (and/or guitar), bass, and finally drums (which either trade 4's with other instruments or play alone), concluding with a repeat statement of the head.

21. Taylor (1993:153).

22. Such (1993:146–47).

23. Experiments in cognitive science show that subjects' recall for items serially presented is superior for the first items (the "primacy effect") and the last items (the "recency effect"). See Ebbinghaus (1913).

24. At this point in their careers, Hunter and Amendola had been playing together for over ten years, so they had many songs in their collective repertoire.

25. Cf. Leonard Meyer's argument that emotional reaction to music depends on the opposition of and fluctuation between the creation and destruction of expectations (1961:118).

26. See Ch. 1: "Sounds of Surprise"; see also Kernfeld (1988a:562).

27. See Ch. 1: "Creating Contexts" and n. 20.

28. Ellington was famous for constantly rearranging and updating his pieces, perhaps so that they'd stay fresh for himself and the band; see Hasse (1995) and Tucker (1989, 1993).

29. Such (1993:76–77).

30. See Introduction, n. 20.

31. Wilmer (1970:195).

32. Ellison (1964:38).

33. Some material in this chapter has previously appeared in Greenland (2004; 2006b,c; 2007a; 2014).

34. See Sarath (1996) and Borgo (2005:26).

35. Fischlin and Heble (2004:73).

36. Bailey (1992:44).

37. Douglas Daniels, pers. comm.

38. See Introduction, n. 18.

39. See Introduction, n. 20.

40. Lomax (1973:xiii).

41. Now deceased, Hank Jones was at the time a "living legend," the last survivor of an influential jazz dynasty that included his brothers Elvin (drummer) and Thad (trumpeter/composer/arranger).

42. See Somoroff (2014:145–47, 163–67) for examples of how avant-jazz audiences "perform" their acts of listening: through body language that telegraphs a state of "interiority," by "reciprocat[ing] the concentration" of performing musicians, and/or by showing their familiarity with inserted musical quotes.

43. Maria Schneider is a multiple Grammy award winner; Ingrid Jensen is one of her featured soloists. The concert Adler describes featured pianist Renee Rosnes and vibraphonist Joe Locke.

44. At the time, Patrick Frisco was also a (jazz) music director/programmer for WHFR-FM, at Henry Ford Community College, Dearborn, Mich. (see http://whfr.hfcc.net/; accessed Sept. 1, 2012).

45. Douglas is a trumpeter/composer/bandleader/independent label head whose music straddles mainstream and avant-jazz.

46. See Lomax (1973:124).

47. Jackson (2012:82, 152) describes similar acknowledgments between listeners of when performers are "going to the next level" through ritualized expressions of the "blues aesthetic" and alludes to the spiritual dimensions of jazz through statements by saxophonists Antonio Hart and Steve Wilson (122–25).

48. Schlanger, pers. comm.

49. Grimes, a foundational figure in early free jazz, vanished from the New York scene in the late 1960s, only to be discovered in 2003 living in less-than-favorable circumstances in Los Angeles. With the help of bassist William Parker, Margaret Davis Grimes, and others, Grimes was provided with a bass and brought back to New York, where he was again championed by the avant-jazz community, revitalizing his career. The painting was made shortly after Grimes's return to the scene.

50. The people mentioned are Margaret Davis Grimes, Irving and Stephanie Stone, Harold Meiselman, and Peter Cox.

51. After reviewing a draft of this book, in which I had described his painting as an "abstract" image of Henry Grimes, Schlanger asked me to remove the adjective, asserting that his image "is the actual spirit of Henry Grimes listening!" He also wrote that "the painting is actually an 'orienteered' map of the whole development of musical energy during this performance" (pers. email comm., July 8, 2014).

52. See Ch. 3: "What Is Hip? Social Determinants of Taste."

53. See Berliner (1994:485–504).

54. Wilmer (1970:258).

55. Berger and DeNicola have shown no signs of slackening their pace in the ten years since our interview, so Berger's estimate should be revised to *thirty* years of active concertgoing. See also Somoroff's (2014) conversations with Berger and DeNicola (referred to as the Bergers), which reveal similar zeal; and Ch. 3, n. 56.

56. Cf. Richard Berger's comment about oxygen in the Prologue.

57. From an email by publicist Kim Smith, Mar. 31, 2015.

58. Jackson (2012:206).

59. Impulse!: AS-9191, 1969.

60. Speaking in Apr. 2003, DeNicola was referring to the U.S. invasion of Iraq.

61. Bubba Brooks plays tenor sax; the incident took place in Pumpkins, now defunct.

62. On June 8, 2013, a decade after she'd made this statement, Leonard was ordained as an Interfaith/Interspiritual Minister.

63. See Ch. 4: "For Love or Money? The Business of Jazz."

64. Cf. Jonathan Daniel's comment in the previous section.

65. Note that musicians such as the late Yusef Lateef would take issue with the idea of improvisation because it suggests that musical ideas happen by chance, rather than by intention. See Greenland (2006a).

66. Dass (1971).

67. Jackson (2012:206) describes this as a "second register" of musical meaning, accessible when ritualized jazz events become "transcendent experience[s]" through participant interactions.

68. See Ch: 2: "Listening Out" and n. 86.

69. James (1997:59–60).

70. Rouget (1985:73–75).

71. Friedson (1996:5–6).

72. Turner and Turner (1978:250); cf. Introduction, n. 16.

73. Taylor (1993:182).

74. See Ch. 4: "Curating Creativity: Relating to Musicians."

75. Interview with Wilmer (1970:17).

76. Ibid. (62).

77. Gillespie and Fraser (1979:474). Gillespie lists trumpeters Buddy Bolden, King Oliver, Louis Armstrong, Roy Eldridge, Miles Davis, Fats Navarro, Clifford Brown, Lee Morgan, Freddie Hubbard, and himself as messengers (or prophets) of jazz.

78. Ibid. (476).

79. Taylor (1993:182).

80. I previously investigated artist-audience interactions and the confluence of social and spiritual elements at Marjorie Eliot's Parlor Jazz concerts in Greenland (2003). See also Ch. 6, n. 33.

81. See Ch. 1: "Sounds of Surprise."

82. Compare Stone's and Maris's use of "blood" with pianist Cecil Taylor's characterization of "the dilettantish cliques that had recently adopted him": "If you get to know or feel the emotional fibres of these people and you listen to them talk, the talk is always very quiet, very soft and refined, and the taste, oh, the finest taste in books and so on. They're very gentle, they look so pale and anaemic, but they're very bright and they're very witty, and they can't do much of anything really. They can think, but they don't *live!* . . . [*hissing*] There's no fucking *blood!*" in Wilmer (1970:24).

83. Somoroff (2014:145–46), emphasis in original.

84. Otomo was referring to Irving and Stephanie Stone and Steve Dalachinsky.

85. See Ch. 5: "Channeling the Muse: Professionals as Co-improvisers."

EPILOGUE

1. Cf. Ch. 1: "Creating Contexts" and "Sounds of Surprise."

2. Ch. 4: "For Love or Money? The Business of Jazz" and nn. 20–21; see also Wein (2012).

3. Baraka made these comments in reference to Obama's presidency at a Vision Festival panel discussion, "Decolonizing the Music: Reclaiming the Power of Creative Music in Communities of Color," on June 16, 2013; Baraka died on Jan. 9, 2014; see also Ch 4 of this book, nn. 4–10.

4. See Ch. 4: "For Love or Money?"

5. See Introduction, n. 53; Ch. 4: "For Love or Money?" and nn. 13–14.

6. See Ch. 3: "Musical Chairs: In Search of a Club/house," "Fan versus Himself: Divided Nights," and n. 17; Ch. 4: "For Love or Money?" and n. 17.

7. See Ch. 5: "Professional as Amateurs."

8. See Ch. 4: "For Love or Money?" and Figures 12 and 13.

9. See Ch. 4: "For Love or Money?"

10. See Ch. 4: "Cultivating Clientele: Relating to Audiences" and nn. 73–75.

11. I addressed jazz's interaction with global music-cultures in Greenland (2011). In my "Globe Unity" column in the *New York City Jazz Record*, I've reviewed jazz recordings by

artists from different countries (and/or cultures) around the world, including Argentina, Australia, Austria, Belgium, Brazil, Chile, China, Columbia, Cuba, the Czech Republic, Denmark, Finland, France, Germany, Greece, Hawaii, Hungary, Iceland, India, Iran, Israel, Italy, Japan, Korea, Mexico, the Netherlands, New Zealand, Norway, Poland, Portugal, Russia, Scotland, Serbia, Slovenia, South Africa, Spain, Sweden, Switzerland, and Turkey.

12. I discussed these developments in Greenland (2012a,b).

13. See Introduction: "Roots and Shoots."

14. In jazz parlance, up-and-coming musicians are "young lions"; established veterans are "cats."

15. See Introduction: "Roots and Shoots" and n. 50.

APPENDIX

All interviewees from 2002–2004 signed a release permitting the use of their statements and photographs for research purposes; interviewees from 2005 onward were the subjects of articles for *AllAboutJazz: New York* (which became *The New York City Jazz Record* in March 2011), or Ted Gioia's Jazz.com website.

1. *Occupation* refers to each consultant's jazz-related activities at the time of the interview; it does not include "day jobs." Some interviewees have retired or switched occupations since then.

2. Now deceased.

3. See Ch. 4, n. 2.

4. Cox passed away in March 2013.

5. Irving Stone passed away on June 18, 2003, Stephanie Stone on Apr. 11, 2014.

6. Margaret Davis married Henry Grimes in 2007.

7. Ousley passed away on Aug. 13, 2015.

8. Campbell passed away on Jan. 9, 2014.

9. Lateef passed away on Dec. 23, 2013.

10. The International Association for Jazz Education filed for bankruptcy in April 2008.

11. Dorn passed away on Dec. 12, 2007.

REFERENCES

Adams, Rebecca G., and Robert Sardiello, eds. 2000. *Deadhead Social Science: You Ain't Gonna Learn What You Don't Want to Know*, 3rd ed. Walnut Creek, Calif.: AltaMira Press.

Adler, David. 2005. "Jazz Beat: The Bad Plus and the State of Jazz." *New Republic Online*. http://adlermusic.com/C119771372/E1963307061/Media/Bad%20Plus%20TNR.pdf (Feb. 14, 2005; accessed July 10, 2012).

Adorno, Theodor W. 1941. "On Popular Music." *Studies in Philosophy and Social Science* 9(1):17–48; reprinted in: *On Record: Rock, Pop and the Written Word*, ed. Simon Frith and Andrew Goodwin, 301–19. 1990. New York: Pantheon.

Anderson, Benedict. 1991 (c. 1983). *Imagined Communities: Reflections on the Origin and Spread of Nationalism*, rev. ed. London: Verso.

Appadurai, Arjun. 1993. "Disjuncture and Difference in the Global Cultural Economy." *The Cultural Studies Reader* 2nd ed., ed. Simon During, 220–30. New York: Routledge.

Bailey, Derek. 1992 (c. 1980). *Improvisation: Its Nature and Practice in Music*. New York: Da Capo.

Bailey, Phil. 1976. *Charlie Parker: All Bird*, ed. Jamey Aebersold. New Albany, Ind.: Jamey Aebersold Jazz, Inc.

Baker, Alan. 2003. "An Interview with Pauline Oliveros," recording and transcript. *American Mavericks*. American Public Media, online archives. http://musicmavericks.publicradio.org/features/interview_oliveros.html (Jan. 2003; accessed Aug. 23, 2013).

Baker, Houston A., Jr. 1984. *Blues, Ideology and Afro-American Literature: A Vernacular Theory*. Chicago: University of Chicago Press.

Baldwin, James. 1961. "The Black Boy Looks at the White Boy." *Nobody Knows My Name: More Notes of a Native Son*. 1992 (c. 1954–1961). New York: Dial Press.

Balliett, Whitney. 1959. *The Sound of Surprise: 46 Pieces on Jazz*. New York: Dutton.

———. 2002 (c. 2000). *Collected Works: A Journal of Jazz 1954–2001*. New York: St. Martin's Griffin.

Baraka, Amiri (LeRoi Jones). 1963. *Blues People: Negro Music in White America*. New York: William Morrow and Company, Inc.

———. 1967. *Black Music*. New York: Quill.

———. 1991. "The 'Blues Aesthetic' and the 'Black Aesthetic': Aesthetics as the Continuing Political History of a Culture." *Black Music Research Journal* 11(2):101–9.

Barlow, Sean, Banning Eyre, and Jack Vartoogian. 1995. *Afropop: An Illustrated Guide to Contemporary African Music*. New York: Book Sales.

Barry, Dan. 2003. "Sweet Sounds Ease the Pain, Then and Now." *New York Times*, Nov. 1, 2003.

Barthes, Roland. 1991. "Listening." *The Responsibility of Forms: Critical Essays on Music, Art and Representation*, trans. Richard Howard, 245–47. Berkeley: University of California Press.

Barzel, Tamar. 2000. "Jewsapalooza: Postmodern Jazz Meets New York's Jewish Alternative Movement," paper given at Toronto 2000: Joint Intersections/Annual Meeting of the American Musicological Society (Nov. 2, 2000).

———. 2002. "If Not Klezmer, Then What? Jewish Music and Modalities on New York City's 'Downtown' Music Scene." *Michigan Quarterly Review* (Winter 2002).

———. 2005. "'Rootless Cosmopolitans,' 'Selfhaters' Orchestra,' 'Jews and the Abstract Truth': Theorizing Jewish Identity on New York City's 1990's Downtown Scene," paper given at "Improvising American," the 2nd Annual Kansas University Interdisciplinary Jazz Colloquium (Mar. 3, 2005).

———. 2012. "The Praxis of Composition-Improvisation and the Poetics of Creative Kinship." *Jazz/Not Jazz: The Music and Its Boundaries*, ed. David Ake, Charles Hiroshi Garrett, and Daniel I. Goldmark, 171–89. Berkeley: University of California Press.

Bauman, Richard. 1984 (c. 1977). *Verbal Art as Performance*. Prospect Heights, Ill.: Waveland Press, Inc.

Becker, Howard S. 1982. *Art Worlds*. Berkeley: University of California Press.

Bell, Catherine. 1992. *Ritual Theory, Ritual Practice*. New York: Oxford University Press.

Bendix, Regina. 2000. "The Pleasures of the Ear: Toward an Ethnography of Listening." *Cultural Analysis* 1:33–50.

Bennett, Andy. 2000. *Popular Music and Youth Culture: Music, Identity and Place*. New York: St. Martin's Press.

———. 2002. "Music, Media and Urban Mythscapes: A Study of the Canterbury Sound." *Culture and Society* 24(1):107–20.

Bennett, Andy, and Richard A. Peterson, eds. 2004. *Music Scenes: Local, Translocal and Virtual*. Nashville: Vanderbilt University Press.

Berger, Peter, and Thomas Luckmann. 1967. *The Social Construction of Reality: A Treatise in the Sociology of Knowledge*. Harmondsworth, England: Penguin Books.

Berliner, Paul F. 1994. *Thinking in Jazz: The Infinite Art of Improvisation*. Chicago: University of Chicago Press.

Blowers, Geoffrey, and John Bacon-Shone. 1994. "On Detecting Differences in Jazz: A Reassessment of Comparative Methods of Measuring Perceptual Veridicality." *Empirical Studies of the Arts* 12(1):41–58.

Bogdanov, Vladimir, Chris Woodstra, and Stephen Thomas Erlewine. 2002. *All Music Guide to Jazz*, 4th ed. Milwaukee: Backbeat Books.

Bohlman, Philip V., Edith L. Blumhofer, and Maria M. Chow. 2006. *Music in American Religious Experience*. New York: Oxford University Press.

Borgo, David. 2005. *Sync or Swarm: Improvising Music in a Complex Age*. New York: Continuum Publishing.

Bourdieu, Pierre. 1984. *Distinction: A Social Critique of the Judgment of Taste*, trans. Richard Nice. Cambridge: Harvard University Press.

Brackett, John. 2008. *John Zorn: Tradition and Transgression*. Bloomington: Indiana University Press.

Brand, Gail, John Sloboda, Ben Saul, and Martin Hathaway. 2012. "The Reciprocal Relationship between Jazz Musicians and Audiences in Live Performances: A Pilot Qualitative Study." *Psychology of Music* (Sept.) 40(5):634–51.

Bregman, Albert. 1990. *Auditory Scene Analysis: The Perceptual Organization of Sound*. Cambridge: MIT Press.

Brinker, Helmut. 1996. *Zen: Masters of Meditation in Images and Writing*. Honolulu: University of HI Press.

Brooker, Will, and Deborah Jermyn, eds. 2003. *The Audience Studies Reader*. New York: Routledge.

Brown, Rex H. 2012. "DocuDrama: 5C Cultural Center Avoids Eviction, but at a Price." *Local East Village*. http://eastvillage.thelocal.nytimes.com/2012/03/29/the-war-is-over-5c-cultural-center-no-longer-under-threat-of-eviction/ (Mar. 29, 2012; accessed Aug. 20, 2012).

Burkhalter, Thomas. 2013. *Local Music Scenes and Globalization: Transnational Platforms in Beirut*. New York: Routledge.

Burland, Karen, and Stephanie E. Pitts. 2010. "Understanding Jazz Audiences: Listening and Learning at the Edinburgh Jazz and Blues Festival." *Journal of New Music Research* 39(2):125–34.

———, eds. 2014. *Coughing and Clapping: Investigating Audience Experience*. London: Ashgate Press.

Butterfield, Matthew W. 2010a. "Participatory Discrepancies and the Perception of Beats in Jazz." *Music Perception: An Interdisciplinary Journal* 27(3):157–76.

———. 2010b. "Race and Rhythm: The Social Component of the Swing Groove." *Jazz Perspectives* 4(3):301–35.

————. 2011. "Why Do Jazz Musicians Swing Their Eighth Notes?" *Music Theory Spectrum—The Journal for the Society for Music Theory* 33(1):3–26, 107.

Cameron, William Bruce. 1954. "Sociological Notes on the Jam Session." *Social Forces* 33(2):177–82.

Cavicchi, Daniel. 1998. *Tramps like Us: Music and Meaning among Springsteen Fans.* New York: Oxford University Press.

Chaney, David. 1996. *Lifestyles.* New York: Routledge.

Clifford, Amber. 2007. "Queering the Inferno: Space, Identity and Kansas City's Jazz Scene." PhD diss., University of Kansas.

Cohen, Sara. 1991. *Rock Culture in Liverpool: Popular Music in the Making.* Oxford, U.K.: Oxford University Press.

Cook, Richard, and Brian Morton. 1993. "Ethnography and Popular Music Studies." *Popular Music* 12(2):123–38.

————. 2004. *The Penguin Guide to Jazz on CD,* 7th ed. New York: Penguin Books.

Crafts, Susan D., Daniel Cavicchi, Charles Keil, and the Music in Daily Life Project. 1993. *My Music: Explorations of Music in Daily Life.* Middletown, Conn.: Wesleyan University Press.

Cross, Ian. 2011. "Music as Social and Cognitive Process." *Language and Music as Cognitive Systems,* ed. P. Rebuschat, M. Rohrmeier, J. Hawkins, and I Cross, 315–28. Oxford, U.K.: Oxford University Press.

Cross, Ian, and Irène Deliège. 1993. "Cognitive Science and Music: An Overview." *Contemporary Music Review, Special Issue: Music and the Cognitive Sciences* 9:1–6.

Cruz, John, and Justin Lewis, eds. 1994. *Viewing, Reading, Listening: Audiences and Cultural Reception.* Boulder: Westview Press.

Currie, Scott. 2009. *Sound Visions: An Ethnographic Study of Avant-garde Jazz in New York City.* PhD diss., New York University.

Curtis, Helena, and N. Sue Barnes. 1989. *Biology,* 5th ed. New York: Worth Publishers, Inc.

Dahl, Linda. 1984. *Stormy Weather: The Music and Lives of a Century of Jazzwomen.* New York: Pantheon.

————. 2000. *Morning Glory: A Biography of Mary Lou Williams.* New York: Pantheon.

Dance, Stanley. 1994. "The Assault on Marsalis." *Jazz Journal* 47(5):14–15 (May 1994).

————. 2000 (c. 1970). *The World of Duke Ellington.* New York: Da Capo.

Daniels, Douglas Henry. 2002. *Lester Leaps In: The Life and Times of Lester "Pres" Young.* Boston: Beacon Press.

Dannen, Fredric. 1991 (c. 1990). *Hitmen: Power Brokers and Fast Money inside the Music Business.* New York: Vintage.

Dass, Ram. 1971. *Be Here Now.* San Cristobal, N.M.: Lama Foundation.

Davis, Angela. 1998. *Blues Legacies and Black Feminism: Gertrude "Ma" Rainey, Bessie Smith and Billie Holiday.* New York: Random House.

Davis, Francis. 1986. "In the Macho World of Jazz, Don't Ask, Don't Tell." *New York Times,* Sept. 1, 1986, Sec. 1:19, 21.

———, moderator. 2001. "Destination Out." Talking Jazz: Three Conversations. Panelists Gary Burton, Andy Bey, Fred Hersch, Charlie Kohlhase, Grover Sales. National Arts Journalism Program. Village Vanguard, New York. http://www.najp.org/events/talkingjazz/transcript1.html (Apr. 26, 2001; accessed Aug. 9 2013).

———. 2002. "Music: In the Macho World of Jazz, Don't Ask, Don't Tell." *New York Times*. http://www.nytimes.com/2002/09/01/arts/music-in-the-macho-world-of-jazz-don-t-ask-don-t-tell.html (Sept. 1, 2002; accessed Aug. 9, 2013).

Deutsch, Diana, ed. 1982. *Psychology of Music*. New York: Academic Press.

DeVeaux, Scott. 1995. *Jazz in America: Who's Listening*. Research Division Report #31. National Endowment for the Arts. Carson, Calif.: NEA/Seven Locks Press.

———. 1997. *The Birth of Bebop: A Social and Musical History*. Berkeley: University of California Press.

———. 1999. "Jazz: Who's Listening." *Jazz Journalists of America*. http://www.jazzhouse.org/library/?read=deveaux1 (accessed July 11, 2014).

Donohue-Greene, Laurence. 2004. "Vision of the musicWitness®." *AllAboutJazz*, online archives. http://www.allaboutjazz.com/php/article.php?id=2009 (May 9, 2004; accessed Aug. 6, 2004).

———. 2008. "musicWitness®: The Other Dimension of Sound." *Signal to Noise: The Journal of Improvised and Experimental Music* 49:28–35.

Dorf, Michael. 2000. Letter to the Editor. *New Times–L.A.*, Sept. 7, 2000.

Dowling, W. Jay, and Dane Harwood. 1986. *Music Cognition*. New York: Academic Press.

Duranti, Alessandro. 1986. "The Audience as Co-author." *Text* 6 (3):239–47.

Dyson, Michael Eric. 2003. *Open Mike: Reflections on Philosophy, Race, Sex, Culture and Religion*. New York: Basic Civitas Books.

Ebbinghaus, Herman. 1913 (c. 1885). *Memory: A Contribution to Experimental Psychology*, trans. Henry A. Ruger and Clara E. Bussenius. New York: Teachers College, Columbia University.

Ellington, Edward Kennedy ("Duke"). 1973. *Music Is My Mistress*. New York: Da Capo.

Ellison, Ralph. 1964 (c. 1953). *Shadow and Act*. New York: Random House.

———. 2001 (c. 1955). "The Art of Fiction: An Interview." *Living with Music: Ralph Ellison's Jazz Writings*, ed. Robert G. O'Meally, 167–83. New York: The Modern Library.

Enstice, Wayne, and Janis Stockhouse. 2004. *Jazzwomen: Conversations with Twenty-One Musicians*. Bloomington: Indiana University Press.

Fabre, Geneviève, and Robert G. O'Meally, eds. 1994. *History and Memory in African American Culture*. New York: Oxford University Press.

Farnbauch, Christy, Alan Brown, and Jerry Yoshitomi. 2011. "Jazz Audiences Initiative National Convening." *Jazz Arts Group*. http://www.jazzartsgroup.org/wp-content/uploads/2011/10/JAINationalConvening_FinalReport.pdf (accessed July 16, 2014).

Faulkner, Robert R., and Howard S. Becker. 2009. *Do You Know . . . ? The Jazz Repertoire in Action*. Chicago: University of Chicago Press.

Finnegan, Ruth. 1989. *The Hidden Musicians: Music-Making in an English Town*. Cambridge: Cambridge University Press.

Fischlin, Daniel, and Ajay Heble, eds. 2004. *The Other Side of Nowhere: Jazz Improvisation and Communities in Dialogue*. Middletown, Conn.: Wesleyan University Press.

Fishbein, Jennifer. 2003. "The City's Jazz Mecca—Smalls—Will Close Its Doors for Good." *New York Sun*, May 30, 2003.

Floyd, Samuel A., Jr. 1991. "Ring Shout! Literary Studies, Historical Studies and Black Music Inquiry." *Black Music Research Journal* 11(2):265–87.

———. 1995. *The Power of Black Music: Interpreting Its History from Africa to the United States*. New York: Oxford University Press.

Friedson, Steven M. 1996. *Dancing Prophets: Musical Experience in Tumbuka Healing*. Chicago: University of Chicago Press.

Frith, Simon, and Andrew Goodwin, eds. 1990. *On Record: Rock, Pop and the Written Word*. New York: Pantheon.

Gann, Kyle. 1997. *American Music in the Twentieth* Century. New York: Schirmer.

———. 2005. "Downtown Music and Its Misrepresentations." http://www.artsjournal.com/postclassic/archives20050301.shtml (Mar. 8, 2005; accessed Mar. 21, 2005).

———. 2006. *Music Downtown: Writings from the Village Voice*. Berkeley: University of California Press.

Garofalo, Reebee. 1997. *Rockin' Out: Popular Music in the USA*. Boston: Allyn and Bacon.

Gates, Henry Louis, Jr. 1988. *The Signifying Monkey: A Theory of Afro-American Literary Criticism*. New York: Oxford University Press.

Gavin, James. 2001. "Gay and Unhappy" (cover title); "The Most Democratic Music? Homophobia in Jazz" (inside title). *Jazz Times*, Dec. 2001, 66–70.

Geertz, Clifford. 1973. "Thick Description: Toward an Interpretive Theory of Culture." *The Interpretation of Cultures*, 3–30. New York: Basic Books.

Gennari, John. 2006. *Blowin' Hot and Cool: Jazz and Its Critics*. Chicago: University of Chicago Press.

Giddens, Anthony. 1979. *Central Problems in Social Theory: Action, Structure and Contradiction in Social Analysis*. Berkeley: University of California Press.

———. 1984. *The Constitution of Society: Outline of a Theory of Structuration*. Berkeley: University of California Press.

———. 1993. *New Rules of Sociological Method: A Positive Critique of Interpretive Sociologies*, 2nd ed. Stanford: Stanford University Press.

Giddins, Gary. 1985. *Rhythm-a-ning: Jazz Tradition and Innovation in the '80s*. New York: Oxford University Press.

———. 1998. *Visions of Jazz: The First Century*. New York: Oxford University Press.

———. 2003. "Out of the Territories: Steven Bernstein's Old-Timey Jazz Comes In from the Cold." *Village Voice*, Jan. 22–28, 2003, 99–100.

Gilbert, Jeremy. 1999. "White Light/White Heat: *Jouissance* beyond Gender in the Velvet Underground." *Living through Pop*, ed. Andrew Blake, 31–48. London: Routledge.

Gillespie, Dizzy, and Al Fraser. 1979. *To Be or Not to Bop: Memoirs of Dizzy Gillespie with Al Fraser*. New York: Da Capo.

Gioia, Ted. 1988. *The Imperfect Art: Reflections on Jazz and Modern Culture*. Stanford, Calif.: Stanford Alumni Association.

Gitler, Ira. 1958. Liner Notes to *Soultrane*. John Coltrane. Prestige 7142, LP.

Goffman, Irving. 1986 (c. 1974). *Frame Analysis: An Essay on the Organization of Experience*. Boston: Northeastern University Press.

Gordon, Lorraine. 2002. "Cold School Flow" (letter to the editor). *Jazz Times*, May 2002, 22.

Gordon, Max. 1980. *Live at the Village Vanguard*. New York: Da Capo.

Grahn, Jessica A., and Matthew Brett. 2007. "Rhythm and Beat Perception in Motor Areas of the Brain." *Journal of Cognitive Neuroscience* 19(5):893–906.

Gray, John. 2007. *Fandom: Identities and Communities in a Mediated World*. New York: New York University Press.

Grazian, David. 2003. *Blue Chicago: The Search for Authenticity in Urban Blues Clubs*. Chicago: University of Chicago Press.

———. 2004. "The Symbolic Economy of Authenticity in the Chicago Blues Scene." *Music Scenes: Local, Trans-Local and Virtual*, ed. Andy Bennett and Ralph A. Peterson, 31–47. Nashville: University of Vanderbilt Press.

Greenland, Thomas H. 2002. "Mutiny on the Boundary or Microcosmopolitanism? Theorizing Transience in Cruise Ship Communities," paper given at the 47th Annual Meeting of the Society for Ethnomusicology, Estes Park, Colo. (Oct. 26, 2002).

———. 2003. "We Hear Ya Talkin': Audience-Artist Dynamics in Jazz Performance," paper given at the 48th Annual Meeting of the Society for Ethnomusicology, SEM/CMS/ATMI Joint Association Meeting, Miami, Fla. (Oct. 4, 2003).

———. 2004. "Hearing the Listeners and Performing the Players: "Socio-musical Intercourse in the Jazz Village," paper given at the 49th Annual Meeting of the Society for Ethnomusicology, Tucson, Ariz. (Nov. 7, 2004).

———. 2006a. "Yusef Lateef: Roots and Routes." *All about Jazz: New York* 45 (Jan. 2006):1, 9.

———. 2006b. "Uniquely New York: Collective Improvisation in the Jazz Village," invited lecture at the University of Wisconsin, Eau Claire, Wis. (Feb. 24, 2006).

———. 2006c. "Social Synergy and Mutual Musicking: Audience-Artist Interaction, Intermediation and Improvisation in Jazz Performances," paper given at the Northeast Chapter of the Society for Ethnomusicology's annual conference, Trinity College, Hartford, Conn. (Apr. 8, 2006).

———. 2006d. "Comping the Changes: Musical Professionals in the New York City Jazz Scene," paper given at the Society for Ethnomusicology's 51st Annual Conference, Honolulu (Nov. 18, 2006).

———. 2007a. "Improvising Community: Artist-Audience Interaction in Jazz," paper given at the Mid-Atlantic Chapter of the Society for Ethnomusicology and The Mid-Atlantic Folklife Association Joint Conference, College of William and Mary, Williamsburg, Va. (Mar. 30, 2007).

———. 2007b. *Pilgrims in the Big Apple: Improvisation, Interaction and Inspiration in the Jazz Village*. PhD diss., University of California, Santa Barbara.

———. 2010a. "Jazz Internet-works: Improvising Imagined Communities," paper given at the annual meeting of the Mid-Atlantic Chapter of the Society for Ethnomusicology, Charlottesville, Va. (Mar. 13, 2010).

———. 2010b. "Pat Metheny: One Man's Band." *All about Jazz: New York* 97 (May 2010):1, 9.

———. 2011. "Lingua Franca or Local Vernaculars? Jazz Hybridity in a World of Music," paper given at the 56th annual meeting of the national Society for Ethnomusicology, Philadelphia, Pa. (Nov. 17, 2011).

———. 2012a. "Colorizing the 'Classics': Hybrid Identities in *Hindustānī, Karṇāṭic* and Jazz Musi-cultures," paper given at the annual meeting of the Mid-Atlantic Chapter of the Society for Ethnomusicology in Williamsburg, Va. (Apr. 1, 2012).

———. 2012b. "When *Rāga* Meets Jazz: Contemporary Fusions of *Hindustānī, Karṇāṭic* and Jazz Improvisation," paper given at the annual meeting of the Northeast Chapter of the Society for Ethnomusicology in Medford, Mass. (Apr. 14, 2012).

———. 2013. "Hear and Now: Creating Shared Improvisational Spaces," paper given at the Northeast Chapter of the Society for Ethnomusicology's annual meeting, Brunswick, Maine (Apr. 20, 2013).

———. 2014. "The Sound of Listening: Audiences as Co-improvisers," paper given at the Northeast Chapter of the Society for Ethnomusicology's annual conference, Wheaton College, Norton, Mass. (Apr. 5, 2014).

Griffin, Farah Jasmine. 2001. *If You Can't Be Free, Be a Mystery: In Search of Billie Holiday.* New York: Free Press.

Grossman, William L., and Jack W. Farrell. 1956. *The Heart of Jazz,* 1st ed. New York: New York University Press.

Hajdu, David. 1996. *Lush Life: A Biography of Billy Strayhorn.* New York: North Point Press.

Hall, Stuart. 1980 (c. 1973). "Encoding/Decoding." *Culture, Media, Language: Working Papers in Cultural Studies, 1972–79,* ed. Stuart Hall, Dorothy Hobson, Andrew Lowe, and Paul Willis, 128–38. London: Hutchinson.

Hall, Stuart, and Tony Jefferson, eds. 1976. *Resistance through Rituals.* London: Routledge.

Hallam, Susan, Ian Cross, and Michael Thaut. 2009. *The Oxford Handbook of Musical Psychology.* Oxford, U.K.: Oxford University Press.

Handy, D. Antoinette. 1998. *Black Women in American Bands and Orchestras,* 2nd ed. Lantham, Md.: Scarecrow Press.

Hanna, Judith Lynne. 1983. *The Performer-Audience Connection: Emotion to Metaphor in Dance and Society.* Austin, Tex.: University of Texas Press.

Harris, Keith. 2000. "Roots? The Relationship between the Global and the Local within the Extreme Metal Scene." *Popular Music* 19:13–30.

Hasse, John Edward. 1995. *Beyond Category: The Life and Genius of Duke Ellington.* New York: Da Capo.

Hebdige, Dick. 1979. *Subculture: The Meaning of Style.* London: Routledge.

Heble, Ajay, and Gillian Siddall. 2000. "Nice Work if You Can Get It." *Landing on the Wrong Note: Jazz, Dissonance and Critical Practice,* 141–65. London: Routledge.

Hecht, Paul. 1968. *The Wind Cried: An American's Discovery of the World of Flamenco.* New York: The Dial Press, Inc.

Heckathorn, Douglas D. 1997. "Respondent-Driven Sampling: A New Approach to the Study of Hidden Populations." *Social Problems* 44(2):174–99.

———. 2002. "Performance-Driven Sampling II: Deriving Valid Population Estimates from Chain-Referral Samples of Hidden Populations." *Social Problems* 49(1):11–34.

Heckathorn, Douglas, and Joan Jeffri. 2001. "Finding the Beat: Using Respondent-Driven Sampling to Study Jazz Musicians." *Poetics* 28:307–29.

Heimlich, Joe E. 2011. "Jazz Audiences Initiative: Report #1: Music Listening Study." *Jazz Arts Group.* http://www.jazzartsgroup.org/wp-content/uploads/2011/01/JAIListening Study_FinalReport.pdf (accessed July 16, 2014).

Heller, Michael. 2005. "Loft Jazz." *Vision Festival: Peace,* ed. Patricia Parker. New York: Art for Arts.

———. 2011. "Complaining Time Is Over: Network and Collective Strategies of the New York Musicians Organization." *Jazz Research Journal* 5(1–2):21–41.

———. 2012. *Reconstructing We: History, Memory and Politics in a Loft Jazz Archive.* PhD diss., Harvard University.

Hentoff, Nat. 2001. "Testosterone Is Not an Instrument." *JazzTimes* 31(6):166.

Herskovits, Melville J. 1970 (c. 1941). *The Myth of the Negro Past.* Boston: Beacon Press.

Hills, Matt. 2002. *Fan Cultures.* New York: Routledge.

Hodkinson, Paul. 2002. *Goth, Identity, Style and Subculture.* Oxford, U.K.: Berg.

Holbrook, Morris B., and Joel Huber. 1983. "Detecting the Differences in Jazz: A Comparison of Methods for Assessing Perceptual Veridicality in Applied Aesthetics." *Empirical Studies of the Arts* 1(1):35–53.

Isoardi, Steven L. 2006. *The Dark Tree: Jazz and the Community Arts in Los Angeles.* Berkeley: University of California Press.

Iyer, Vijay. 1998. "Microstructures of Feel, Macrostructures of Sound: Embodied Cognition in West African and African-American Musics." PhD diss., University of California, Berkeley.

Jackson, Travis. 2003. "Jazz Performance as Ritual: The Blues Aesthetic and the African Diaspora." *The African Diaspora: A Musical Perspective,* ed. Ingrid Monson, 23–82. New York: Routledge.

———. 2012. *Blowin' the Blues Away: Performance and Meaning on the New York Jazz Scene.* Berkeley: University of California Press.

James, William. 1997 (c. 1912). *The Varieties of Religious Experience: A Study in Human Nature.* New York: Simon and Schuster.

Jeffri, Joan. 2003. *Changing the Beat: A Study of the Worklife of Jazz Musicians,* 3 vols. Research Center for Arts and Culture. Washington, D.C.: NEA Research Division Report #43.

Johnson, James Weldon. 1927. *Autobiography of an Ex-Coloured Man.* New York: Alfred A. Knopf.

Jost, Ekkehard. 1975. *Free Jazz.* Graz, Vienna: Universal Edition.

Juslin, Patrik N., and John A. Sloboda. 2010. *Handbook of Music and Emotion: Theory, Research, Applications.* Oxford, U.K.: Oxford University Press.

Kassel, Matthew. 2014. "What Is the Future of Jazz in New York?" *Observer/Culture.* http://observer.com/2014/02/what-is-the-future-of-jazz-in-new-york/ (accessed Apr. 11, 2015).

Kassell, Dan. 2011. "George Wein's Foundation Already Set for Newport Festivals in 2012," article on *All about Jazz* website: www.allaboutjazz.com/php/news.php?id=84988 (July 30, 2011; accessed Aug. 24, 2011).

Keil, Charles M. 1994a (c. 1966). "Motion and Feeling through Music." *Music Grooves: Essays and Dialogues,* Charles Keil and Steven Feld, 53–76. Chicago: University of Chicago Press.

———. 1994b (c. 1987). "Participatory Discrepancies and the Power of Music." *Music Grooves: Essays and Dialogues,* Charles Keil and Steven Feld, 96–108. Chicago: University of Chicago Press.

Kernfeld, Barry D. 1988a. "Improvisation." *The New Grove Dictionary of Jazz,* 2 vols., 554–63. London: Macmillan Press Ltd.

———, ed. 1988b. *The New Grove Dictionary of Jazz,* 2 vols. London: Macmillan Press Ltd.

Khun, Thomas H. 1996 (c. 1962). *The Structure of Scientific Revolutions,* 3rd ed. Chicago: University of Chicago Press.

Kibby, Marjorie D. 2000. "Home on the Page: A Virtual Place of Music Community." *Popular Music* 19(1):91–100.

Kirshenblatt-Gimblett, Barbara. 2000. "Folklorists In Public: Reflections on Cultural Brokerage in the United States and Germany." *Journal of Folklore Research* 37:1–21.

Kivy, Peter. 1997. *Philosophies of Arts: An Essay on Differences.* Oxford, U.K.: Oxford University Press.

———. 2002. *Introduction to a Philosophy of Music.* Oxford, U.K.: Oxford University Press.

Koopman, Constantijn. 2005. "The Nature of Music and Musical Works." *Praxial Music Education: Reflections and Dialogues,* ed. David J. Elliott, 79–97. New York: Oxford University Press.

Krumhansl, Carol L. 1990. *The Cognitive Foundations of Musical Pitch.* New York: Oxford University Press.

Kruse, Holly. 1993. "Subcultural Identity in Alternative Music Culture." *Popular Music* 12(1):31–43.

———. 2009. "Local Independent Music Scenes and the Implications of the Internet." *Sound, Society and the Geography of Popular Music,* ed. Thomas L. Bell and Ola Johansson. London: Ashgate.

Lee, Steve S., and Richard A. Peterson. 2004. "Internet Based Virtual Music Scenes: The Case of P2 in Alt. Country Music." *Music Scenes: Local, Trans Local and Virtual,* ed. Andy Bennett and Richard A. Peterson, 187–204. Nashville: University of Vanderbilt Press.

Leonard, Neil. 1987. *Jazz: Myth and Religion.* New York: Oxford University Press.

Lerdahl, Fred, and Ray Jackendoff. 1983. *A Generative Grammar of Tonal Music.* Cambridge: MIT Press.

Levine, Lawrence W. 1988. *Highbrow/Lowbrow: The Emergence of Cultural Hierarchy in America.* Cambridge: Harvard University Press.

Levitin, Daniel J., and Vinod Menon. 2003. "Musical Structure Is Processed in 'Language' Areas of the Brain: A Possible Role for Brodmann Area 47 in Temporal Coherence." *NeuroImage* 20(4):2142–52.

Lewis, George. 2004. "Afterword to 'Improvised Music after 1950': The Changing Same." *The Other Side of Nowhere: Jazz, Improvisation and Communities in Dialogue*, ed. Fischlin and Heble, 131–62. Middleton, Conn.: Wesleyan University Press.

———. 2008. *A Power Stronger than Itself: The AACM and American Experimental Music*. Chicago: University of Chicago Press.

Lieberman, Fredric. "Zen Buddhism and Its Relationship to Elements of Eastern and Western Arts," *Fredric Lieberman: Selected Publications*, online archive. http://arts.ucsc.edu/faculty/lieberman/zen.html (accessed Aug. 8, 2006).

Litweiler, John. 1984. *The Freedom Principle: Jazz after 1958*. New York: Da Capo.

Lomax, Alan. 1973. *Mister Jelly Roll: The Fortunes of Jelly Roll Morton, New Orleans Creole and 'Inventor' of Jazz*, 2nd ed. Berkeley: University of California Press.

Lopes, Paul. 2002. *The Rise of a Jazz Art World*. Cambridge: Cambridge University Press.

Love, Preston. 1997. *A Thousand Honey Creeks Later: My Life in Music from Basie to Motown—And Beyond*. Hanover, N.H.: University Press of New England.

Lurie, John. 2000. Letter to the editor, *New Times–L.A.*, July 6, 2000.

MacLeod, Bruce A. 1993. *Club Date Musicians: Playing the New York Party Circuit*. Urbana: University of Illinois Press.

Maitland, Heather. 2009. *Understanding Audiences for Jazz: Briefing 3e: What Kind of People Attend Nottingham Jazzsteps Gigs*. http://www.jazzsteps.co.uk/emjazz_report/3e%20Mosaic%20report%20Nottingham.pdf (accessed July 16, 2014).

Maritain, Jacques. 1953. *Creative Intuition in Art and Poetry*. New York: Pantheon Books.

Martin, Peter J. 2005. "Jazz Community as an Art World." *The Source: Challenging Jazz Criticism* 2:5–13.

McIntyre, Morris Hargreaves, and the Jazz Development Trust. 2001. *How to Develop Audiences for Jazz*. Report prepared for the Arts Council of England. http://www.creativenorthyorkshire.com/documents/DevAudJazz1.pdf (accessed July 16, 2014).

Meizel, Katherine. 2011. *Idolized: Music, Media and Identity in American Idol*. Bloomington: Indiana University Press.

Meyer, Leonard. 1961 (c. 1956). *Emotion and Meaning in Music*. Philadelphia: University of Philadelphia Press.

Middlebrook, Diane Wood. 1998. *Suits Me: The Double Life of Billy Tipton*. Boston: Houghton Mifflin.

Milkowski, Bill. 2001. "Family Jazz." "Family Life and Sex Special Issue." *JazzTimes* (Dec. 2001):72–79.

———. 2001. "Timeless Tales (for Changing Times)." *JazzTimes*. http://jazztimes.com/articles/7868-timeless-tales-for-changing-times-joshua-redman (Jan./Feb. 1999; accessed July 19, 2012).

Miller, Norma, and Evette Jensen. 1996. *Swingin' at the Savoy: The Memoir of a Jazz Dancer*. Philadelphia: Temple University Press.

Miller, Terry E., and Andrew Shahriari. 2012. *World Music: A Global Journey*, 3rd ed. New York: Routledge.

Millett, Maya. 2010. "Court Delays Eviction of Nonprofit." *The Local East Village*. http://eastvillage.thelocal.nytimes.com/2010/10/06/court-delays-eviction-of-nonprofit/ (Oct. 6, 2010; accessed Aug. 20, 2012).

Mirkin, Steven. 2000. "Smart Club?" *New Times–L.A.*, Music section, June 8–14, 2000.

Mitchell, Tony. 1996. *Popular Music and Local Identity: Rock, Pop and Rap in Europe and Oceania*. London: Leicester University Press.

Mockus, Martha. 2007. *Sounding Out: Pauline Oliveros and Lesbian Musicality*. New York: Routledge.

Moehn, Frederick J. 2013. "Curating Community at the National Jazz Museum in Harlem." *Jazz Perspectives* 7(1):3–29.

Molino, Jean. 1975. "Fait Musical et Sémiologie de la Musique." *Musique en Jeu* 17:37–62.

Molino, Jean, J. A. Underwood, and Craig Ayrey. 1990. "Musical Fact and the Semiology of Music." *Musical Analysis* 9(2):105–11, 113–56.

Monson, Ingrid T. 1995. "The Problem with White Hipness: Race, Gender and Cultural Conceptions in Jazz Historical Discourse." *Journal of the American Musicological Society* 48(3):396–42.

Mueller, Darren. 2013. "Music Scenes: Listening for Liveness." *IASPM-US*. http://iaspm-us.net/listening-for-liveness-by-darren-mueller/ (accessed July 25, 2014).

Muller, Carol Ann, and Sathima Bea Benjamin. 2011. *Musical Echoes: South African Women Thinking in Jazz*. Durham: Duke University Press.

Murph, John. 2002. "Jazz, Blues and the Abstract's Truth." *JazzTimes* 32(2):32–38, 97 (Mar. 2002).

Murray, Albert. 1976. *Stomping the Blues*. New York: McGraw.

Murray, Albert, with Count Basie. 1985. *Good Morning Blues: The Autobiography of Count Basie*. New York: Random House.

Nachmanovitch, Stephen. 1990. *Free Play: The Power of Improvisation in Life and the Arts*. New York: J. P. Putnam and Sons.

Narmour, Eugene. 1990. *The Analysis and Cognition of Basic Melodic Structures: The Implication-Realization Model*. Chicago: University of Chicago Press.

National Endowment for the Arts (NEA). 2009. *Arts Participation 2008—Highlights from a National Survey*, Research Division Report #49. Washington, D.C.: NEA. http://www.arts.gov/research/NEA-SPPA-brochure.pdf (accessed Aug. 22, 2013).

———. 2013. *How a Nation Engages with Art: Highlights from the 2012 Survey of Public Participation in the Arts*. Washington, D.C.: NEA Research Division Report #57. http://arts.gov/sites/default/files/highlights-from-2012-SPPA-rev.pdf (accessed July 23, 2014).

Nattiez, Jean-Jacques. 1990. *Music and Discourse: Toward a Semiology of Music*. Princeton: Princeton University Press.

Negus, Keith. 1996. "Audiences." *Popular Music in Theory: An Introduction*, 7–35. Hanover, N.H.: Wesleyan University Press.

Nettl, Bruno. 1974. "Thoughts on Improvisation: A Comparative Approach." *Musical Quarterly* 60(1):1–19.

Nicholls, David. 1998. "Avant-garde and Experimental Music." *Cambridge History of American Music*. New York: Cambridge University Press.

Nicholson, Stuart, Emma Kendon, and Chris Hodgkins. 2009. *The BBC—Public Sector Radio, Jazz Policy and Structure in the Digital Age*. Jazz Services Ltd. http://www.jazz services.org.uk/Portals/0/BBC%20%20Jazz%20policy%20and%20-Structure%20V7 .pdf (accessed July 16, 2014).

Okamoto, Naomi. 1996. *Japanese Ink Painting: the Art of Sumi-e*. New York: Sterling Publishing Co., Inc.

Oliveros, Pauline. 1998. *The Roots of the Moment*. New York: Drogue Press.

———. 2004. "Harmonic Anatomy: Women in Improvisation." *The Other Side of Nowhere: Jazz, Improvisation and Communities in Dialogue*, ed. Daniel Fischlin and Ajay Heble. Middletown, Conn.: Wesleyan University Press.

Orgren, Kathy. 1989. *The Jazz Revolution: Twenties America and the Meaning of Jazz*. New York: Oxford University Press.

Ostrower, Francie. 2005. *The Diversity of Cultural Participation: Findings from a National Survey*. The Urban Institute. http://www.urban.org/UploadedPDF/311251_cultural _participation.pdf (accessed July 16, 2014).

Otis, Johnny. 1993. *Upside Your Head! Rhythm and Blues on Central Avenue*. Hanover, N.H.: University Press of New England.

Panish, Jon. 1997. *The Color of Jazz: Race and Representation in Postwar American Culture*. Jackson, Mich.: University Press of Michigan State.

Papenbrok, Marion. 1985. "The Spiritual World of Flamenco." *Flamenco*, ed. Claus Schreiner, 49–56. Portland, Ore.: Amadeus Press.

Patel, Aniruddh D. 2008. *Music, Language and the Brain*. New York: Oxford University Press.

Peirce, Charles S. 1931–1935. *Collected Papers of Charles Sanders Peirce*, vols. 1–6, ed. Charles Hartshorne and Paul Weiss; vols. 7–8, 1958, ed. Arthur W. Burks. Cambridge: Harvard University Press.

———. 1958. *Collected Papers of Charles Sanders Peirce*, vols. 7–8, ed. T. Burks. Cambridge: Harvard University Press.

Pellegrinelli, Lara. 2000. "Dig Boy, Dig: Jazz at Lincoln Center Breaks New Ground, but Where Are the Women?" *Village Voice*, 8–14. www.villagevoice.com/issues/0045/ pellegrinelli.shtml (Nov. 8, 2000); accessed Sept. 3, 2012).

———. 2001. "I Guess I Would Notice, but That Doesn't Mean You Should." *Jazz Times*. http://jazztimes.com/articles/20352-i-guess-i-would-notice-but-that-doesn-t-mean -you-shouldn-t (Mar. 2001, 23; accessed Sept. 3, 2012); updated as: "Tackling the Gender Divide." *Jazz Journalists Association*, online archives. www.jazzhouse.org/library/ index.php3?read=pellegrinelli2 (accessed Sept. 3, 2012).

Peretti, Burton W. 1992. *The Creation of Jazz: Music, Race and Culture in Urban America*. Urbana: University of Illinois Press.

Perrenoud, Marc. 2007. *Les musicos: Enquête sur des musiciens ordinaires*. Paris: La Découverte.

Peterson, Richard A., Pamela Hull, and Roger Kern. 2000. *Age and Arts Participation: 1982–1997*. Washington, D.C.: NEA Research Division Report #42.

Placksin, Sally. 1992. *American Women in Jazz: 1900 to the Present: Their Words, Lives and Music.* New York: Wideview Books.

Pohren, Donn E. 1999 (c. 1979). *A Way of Life.* Westport, Conn: The Bold Strummer, Ltd.

Powell, Richard J., ed. 1989. *The Blues Aesthetic: Black Culture and Modernism.* Washington, D.C.: Washington Project for the Arts.

Prögler, J. A. 1995. "Searching for Swing: Participatory Discrepancies in the Jazz Rhythm Section." *Ethnomusicology* 39(1):21–54.

Prouty, Ken. 2012a. *Knowing Jazz: Community, Pedagogy and Canon in the Information Age.* Jackson, Mich.: University Press of Michigan State.

———. 2012b. "Creating Boundaries in the Virtual Jazz Community." *Jazz/Not Jazz: The Music and Its Boundaries,* ed. David Ake, Charles Hiroshi Garrett, and Daniel I. Goldmark, 70–88. Berkeley: University of California Press.

Qureshi, Regula Burckhardt. 1995. *Sufi Music of India and Pakistan: Sound, Context and Meaning in Qawwali.* Chicago: University of Chicago Press.

Racy, Ali Jihad. 1991. "Creativity and Ambience: An Ecstatic Feedback Model from Arab Music." *World of Music* 33(3):7–28.

———. 1998. "Improvisation, Ecstasy and Performance Dynamics in Arabic Music." *In the Course of Performance: Studies of the World of Musical Improvisation,* ed. Bruno Nettl with Melinda Russell, 95–112. Chicago: University of Chicago Press.

———. 2003. *Making Music in the Arab World: The Culture and Artistry of Ṭarab.* Cambridge, U.K.: Cambridge University Press.

Ramsey, Guthrie. 2003. *Race Music: Black Cultures from Bebop to Hip-Hop.* Berkeley: University of California Press.

Ratliff, Ben. 2003a. "The Lesson of Smalls, A Place with a Big Heart." *New York Times,* May 31, 2003.

———. 2003b. "Irving Stone, Ardent Fan of the Downtown Music Scene, Dies at 80." *New York Times,* June 1, 2003.

Rhiannon. 2013. *Vocal River: The Skill and Spirit of Improvisation.* Hakalau, Hawaii: Rhiannon Music.

Riesman, David. 1990 (c. 1950). "Listening to Popular Music." *On Record: Rock, Pop, and the Written Word,* ed. Simon Frith and Andrew Goodwin, 5–13. New York: Pantheon.

Riley, Mykaell, and Dave Laing. 2006. *The Value of Jazz in Britain.* Commissioned by Jazz Services Ltd. http://www.jazzservices.org.uk/Portals/0/ValueofJazzReportDec2006.pdf (accessed July 16, 2014).

Robinson, Greg. 1994. "Fred Hersch: Trials and Rewards." *Jazz Times,* Sept. 1994, 43–44.

Rouget, Gilbert. 1985. *Music and Trance: A Theory of the Relations between Music and Possession,* trans. and rev. B. Biebuyck. Chicago: University of Chicago Press.

Rubolino, Frank. 2000. "The Compelling Interrelationship of Music and the Visual Arts: Discussions with Artist Jeff Schlanger." *One Final Note: Jazz and Improvised Music Webzine,* online archives. http://www.onefinalnote.com/features/2000/witness (Sept. 2000; accessed Aug. 6, 2004).

Ruesch, Jürgen, and Gregory Bateson. 2008 (c. 1951). *Communication: The Social Matrix of Psychiatry.* New Brunswick, N.J.: Transaction Publishers.

Rustin, Nichole T., and Sherrie Tucker, eds. 2008. *Big Ears: Listening for Gender in Jazz Studies*. Durham: Duke University Press.

Ryukyu, Saito. 2001 (c. 1959). *Japanese Ink-Painting: Lessons in Suiboku Techniques*. North Clarendon, Vt.: Tuttle Publishing.

Salamone, Frank A. 1988. "The Ritual of Jazz Performance." *Play and Culture* 1:85–104.

Sarath, Ed. 1996. "A New Look at Improvisation." *Journal of Music Theory* 40(1):1–38.

Saul, Scott. 2003. *Freedom Is, Freedom Ain't: Jazz and the Making of the Sixties*. Cambridge: Harvard University Press.

Saussure, Ferdinand de. 1959 (c. 1916). *Course in General Linguistics*, ed. Charles Baily and Albert Sechehave, with Albert Riedlinger; trans. Wade Baskin. New York: McGraw-Hill Book Co.

Schreiner, Claus, ed. 1990. *Flamenco*. Portland, Ore: Amadeus Press.

Schütz, Alfred. 1976. "Fragments on the Phenomenology of Music." *Music and Man: An Interdisciplinary Journal of Studies on Music* 2(1–2):5–72.

Seeger, Charles. 1977. *Studies in Musicology 1935–1975*. Berkeley: University of California Press.

Shank, Barry. 1994. *Dissonant Identities: The Rock 'n' Roll Scene in Austin, Texas*. Middletown, Conn.: Wesleyan University Press.

Shannon, Jonathan H. 2003. "Emotion, Performance and Temporality in Arab Music: Reflections on *Tarab*." *Cultural Anthropology* 18(1):72–98.

Sidran, Ben. 1981 (c. 1971). *Black Talk*. New York: Da Capo.

Siren, Osvald. 2005 (c. 1936). *The Chinese on the Art of Painting: Texts by the Painter-Critics, from the Han through the Ch'ing Dynasties*. New York: Dover Publishing.

Slobin, Mark. 1993. *Subcultural Sounds: Micro-Musics of the West*. Middletown, Conn.: Wesleyan University Press.

Sloboda, J. A. 1989 (c. 1985). Ch. 3.4: "Expert Performance" and Ch. 4: "Composition and Improvisation." The *Musical Mind: The Cognitive Psychology of Music*, 93–150. Oxford, U.K.: Clarendon Press.

Small, Christopher. 1988 (c.1987). *Music of the Common Tongue: Survival and Celebration in Afro-American Music*. New York: Riverrun Press.

———. 1998. *Musicking: The Meanings of Performance and Listening*. Hanover, N.H.: Wesleyan University Press.

Smith, Chris. 1988. "A Sense of the Possible: Miles Davis and the Semiotics of Improvised Performance." *In the Course of Performance: Studies of the World of Musical Improvisation*, ed. Bruno Nettl with Melinda Russell, 261–89. Chicago: University of Chicago Press.

Smith, Julie Dawn. 2004. "Playing Like a Girl: The Queer Laughter of the Feminist Improvising Group." *The Other side of Nowhere: Jazz, Improvisation and Communities in Dialogue*, ed. Daniel Fischlin and Ajay Heble. Middletown, Conn.: Wesleyan University Press.

Solis, Gabriel. 2008. *Monk's Music: Thelonious Monk and Jazz History in the Making*. Berkeley: University of California Press.

Solis, Gabriel, and Bruno Nettl, eds. 2009. *Musical Improvisation: Art, Education and Society*. Urbana: University of Illinois Press.

227

Somoroff, Matthew A. 2014. *Listening at the Edges: Aural Experience and Affect in a New York Jazz Scene.* PhD diss., Duke University.

Spring, Ken. 2004. "Behind the Rave: Structure and Agency in a Rave Scene." In Bennett and Peterson, *Behind the Rave*, 48–63. Nashville: Vanderbilt University Press.

Stearns, Marshall W. 1956. *The Story of Jazz.* Oxford, U.K.: Oxford University Press.

Stewart, Alex. 2007. *Making the Scene: Contemporary New York City Big Band Jazz.* Berkeley: University of California Press.

Straw, Will. 1991. "Systems of Articulation, Logics of Change: Communities and Scenes in Popular Music." *Cultural Studies* 5(3):368–88.

Such, David. 1993. *Avant-garde Jazz Musicians: Performing 'Out There.'* Iowa City: University of Iowa Press.

Sudnow, David. 1978. *Ways of the Hand: The Organization of Improvised Conduct.* Cambridge: Harvard University Press.

Suzuki, Shunryu. 1970. *Zen Mind, Beginner's Mind.* New York: Weatherhill.

Sylvan, Robin. 2002. *Traces of the Spirit: The Religious Dimensions of Popular Music.* New York: New York University Press.

Taylor, Arthur. 1993 (c. 1977). *Notes and Tones: Musician-to-Musician Interviews*, exp. ed. New York: Da Capo.

Terry, Walter, Jack Vartoogian, and Linda Vartoogian. 1982. *How to Look at Dance.* New York: William Morrow and Co.

Thomas, Lewis. 1979. *The Medusa and the Snail.* New York: Viking Press.

Tirro, Frank. 1967. "The Silent Theme Tradition in Jazz." *Musical Quarterly* 53(3):313–34.

Truax, Barry. 1986. "The Listener." *Musicworks* 35:13–16.

Tucker, Mark. 1989. *Ellington: The Early Years.* Urbana: University of Illinois Press.

———, ed. 1993. *The Duke Ellington Reader.* New York: Oxford University Press.

Tucker, Sherrie. 1997. "Telling Performances: Jazz History Remembered and Remade by the Women in the Band." *Women and Music: A Journal of Gender and Culture* 1(1997):12–23.

———. 2000. *Swing Shift: "All-Girl" Bands of the 1940s.* Durham: Duke University Press.

———. 2004. "Bordering on Community: Improvising Women Improvising Women-in-Jazz." *The Other Side of Nowhere: Jazz, Improvisation and Communities in Dialogue,* ed. Daniel Fischlin and Ajay Heble, 244–67. Middletown, Conn.: Wesleyan University Press.

———. 2008. "When Did Jazz Go Straight? A Queer Question for Jazz Studies." *Critical Studies in Improvisation/Études critiques en improvisation* 4(2). http://www.criticalimprov.com/article/view/845 (accessed Aug. 11, 2013).

Turino, Thomas. 1999. "Signs of Imagination, Identity and Experience: A Peircean Theory for Music." *Ethnomusicology* 43(2):221–55.

———. 2008. *Music as Social Life: The Politics of Participation.* Chicago: University of Chicago Press.

———. 2014. "Peircean Thought as Core Theory for a Phenomenological Ethnomusicology." *Ethnomusicology* 58(2):185–221.

Turner, Victor W. 1995 (c. 1969). *The Ritual Process: Structure and Anti-Structure*. New York: Aldine de Gruyter.

Turner, Victor W., and Edith Turner. 1978. *Image and Pilgrimage in Christian Culture*. New York: Columbia University Press.

Vartoogian, Jack, Linda Vartoogian, and Carol Garey. 1987. *The Living World of Dance: Artistry in Motion*. New York: Smithmark.

Vermorel, Judy. 1989. *Fandemonium! The Book of Fan Cults and Dance Crazes*. London: Omnibus.

Vincent, Ted. 1995. *Keep Cool: The Black Activists Who Built the Jazz Age*. London, Conn.: Pluto Press.

Wallach, Jeremy. 2008. *Modern Noise, Fluid Genres: Popular Music in Indonesia, 1997–2001*. Durham: Duke University Press.

Wallach, Jeremy, Harris M. Berger, and Paul D. Greene. 2011. *Metal Rules the Globe: Heavy Metal Music around the World*. Durham: Duke University Press.

Warner, Bijan. 2010. "Jazz Audiences Initiative: A Literature Review of Research on Jazz Audiences." *Jazz Arts Group*. http://www.jazzartsgroup.org/wp-content/uploads/2011/01/JAILitReview_Final.pdf (accessed July 18, 2014).

Waterman, Ellen. 2008. "Naked Intimacy: Eroticism, Improvisation and Gender." *Critical Studies in Improvisation/Études critiques en improvisation* 4(2). http://www.criticalimprov.com/article/view/845 (accessed Aug. 11, 2013).

Wein, George. 2012. "Producing a Jazz Festival Is Fun, but Never Easy," blog entry on the Newport Jazz Festival website. http://newportjazzfest.net/index.php?pID=51&PR=165 (accessed Aug. 25, 2012).

Weinstein, Deena. 2000. *Heavy Metal: The Music and Its Culture*, 2nd ed. New York: Da Capo.

Werner, Kenny. 1996. *Effortless Mastery: Liberating the Master Musician Within*. New Albany, Ind.: Jamey Aebersold Jazz, Inc.

Williams, Martin T. 1967. *Where's the Melody? A Listener's Introduction to Jazz*. New York: Funk and Wagnalls.

Wilmer, Valerie. 1977. *As Serious as Your Life: The Story of the New Jazz*. London: Quartet.

———. 1989. *Mama Said There'd Be Days like This: My Life in the Jazz World*. London: The Women's Press.

———. 1990 (c. 1970). *Jazz People*. New York: Da Capo.

Wilson, Olly. 1992. "The Heterogeneous Sound Ideal in African-American Music." *New Perspectives on Music: Essays in Honor of Eileen Southern*, ed. Josephine Wright w/Samuel Floyd Jr., 327–38. Warren, Mich.: Harmonie Park Press.

DISCOGRAPHY

Aldana, Melissa. 2012. *Second Cycle*. Inner Circle Music: INCM 029CD, CD.

Armstrong, Louis, and His Hot Five. 1928 (rec. Dec. 1927). *Savoy Blues/Hotter Than That*. Okeh: 8535, 78 rpm disc.

———. 1929. (rec. June 1928). *West End Blues/Fireworks*. Okeh 41078, 78 rpm disc.

Armstrong, Louis, with Earl Hines. 1930. (rec. Dec. 1928). *Weather Bird/Dear Old Southland*. Okeh 41454, 78 rpm disc.

Avital, Omer. 2007. *Arrival*. Fresh Sound/World Jazz: FSWJ 035.

Ayler, Albert. 1969. *Music Is the Healing Force of the Universe*. Impulse!: AS-9191, LP.

Bad Plus, The. 2001. *The Bad Plus*. Fresh Sound/New Talent: FSNT 107, CD.

Bad Plus, The. 2003. *These Are the Vistas*. Columbia: CK 87040, CD.

Barber, Patricia. 1998. "Company." *Modern Cool*. Premonition: PREM-741-2, CD.

Basie, Count, and His Orchestra, with Don Byas. 1942. *Harvard Blues/Coming Out Party*. Okeh: 6564, 78 rpm disc.

Bechet, Sidney, Quintet. 1939 (rec. June 1939). "Summertime." *Pounding Heart Blues/Summertime*. Blue Note: BN 6, 78 rpm disc. Side B.

Blakey, Art, & the Jazz Messengers. 1985. *Live at Sweet Basil*. GNP Crescendo: GNPS-2182, LP.

Blythe, Arthur. 1981. *Blythe Spirit*. Columbia: FC 37427, LP.

Brown, Clifford. 1973. *The Beginning and the End*. Columbia: KC 32284, LP.

Brown, Oscar, Jr. 1960. "Bid 'Em In." *Sin & Soul*. Columbia: CL 1577, LP.

Burns, Ken. 2000. *Jazz: A Film by Ken Burns*. PBS Home Video: 88580/10DVD set.

Carter, Daniel, + Reuben Radding. *Luminescence*. AUM Fidelity: AUM025, CD.

Coltrane, John. 1958. *Soultrane*. Prestige 7142, LP.

————. 1961. "Summertime." *My Favorite Things*. Atlantic 1361, LP.

————. 1965. *A Love Supreme*. Impulse!: A-77, LP.

Davis, Miles. 1957. "'Round Midnight." *'Round About Midnight*. Columbia CL 949, LP.

————. 1958. "Summertime." *Porgy and Bess*. Columbia CS 8085, LP.

————. 1959. "So What," *Kind of Blue*. Columbia: CS 8163, LP.

Dylan, Bob. 1975. *Blood on the Tracks*. Columbia: PC 33235, LP.

Ellington, Duke, and His Orchestra. 1933. *Mood Indigo/The Mooche*. Victor: 24486, 78 rpm disc.

Evans, Gil, & the Monday Night Orchestra. 1987. *Bud and Bird (Live at Sweet Basil)*. Electric Bird: CDJ 671, CD.

Garner, Erroll. *Concert by the Sea* (Columbia CL 883) 1955.

Holiday, Billie, and Her Orchestra. 1936. *Summertime/Billie's Blues*. Vocalion: 3288, 78 rpm disc.

————. 1939. *Fine and Mellow/Strange Fruit*. Commodore: 526, 78 rpm disc.

Indo-Pak Coalition, Rudresh Mahanthappa's. 2008. *Apti*. Innova: 709.

Iyer, Vijay, with Prasanna and Nitin Mitta. 2011. *Tirtha*. ACT: 9503–2.

Jackson, Preston, and His Uptown Band. 1926. *It's Tight Jim/Harmony Blues*. Paramount: 12400, 78 rpm disc.

Kidd Jordan /Joel Futterman/Alvin Fielder Trio. 2004. *Live at the Tampere Jazz Happening 2000*. Charles Lester Music: CLM 26–006.

Mahanthappa, Rudresh. 2008. *Kinsmen*. Pi: PI28.

Mahavishnu Orchestra, The, with John McLaughlin. 1971. *The Inner Mounting Flame*. Columbia: KC 31067, LP.

Mahavishnu Orchestra, The. 1973. *Birds of Fire*. Columbia: KC 31996, LP.

Mathis, Johnny, with Ray Conniff and His Orchestra. 1957. *Chances Are/The Twelfth of Never*. Columbia: 4–40993, 45 rpm disc.

Millennial Territory Orchestra, Steven Bernstein's. 2006. *MTO Volume 1*. Sunnyside: SSC 1158, CD.

Mingus, Charles. 1963. *Mingus Mingus Mingus Mingus Mingus*. Impulse! AS-54, LP

Parker, Charlie. 1948 (rec. Sep. 1944). *Red Cross/Tiny's Tempo*. Savoy: 541, 78 rpm disc.

Parker, Charlie, and Dizzy Gillespie. 1957 (rec. June 1950). *Bird and Diz, The Genius of Charlie Parker #4*. Verve: MGV-8006, LP.

Redman, Joshua. 1998. "Summertime." *Timeless Tales for Changing Times*. Warner Bros 9362–47052–2, CD.

Smithsonian Collection of Classic Jazz, The. 1973. Smithsonian: P6 11891/6LP-set.

Tatum, Art. 1933. *Tiger Rag/St. Louis Blues*. Brunswick: 6543, 78 rpm disc.

Tower of Power. 1973. "What Is Hip?" *Tower of Power*. Warner Bros.: BS-268, LP.

Vaughan, Sarah. 1985. *The Complete Sarah Vaughan on Mercury Vol. 1—Great Jazz Years, 1954–1956*. Mercury: 826 320–1/6LP set.

————. 1986. *The Complete Sarah Vaughan on Mercury Vol. 2—Sings Great American Songs, 1956–1957*. Mercury: 826 327–1/5LP set.

————. 1986. *The Complete Sarah Vaughan on Mercury Vol. 3—Great Show on Stage, 1957–1959*. Mercury: 826 333–1/6LP set.

————. 1986. *The Complete Sarah Vaughan on Mercury Vol. 4 (Part 1)—Live in Europe, 1963–1964*. Mercury: 830 721–1/4LP set.

————. 1987. *The Complete Sarah Vaughan on Mercury Vol. 4 (Part 2)—Sassy Swings Again, 1964–1967*. Mercury: 830 726–1/5LP set.

Wildflowers: The New York City Jazz Loft Sessions. 1999 (rec. May 14–23, 1976). Knit Classics: KCR 3037/3CD set.

Williams, Tony. 1964. *Life Time*. Blue Note: BLP 4180, LP.

Young, Lester, and Charlie Christian. 1978. *Lester Young and Charlie Christian 1939–1940*. Jazz Archives: JA-42, LP.

Young, Neil. 1970. *After the Goldrush*. Reprise: RS 6383.

Zappa, Frank, and the Mothers of Invention. 1969. *Freak Out!* Verve: V-5005–2, LP.

Zorn, John. 1987. *Cobra*. Hat Hut: ART 2034/2LP-set.

Zorn, John, et al. 2004. *Irving Stone Memorial Concert*. Tzadik: TZ7611–2.

INDEX

THOMAS H. GREENLAND is a New York City–based guitarist, pianist, vocalist, composer, arranger, journalist, photographer, and educator.

MUSIC IN AMERICAN LIFE

"Susanna," "Jeanie," and "The Old Folks at Home": The Songs of Stephen C. Foster
    from His Time to Ours (2d ed.)   *William W. Austin*

Songprints: The Musical Experience of Five Shoshone Women   *Judith Vander*

"Happy in the Service of the Lord": Afro-American Gospel Quartets
    in Memphis   *Kip Lornell*

Paul Hindemith in the United States   *Luther Noss*

"My Song Is My Weapon": People's Songs, American Communism,
    and the Politics of Culture, 1930–1950   *Robbie Lieberman*

Chosen Voices: The Story of the American Cantorate   *Mark Slobin*

Theodore Thomas: America's Conductor and Builder of Orchestras,
    1835–1905   *Ezra Schabas*

"The Whorehouse Bells Were Ringing" and Other Songs Cowboys Sing
    Collected and Edited by Guy Logsdon

Crazeology: The Autobiography of a Chicago Jazzman   *Bud Freeman,
    as Told to Robert Wolf*

Discoursing Sweet Music: Brass Bands and Community Life
    in Turn-of-the-Century Pennsylvania   *Kenneth Kreitner*

Mormonism and Music: A History   *Michael Hicks*

Voices of the Jazz Age: Profiles of Eight Vintage Jazzmen   *Chip Deffaa*

Pickin' on Peachtree: A History of Country Music in Atlanta, Georgia   *Wayne W. Daniel*

Bitter Music: Collected Journals, Essays, Introductions, and Librettos   *Harry Partch;
    edited by Thomas McGeary*

Ethnic Music on Records: A Discography of Ethnic Recordings Produced
    in the United States, 1893 to 1942   *Richard K. Spottswood*

Downhome Blues Lyrics: An Anthology from the Post–World War II Era   *Jeff Todd Titon*

Ellington: The Early Years   *Mark Tucker*

Chicago Soul   *Robert Pruter*

That Half-Barbaric Twang: The Banjo in American Popular Culture   *Karen Linn*

Hot Man: The Life of Art Hodes   *Art Hodes and Chadwick Hansen*

The Erotic Muse: American Bawdy Songs (2d ed.)   *Ed Cray*

Barrio Rhythm: Mexican American Music in Los Angeles   *Steven Loza*

The Creation of Jazz: Music, Race, and Culture in Urban America   *Burton W. Peretti*

Charles Martin Loeffler: A Life Apart in Music   *Ellen Knight*

Club Date Musicians: Playing the New York Party Circuit   *Bruce A. MacLeod*

Opera on the Road: Traveling Opera Troupes in the United States,
    1825–1860   *Katherine K. Preston*

The Stonemans: An Appalachian Family and the Music That Shaped
    Their Lives   *Ivan M. Tribe*

Transforming Tradition: Folk Music Revivals Examined   *Edited by Neil V. Rosenberg*

The Crooked Stovepipe: Athapaskan Fiddle Music and Square Dancing
    in Northeast Alaska and Northwest Canada   *Craig Mishler*

Traveling the High Way Home: Ralph Stanley and the World of Traditional
    Bluegrass Music   *John Wright*

Carl Ruggles: Composer, Painter, and Storyteller   *Marilyn Ziffrin*

The Bill Monroe Reader   *Edited by Tom Ewing*

Music in Lubavitcher Life   *Ellen Koskoff*

Zarzuela: Spanish Operetta, American Stage   *Janet L. Sturman*

Bluegrass Odyssey: A Documentary in Pictures and Words, 1966–1986   *Carl Fleischhauer
    and Neil V. Rosenberg*

That Old-Time Rock & Roll: A Chronicle of an Era, 1954–1963   *Richard Aquila*

Labor's Troubadour   *Joe Glazer*

American Opera   *Elise K. Kirk*

Don't Get above Your Raisin': Country Music and the Southern
    Working Class   *Bill C. Malone*

John Alden Carpenter: A Chicago Composer   *Howard Pollack*

Heartbeat of the People: Music and Dance of the Northern Pow-wow   *Tara Browner*

My Lord, What a Morning: An Autobiography   *Marian Anderson*

Marian Anderson: A Singer's Journey   *Allan Keiler*

Charles Ives Remembered: An Oral History   *Vivian Perlis*

Henry Cowell, Bohemian   *Michael Hicks*

Rap Music and Street Consciousness   *Cheryl L. Keyes*

Louis Prima   *Garry Boulard*

Marian McPartland's Jazz World: All in Good Time   *Marian McPartland*

Robert Johnson: Lost and Found   *Barry Lee Pearson and Bill McCulloch*

Bound for America: Three British Composers   *Nicholas Temperley*

Lost Sounds: Blacks and the Birth of the Recording Industry, 1890–1919   *Tim Brooks*

Burn, Baby! BURN! The Autobiography of Magnificent Montague   *Magnificent Montague
    with Bob Baker*

Way Up North in Dixie: A Black Family's Claim to the Confederate Anthem
    Howard L. Sacks and Judith Rose Sacks

The Bluegrass Reader   *Edited by Thomas Goldsmith*

Colin McPhee: Composer in Two Worlds   *Carol J. Oja*

Robert Johnson, Mythmaking, and Contemporary American Culture
    Patricia R. Schroeder

Composing a World: Lou Harrison, Musical Wayfarer   *Leta E. Miller
    and Fredric Lieberman*

Fritz Reiner, Maestro and Martinet   *Kenneth Morgan*

That Toddlin' Town: Chicago's White Dance Bands and Orchestras,
    1900–1950   *Charles A. Sengstock Jr.*

Dewey and Elvis: The Life and Times of a Rock 'n' Roll Deejay   *Louis Cantor*

Come Hither to Go Yonder: Playing Bluegrass with Bill Monroe   *Bob Black*

Chicago Blues: Portraits and Stories   *David Whiteis*

The Incredible Band of John Philip Sousa   *Paul E. Bierley*

"Maximum Clarity" and Other Writings on Music   *Ben Johnston, edited by Bob Gilmore*

Staging Tradition: John Lair and Sarah Gertrude Knott   *Michael Ann Williams*

Homegrown Music: Discovering Bluegrass   *Stephanie P. Ledgin*

Tales of a Theatrical Guru   *Danny Newman*

The Music of Bill Monroe   *Neil V. Rosenberg and Charles K. Wolfe*

Then Sings My Soul: The Culture of Southern Gospel Music   *Douglas Harrison*

The Accordion in the Americas: Klezmer, Polka, Tango, Zydeco, and More!
    Edited by Helena Simonett

Bluegrass Bluesman: A Memoir   *Josh Graves, edited by Fred Bartenstein*

One Woman in a Hundred: Edna Phillips and the Philadelphia Orchestra
    Mary Sue Welsh

The Great Orchestrator: Arthur Judson and American Arts Management
    James M. Doering

Charles Ives in the Mirror: American Histories of an Iconic Composer   *David C. Paul*

Southern Soul-Blues   *David Whiteis*

Sweet Air: Modernism, Regionalism, and American Popular Song   *Edward P. Comentale*

Pretty Good for a Girl: Women in Bluegrass   *Murphy Hicks Henry*

Sweet Dreams: The World of Patsy Cline   *Warren R. Hofstra*

William Sidney Mount and the Creolization of American Culture   *Christopher J. Smith*

Bird: The Life and Music of Charlie Parker   *Chuck Haddix*

Making the March King: John Philip Sousa's Washington Years,
    1854–1893   *Patrick Warfield*

In It for the Long Run   *Jim Rooney*

Pioneers of the Blues Revival   *Steve Cushing*

Roots of the Revival: American and British Folk Music in the 1950s
    Ronald D. Cohen and Rachel Clare Donaldson

Blues All Day Long: The Jimmy Rogers Story   *Wayne Everett Goins*

Yankee Twang: Country and Western Music in New England   *Clifford R. Murphy*

The Music of the Stanley Brothers   *Gary B. Reid*

Hawaiian Music in Motion: Mariners, Missionaries, and Minstrels   *James Revell Carr*

Sounds of the New Deal: The Federal Music Project in the West   *Peter Gough*

The Mormon Tabernacle Choir: A Biography   *Michael Hicks*

The Man That Got Away: The Life and Songs of Harold Arlen   *Walter Rimler*

A City Called Heaven: Chicago and the Birth of Gospel Music   *Robert M. Marovich*

Blues Unlimited: Essential Interviews from the Original Blues Magazine
    Edited by Bill Greensmith, Mike Rowe, and Mark Camarigg

Hoedowns, Reels, and Frolics: Roots and Branches of Southern
    Appalachian Dance   *Phil Jamison*

Fannie Bloomfield-Zeisler: The Life and Times of a Piano Virtuoso
    Beth Abelson Macleod

Cybersonic Arts: Adventures in American New Music   *Gordon Mumma,
    edited with commentary by Michelle Fillion*

The Magic of Beverly Sills   *Nancy Guy*

Waiting for Buddy Guy   *Alan Harper*

Harry T. Burleigh: From the Spiritual to the Harlem Renaissance   *Jean E. Snyder*

Music in the Age of Anxiety: American Music in the Fifties   *James Wierzbicki*

Jazzing: New York City's Unseen Scene   *Thomas H. Greenland*

The University of Illinois Press
is a founding member of the
Association of American University Presses.

University of Illinois Press
1325 South Oak Street
Champaign, IL 61820-6903
www.press.uillinois.edu